TRACES

John Singletary

Cofounder: Michael Itkoff
Creative Director: Ursula Damm
Copy Editor: Gabrielle Fastman

ISBN: 978-1-954119-33-8

Printed by Ofset Yapimevi, Turkey

Daylight Books
E-mail: info@daylightbooks.org
Web: www.daylightbooks.org

John Singletary
Web: www.johnsingletaryimaging.com

Traces was devised as a six-channel film and sound multimedia installation that has been reinterpreted in book format.

The audio component comprised a recording of various anonymous interviews alongside an original score composed by Matt Hollenberg. The perspectives chosen reveal both the universality and individuality of human values, through the intersection of symbolism across cultures, through our lineages, and in the perpetual cycles that inform all of our lives.

—John Singletary

In a world where empathy seems scarce and cruelty often takes center stage, art and music offer a much-needed refuge. This project is an attempt to provide a sense of solace amidst the chaos and uncertainty of our times, aiming to reignite a flicker of hope. My goal is for the music to embody this ambitious vision.

—Matt Hollenberg

John Singletary, whom I first met when I was teaching at the University of the Arts in Philadelphia in 2011, had already been doing photography on his own for years. He later enrolled at the school and earned a degree, but we had previously exhibited his work in the 2013 Best of the *Photo Review* show. The 2013 competition was juried by Paul Roth, then the senior curator and director of photography and media arts at the Corcoran Gallery of Art in Washington, D.C. I mention this because it reinforces the seriousness and commitment that drives John. He'd worked with organizations like the *Photo Review*, and Philadelphia Museum of Art's permanent collection. Mind you, these accomplishments happened while he was still a student, achievements that surpassed many of his faculty.

I find Singletary to be intellectually driven, which is to say that his work, while intensely visual and engaging, is built upon a solid base of theory, observation, history, and art history. His 2017 *Anahata* installation was visually and emotionally stunning. A series of large OLED (Organic Light-Emitting Diode) video screens, in a darkened space, provided a mesmerizing, trance-like experience that was both sensual and spiritual at the same time. His approach was unique. He rented a large studio space, collaborated with dancers and choreographers, and using a digital camera created thousands of frames, then used animation and video software to take these frames and create what seemed to me to be a type of mandala.

While dancers did perform at the openings, the installation was most often experienced by immersing oneself in the room, and absorbing the images and music surrounding you. Most of the work was created in camera, and not a digital collage. Some of the longer pieces were created from only seven exposures, and Singletary created a unique black-light process for the project.

The displays shimmered in the darkened space, while especially ethereal soundtracks provided a directed nuance to the atmosphere. Both the *Anahata* and *Traces* projects were recorded by Singletary's childhood friend Matt Hollenberg, and Singletary also played on the *Anahata* soundtrack. Hollenberg is a renowned musician in his own right, having worked with John Zorn and Cleric.

This combination of still imagery, movement, and dancers all created an environment that I think the great site-specific artist

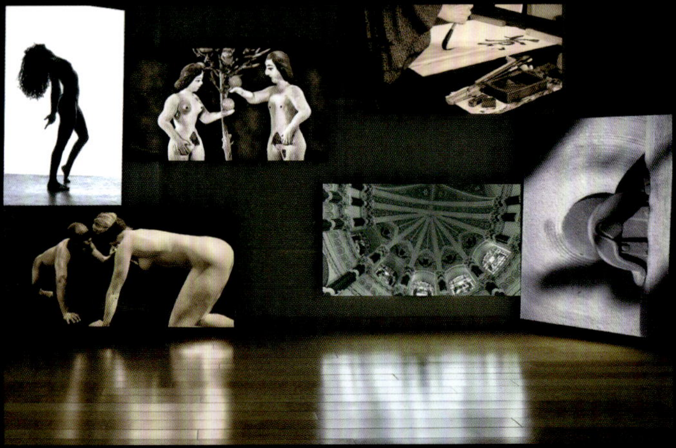

Robert Irwin would have been pleased with. Like Irwin, Singletary is concerned with altering one's perceptual being and experience. Entering into one of his exhibits instantly transports the participants to a different spiritual and emotional space. Irwin was interested in freeing the visitor from the constraints of the object, and while John uses cutting-edge technology, it is to make the technology as invisible as possible.

For example, his choice of OLED display technology isn't really about the medium's resolution, video dynamic range, or gamut (color space) performance; it's really about having completely black blacks. With other video display technologies, the dark shadows, the blacks, are typically dark grey. Not so with OLED; those areas without details are truly black. As the old phrase goes, they are as dark as a black cat in a coal bin at midnight, during a new moon.

A solo show at the Delaware Contemporary art museum in 2019 solidified Singletary's status as an artist to be reckoned with. Draping the exhibit space entirely in black fabric, with large OLED displays set up throughout, the space glowed with kinetic energy, combining dance, choreography, animation, original music, and digital imaging to create a compelling performative experience, not unlike the energy found in a chapel or sanctuary.

This attention to detail surfaces in his newest project, *Traces*, which again utilizes six large OLED screens. Unlike his *Anahata* project, which only utilized images that he personally created, *Traces* draws upon found footage, historical images, digital images, video, and stop-action animation, all woven together via digital video editing, animation, and audio software.

With *Traces*, Singletary is inviting viewers to examine their own altruistic impulses toward one another, and the multimedia aspect of the installation, which this book can't entirely reproduce, is meant to be a transcendent experience, so that viewers can leave their ordinary concerns behind and involve themselves fully in this new environment and context. Replete with interviews, the voices in *Traces* add an additional element not found in his *Anahata* project. I've always known Singletary to be a sincere and profoundly honest artist. He seeks to engage the viewer, allowing them to enter into a consciousness other than what they'd experience in their day-to-day lives. His work succeeds for me on a variety of levels, but it is always invigorating, questioning, and impactful.

Harris Fogel
Porvoo, Finland, 2024

For several years John Singletary has been pushing beyond the bounds of the two-dimensional photographic print into immersive installations on large high-definition monitors. In *Anahata* (2017) he combined still and moving images of dancers in a compelling black-box display, with dance performances within the exhibition's space on special occasions, such as an opening reception or a symposium about his work in conjunction with an exhibition of *Anahata* at the Delaware Contemporary (2019). With evocative costuming and body adornments, the dancers summoned an alternative mystical journey, a modern-day *Rite of Spring*.

Traces is Singletary's most ambitious project to date. A six-screen installation, it metaphorically takes us through terrestrial history from creation to the present. Its references are biblical and metaphysical, historical and mythical, from the opening image of the calmly rolling waves of the ocean—where life began—to a nuclear explosion that could end all life.

In many ways it echoes the book of Genesis, from creation and the beginning of life through the story of the apple and the Fall. What follows is the depiction of the remarkable benefits and the weighty burdens of knowledge and consciousness.

Combining images of the natural world, of scientific studies, of birth and death, of dancers moving in nature and in the studio, of stop motion, of old black-and-white cartoons and silent films, of historical newsreel footage, and of discredited medical treatments, Singletary creates an existential meditation on the human condition, its achievements, and the many wrong turns it has taken along the way. The images subtly confront the dichotomies of existence, from the cellular to the cosmic, from the organic to the mechanical, from deep human connection and sensuality to cartoonish and ultimately real violence.

The images are tied together by an ethereal score by the noted guitarist and composer Matt Hollenberg (a childhood friend of Singletary's) and the spoken words of interviews Singletary conducted with people he recruited through advertisements. The interview questions are both deeply personal and universal, and the subjects included are remarkably revealing and without pretense in discussing their life's problems and joys, their beliefs in a god—or not—and meditations on life and death. Singletary transcribed the interviews, selected excerpts, and had voice actors read the words of his subjects. The recitation lends a gravity that weaves its way into the images and lends them greater depth. The integration of music and voices propels a narrative of human pain and ecstasy, addressing grace, integrity, intimacy, and love—all open-ended questions of human existence.

Singletary asked his dancers the same questions for them to answer in dance, so the movement provides a subconscious echo of the spoken words. Often sensual and sensuous, the mostly naked bodies of the dancers reflect the generative power of creation while celebrating the physicality of the living vessels we inhabit.

Traces is Singletary's most personal work not only in terms of its creation, but within its structure as well. There is a through line of autobiography that appears continually within it, from images of medical scans and monitors that are Singletary's own to a gravestone with the family name that appears near the end of the piece.

As with many people, the pandemic led Singletary to a reevaluation of his life. Making this work, he has said, was a way to get clarity on the issues he confronts in *Traces* for himself. I don't know whether he found answers—nor may viewers of this work—but the questions and the considerations found are a firm step toward knowing oneself and encourage us to be open to what we find in life.

Stephen Perloff

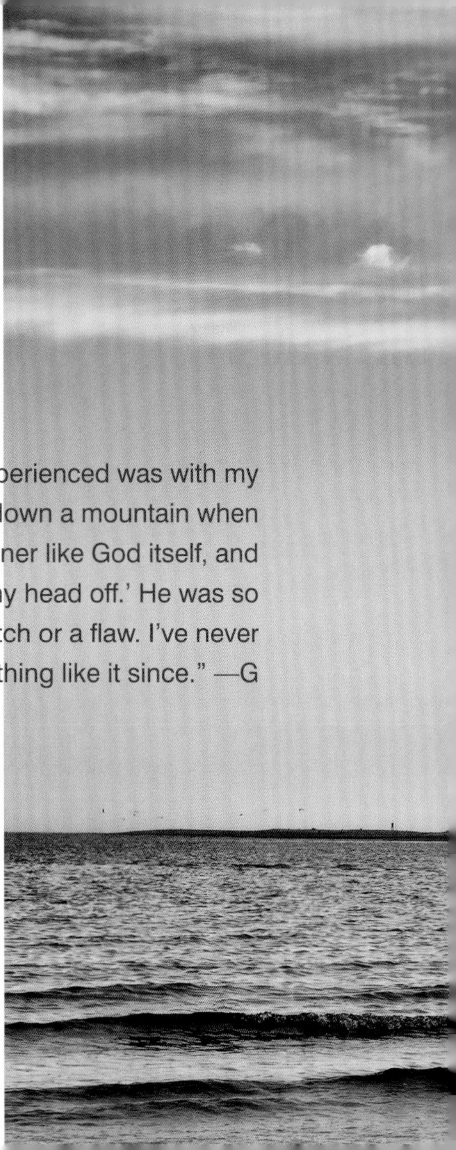

"The most beautiful thing I've ever experienced was with my grandfather in Wyoming. I was climbing down a mountain when this bison came running around the corner like God itself, and I'm thinking, 'This thing is going to rip my head off.' He was so magnificent, so full of life, without a scratch or a flaw. I've never seen anything like it since." —G

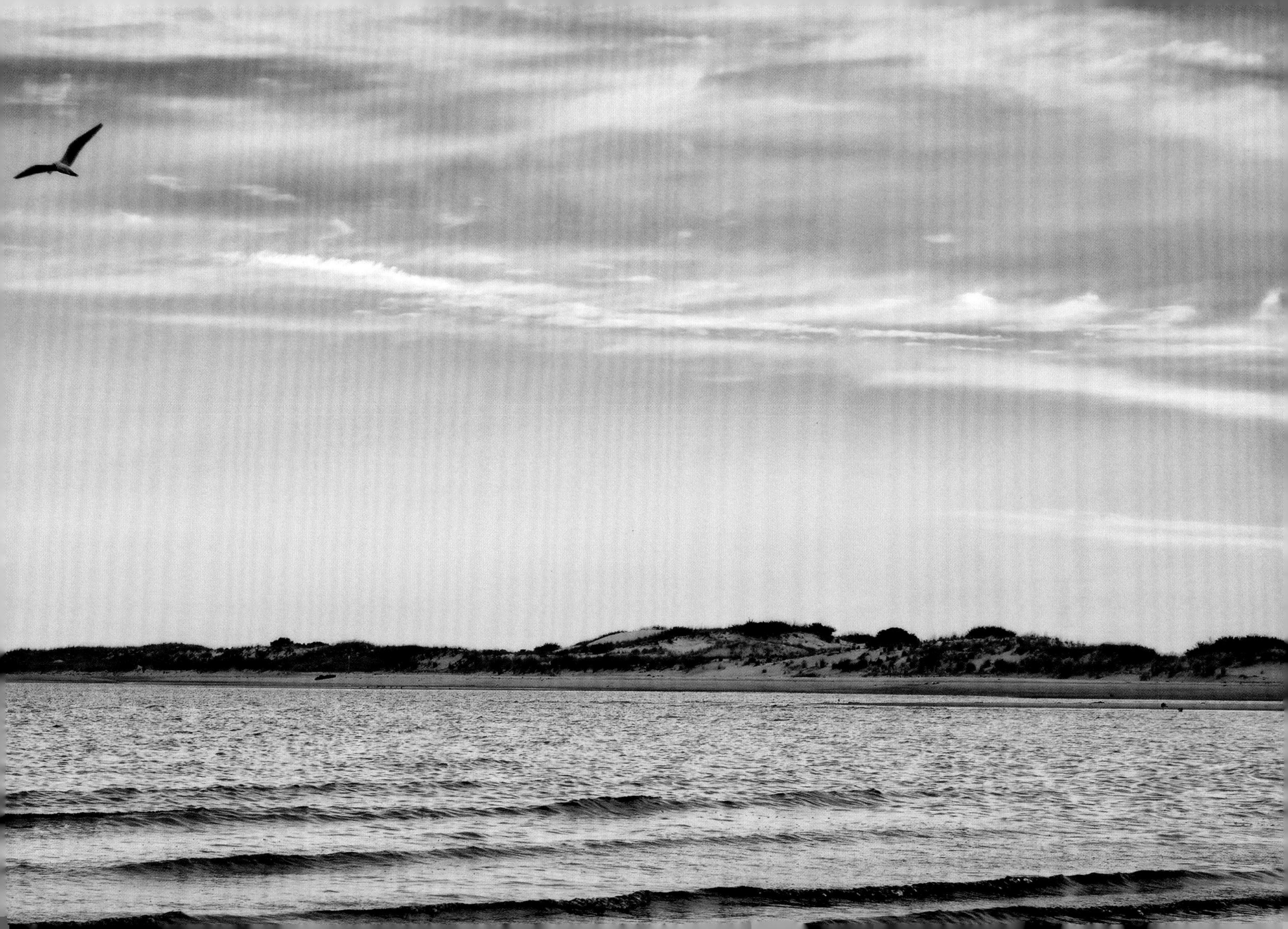

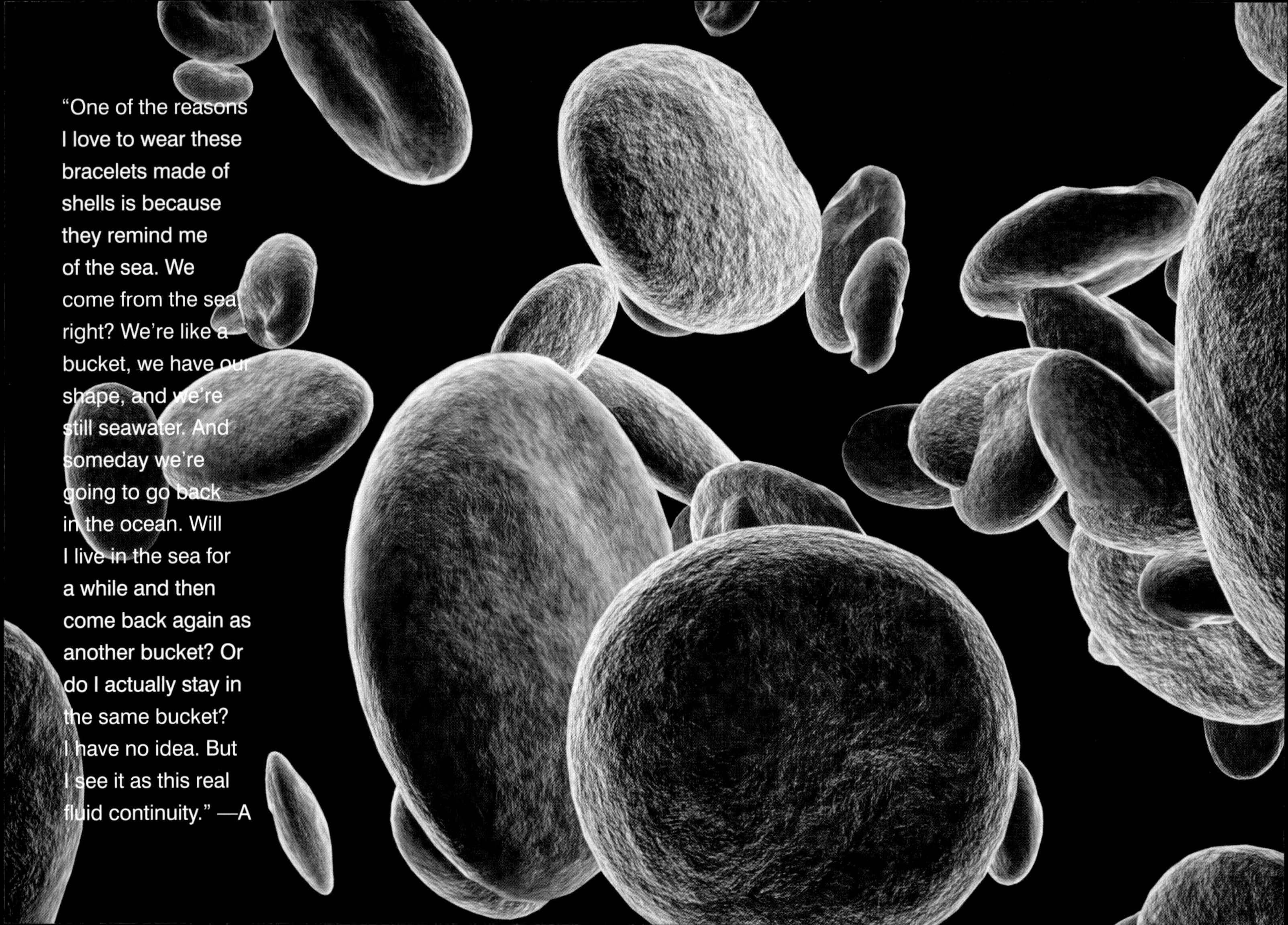

"One of the reasons I love to wear these bracelets made of shells is because they remind me of the sea. We come from the sea, right? We're like a bucket, we have our shape, and we're still seawater. And someday we're going to go back in the ocean. Will I live in the sea for a while and then come back again as another bucket? Or do I actually stay in the same bucket? I have no idea. But I see it as this real fluid continuity." —A

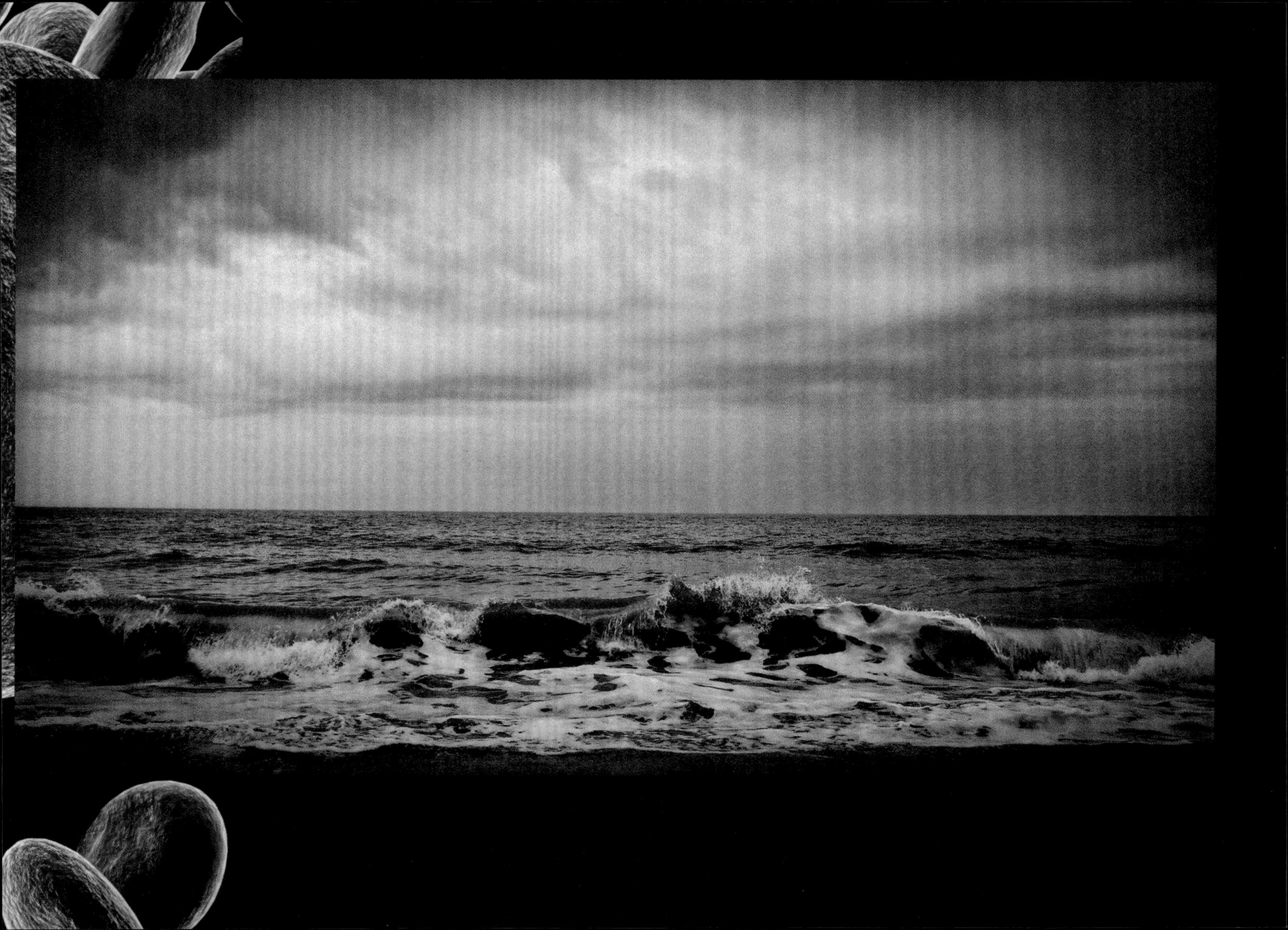

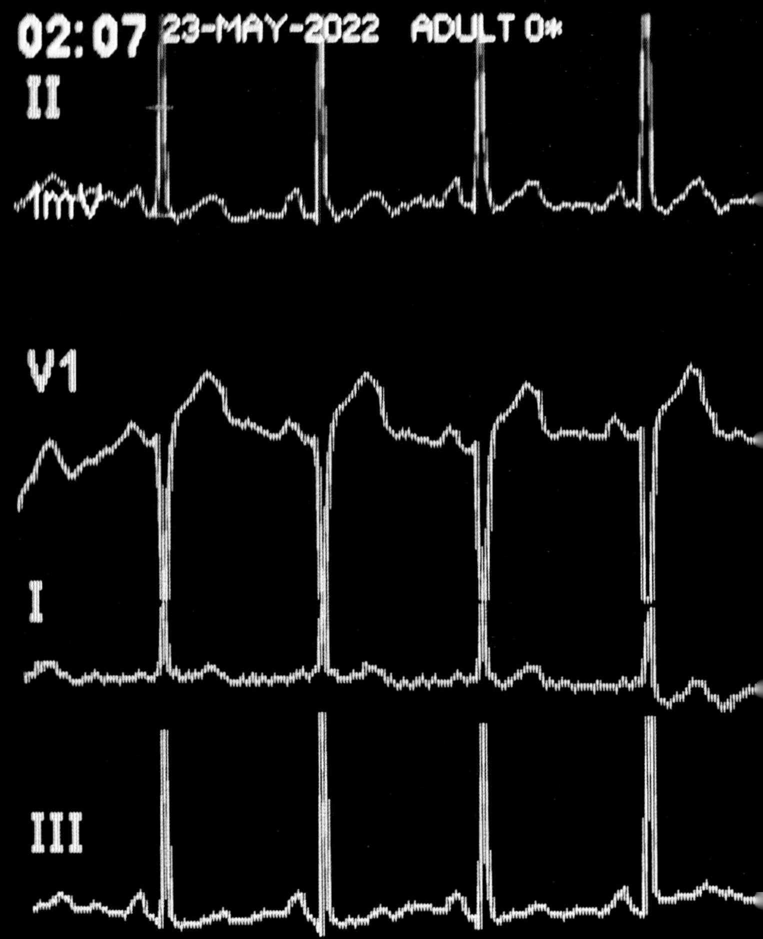
02:07 23-MAY-2022 ADULT 0*
II
1mV
V1
I
III

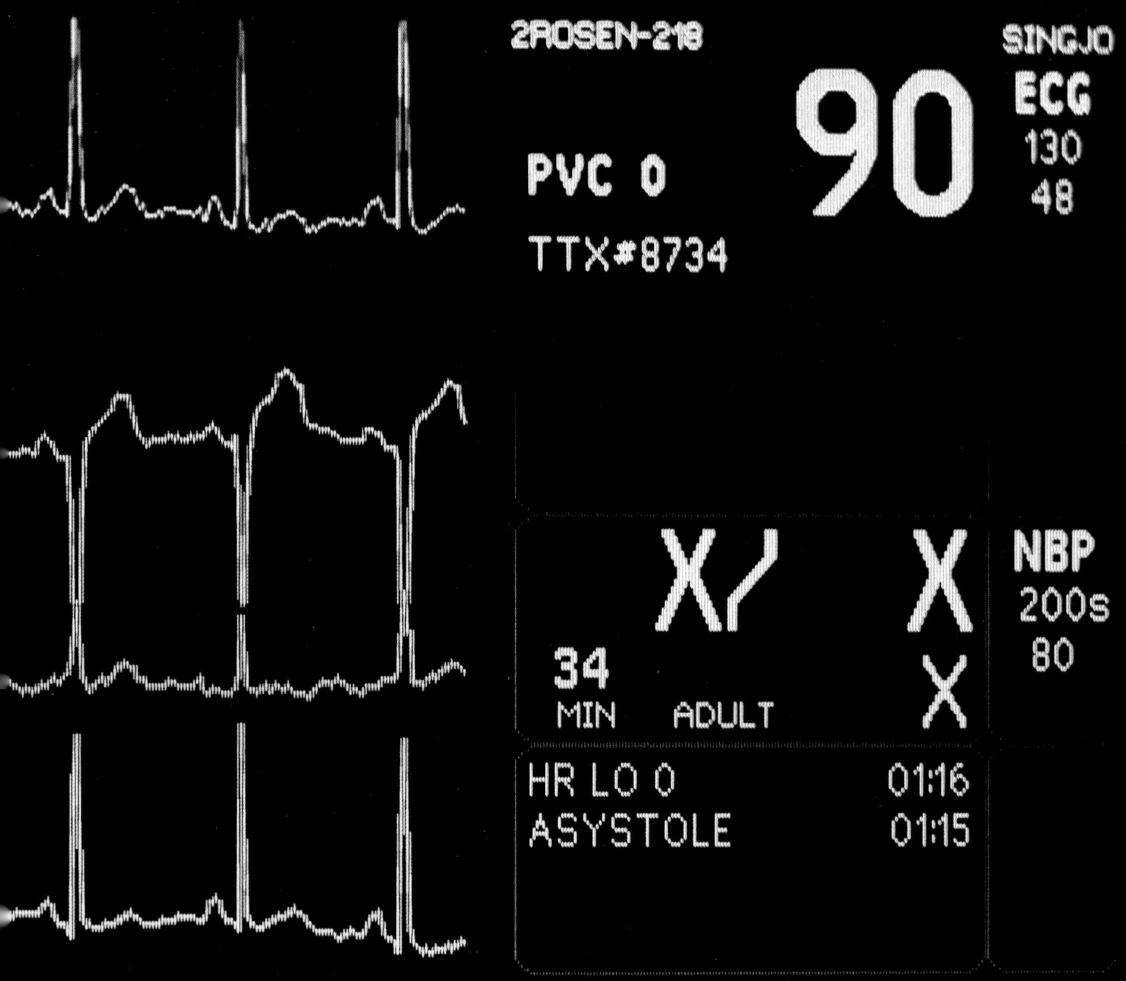
2ROSEN-218
SINGJO
PVC 0
90
ECG
130
48
TTX#8734
X/
X
NBP
200s
80
34
MIN
ADULT
X
HR LO 0
01:16
ASYSTOLE
01:15

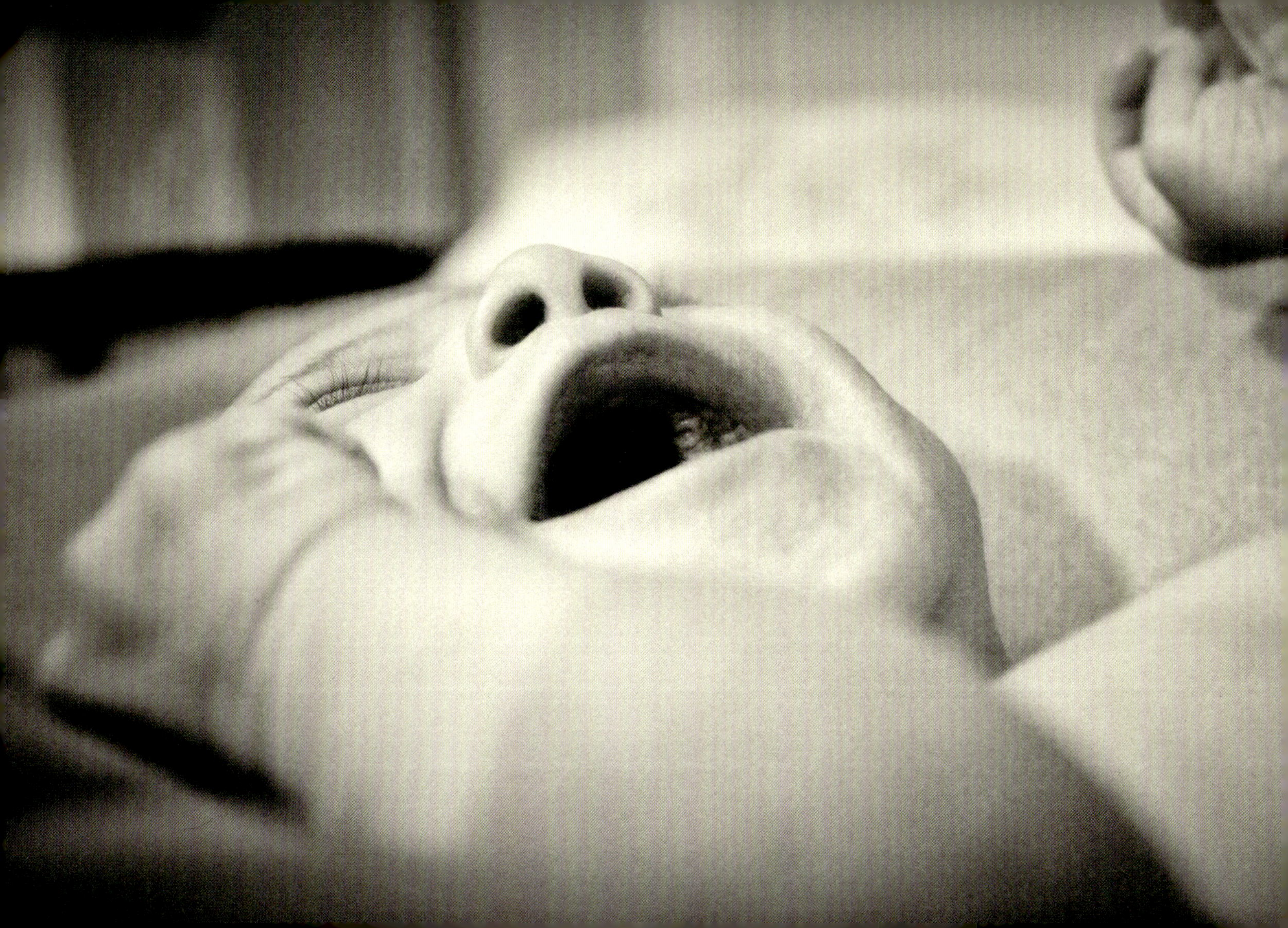

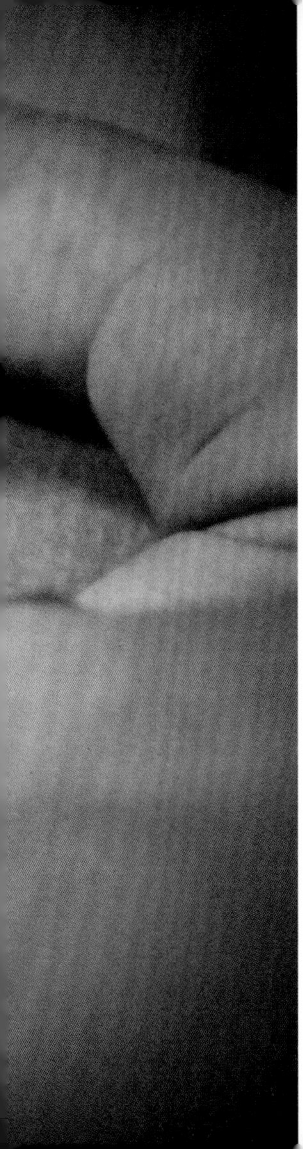

"My earliest memory was more of an experience. It was far more abstract than a memory; it was this sensation of being weightless, suspended in a pale blue light." —JS

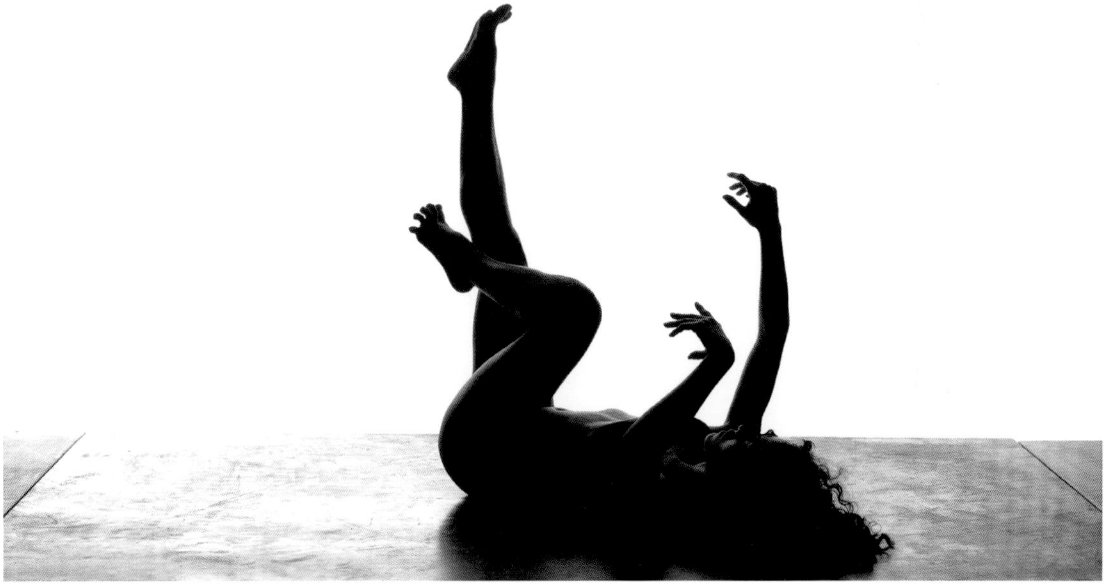

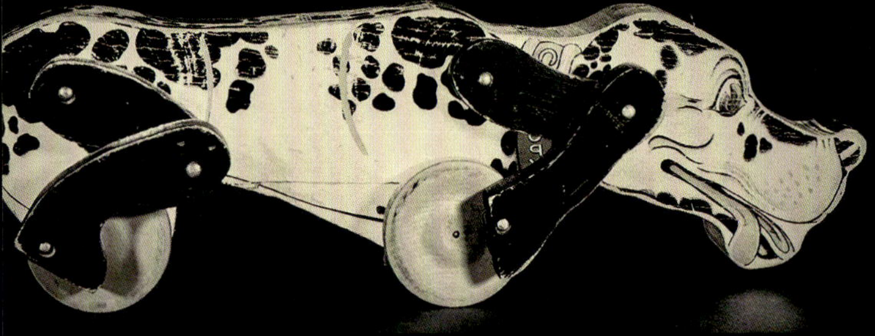

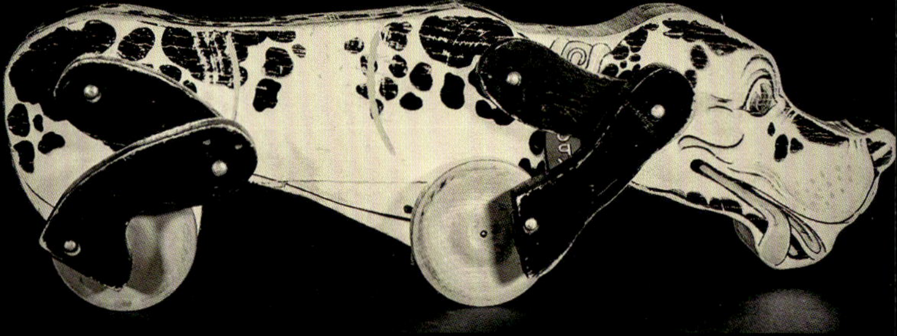

“I really wanted to become a theoretical physicist when I was a kid.

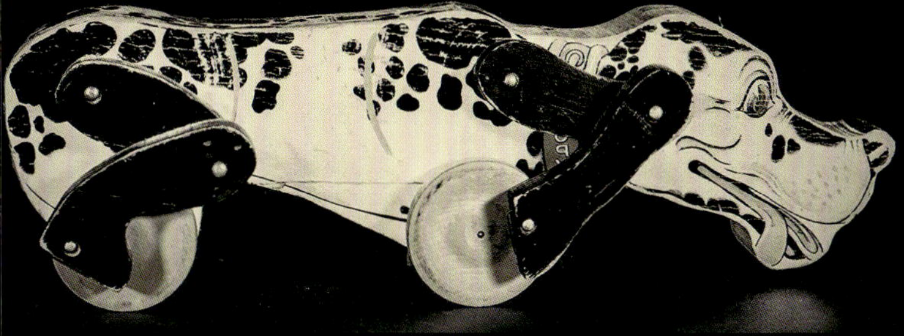

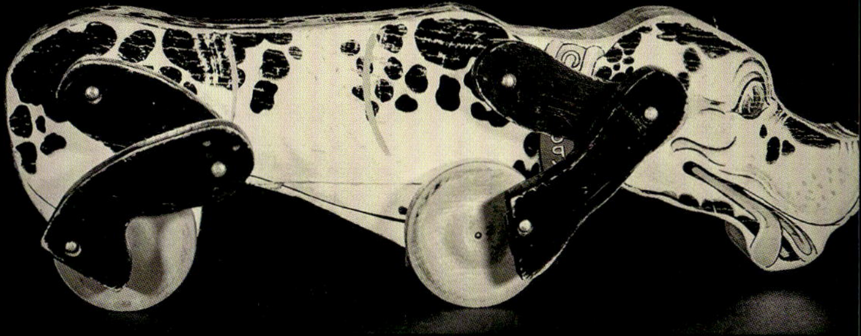

I found that combination of mastery over physics and mathematics together to be extremely fascinating and deeply meaningful."—G

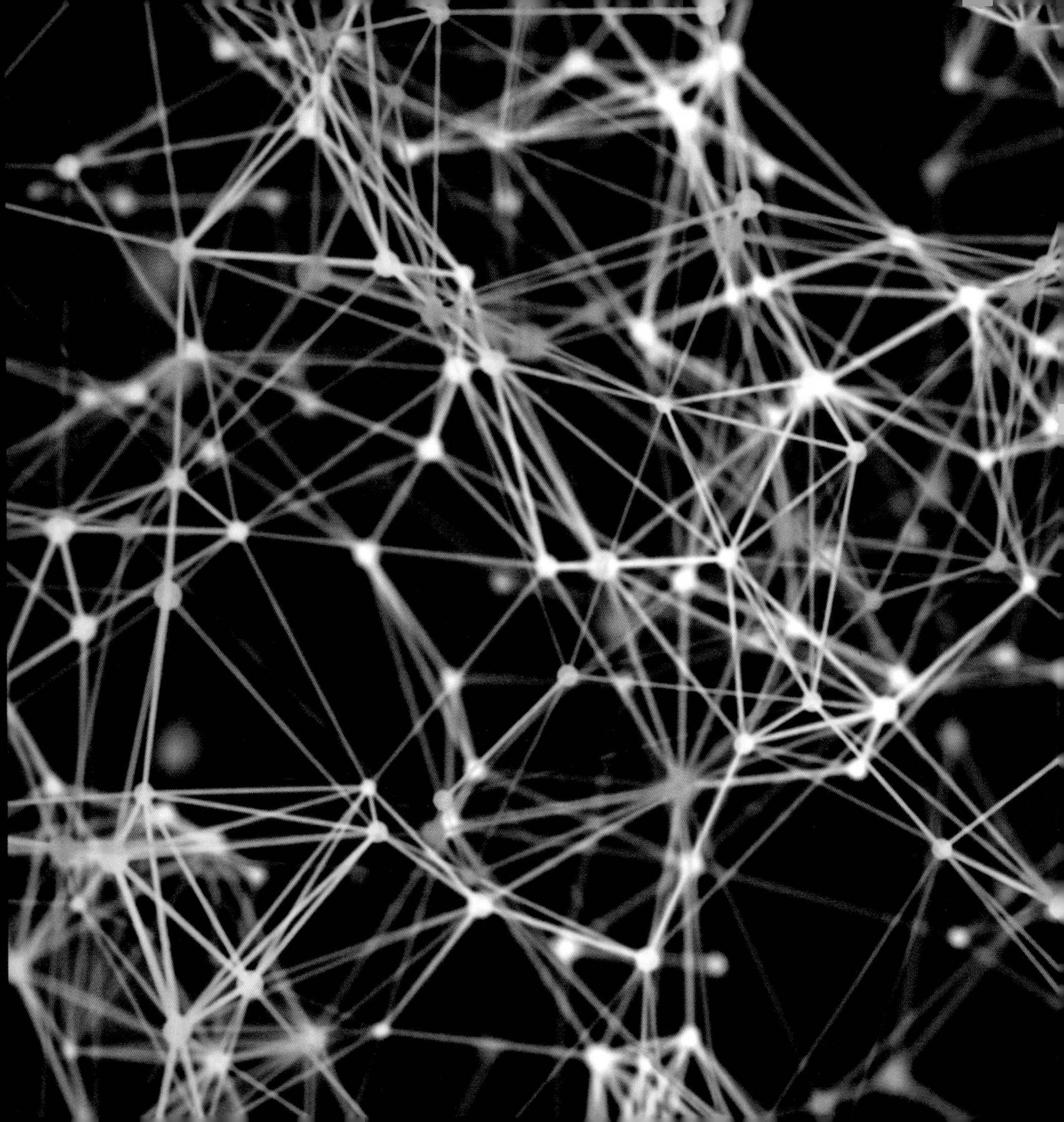

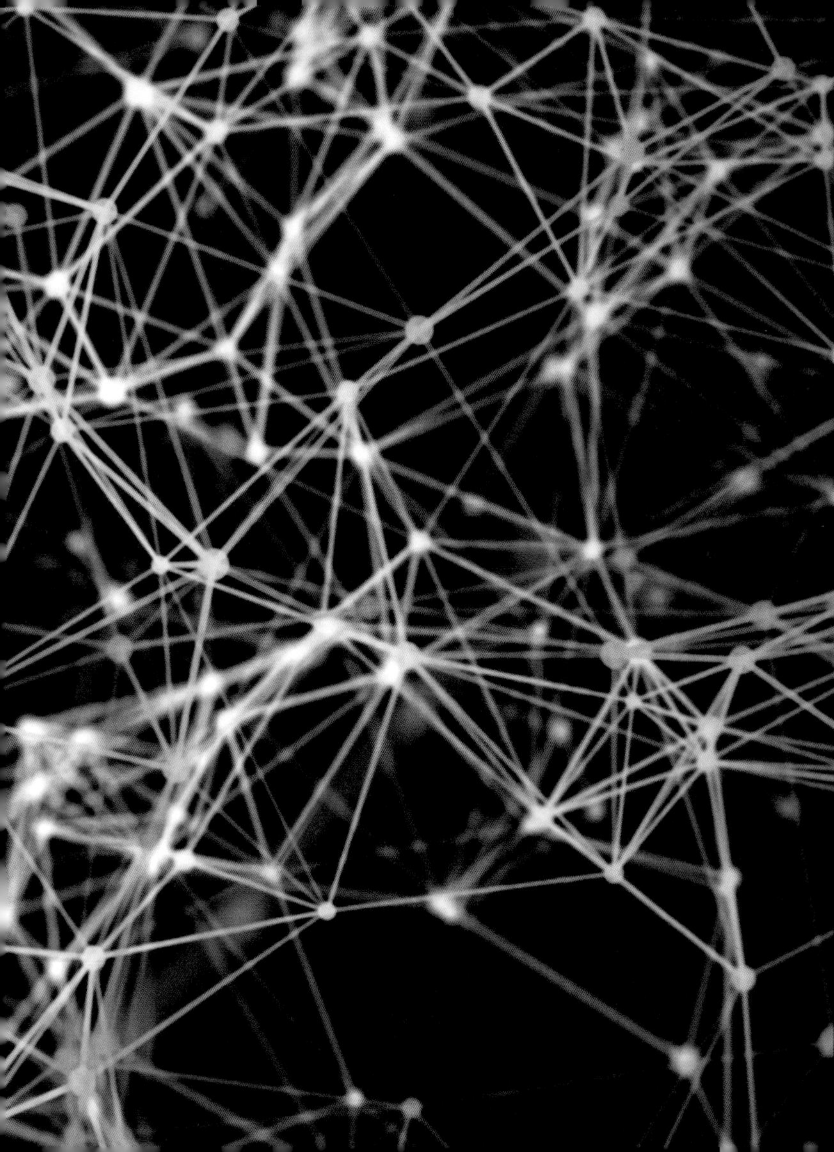

"I didn't really envision what I wanted to be or do with my life when I was a child. All I knew was that I wanted to escape. I remember staring at a painting that my parents had on the wall and thinking, 'Someday I'm going to look at the painting and I'm going to be in a different place.' I just really wanted to be away from there."

—A

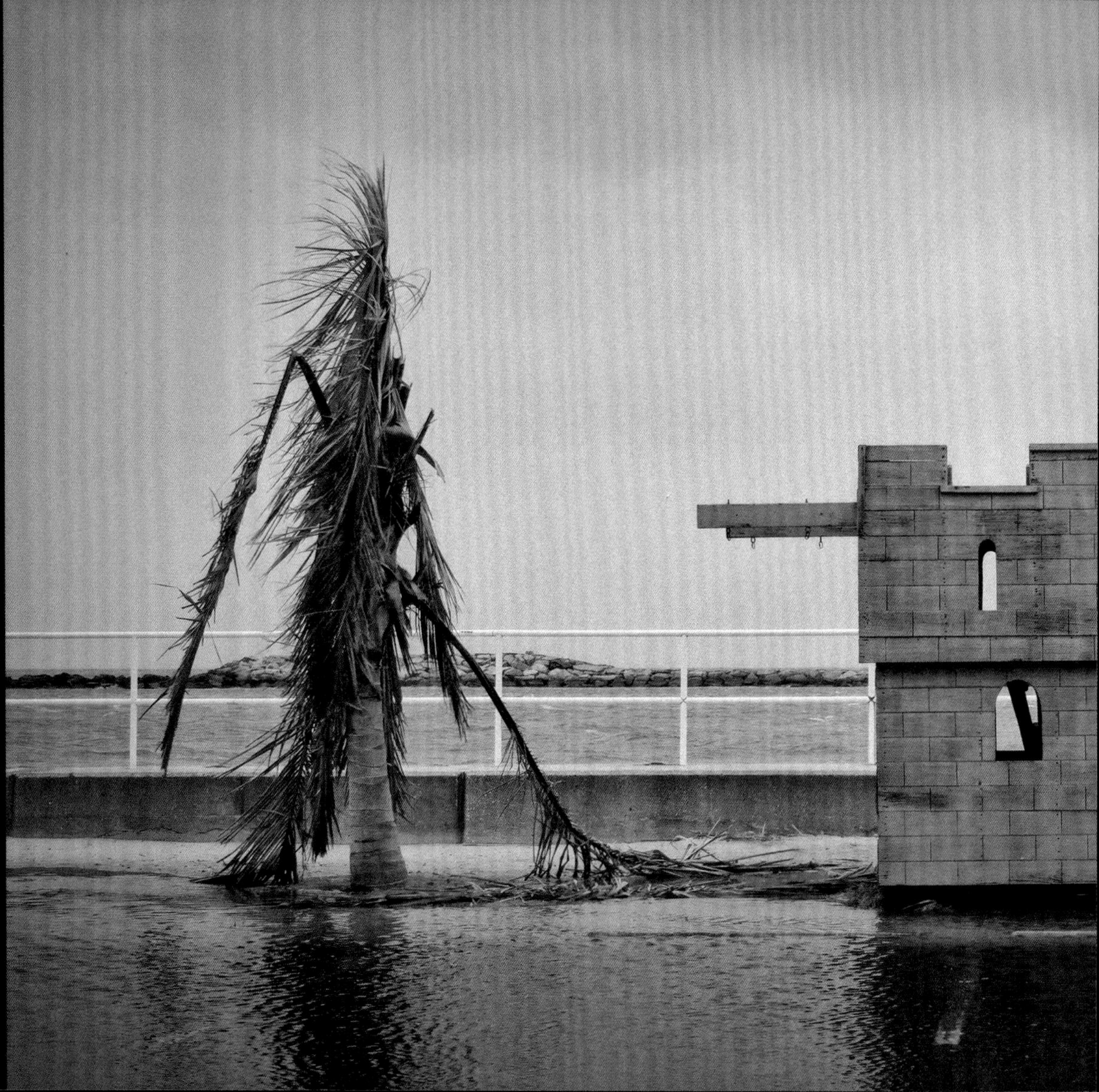

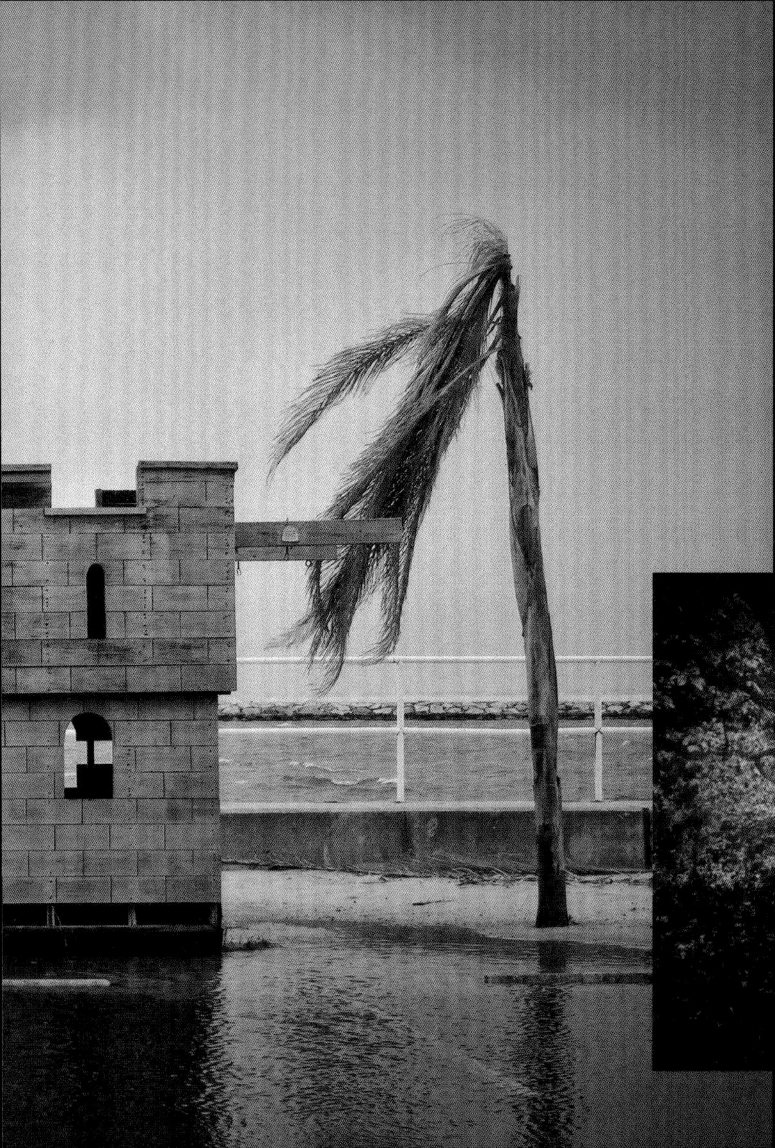
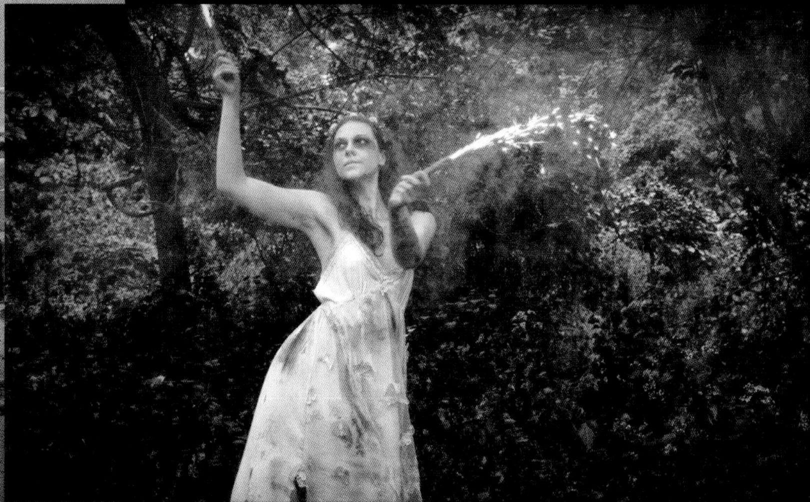

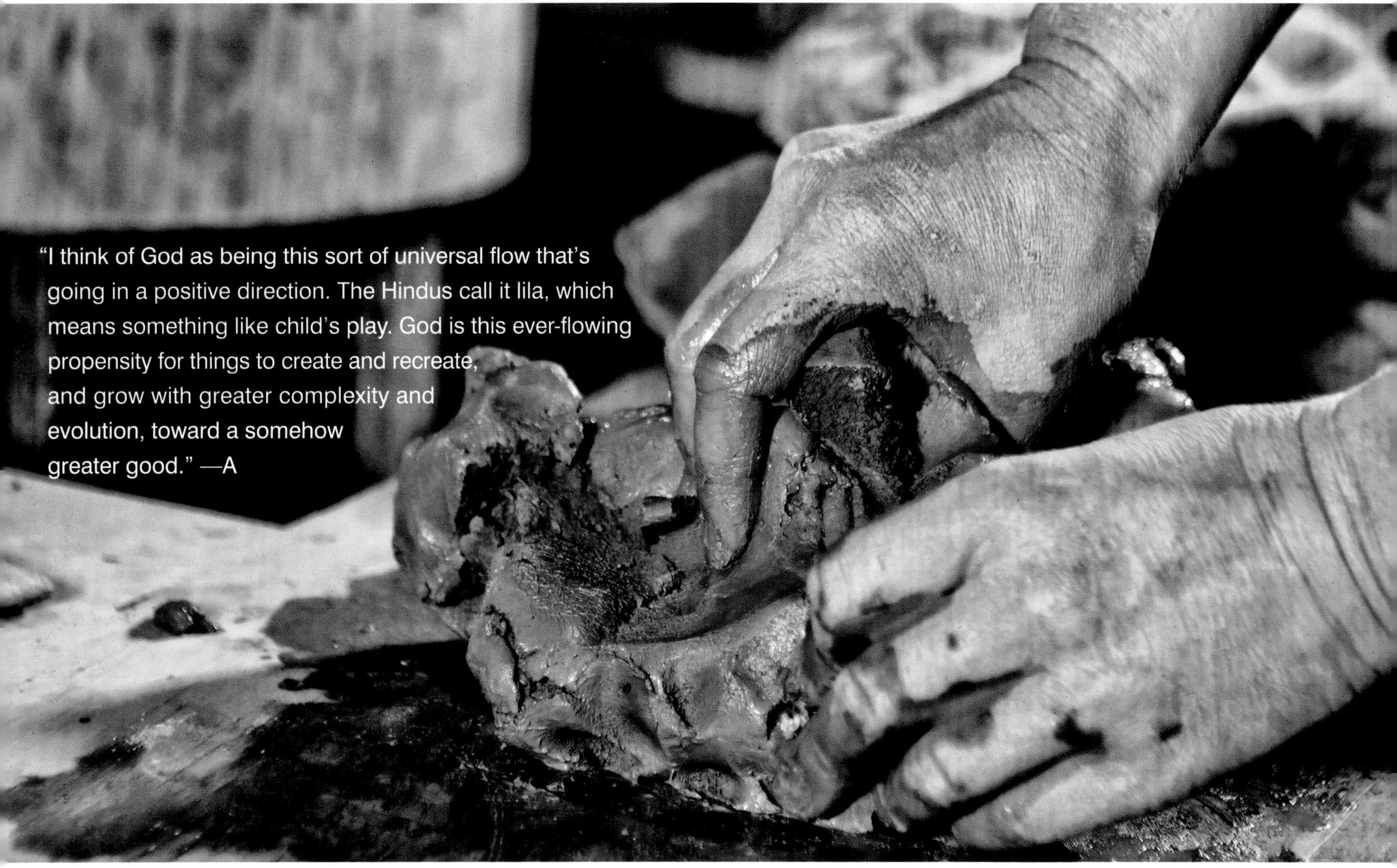

"I think of God as being this sort of universal flow that's going in a positive direction. The Hindus call it lila, which means something like child's play. God is this ever-flowing propensity for things to create and recreate, and grow with greater complexity and evolution, toward a somehow greater good." —A

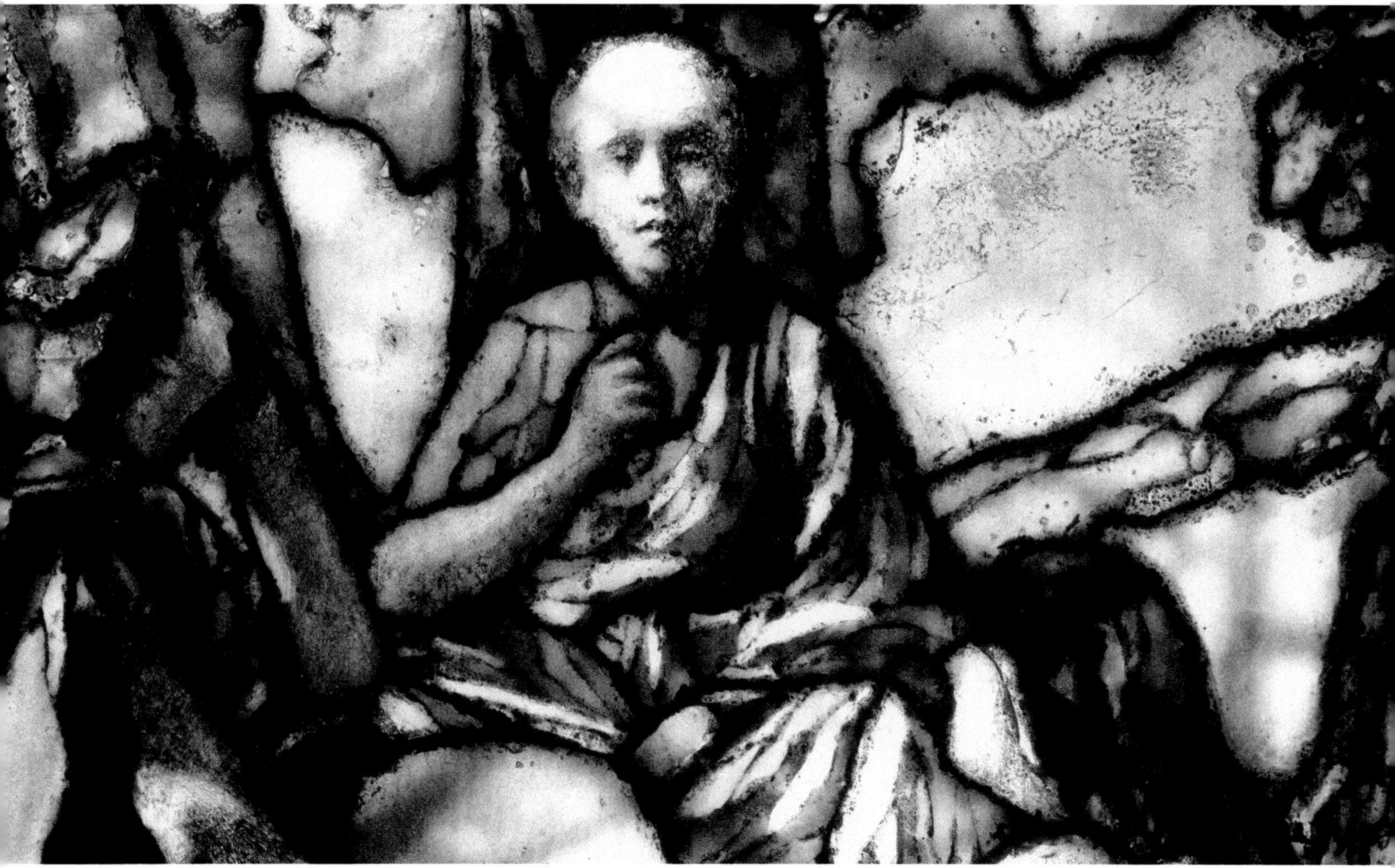

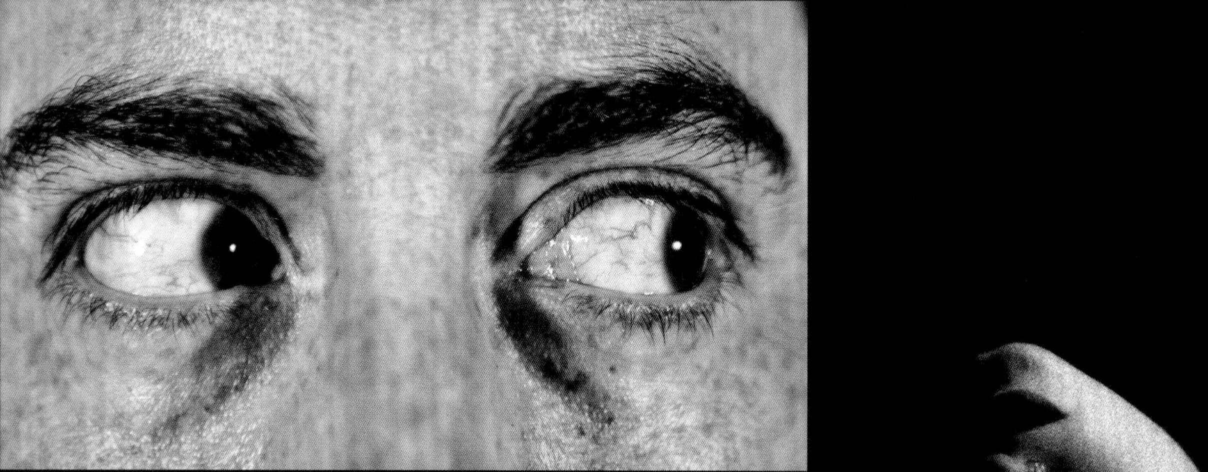

"Young love—that's probably the most beautiful thing I've ever experienced." —CR

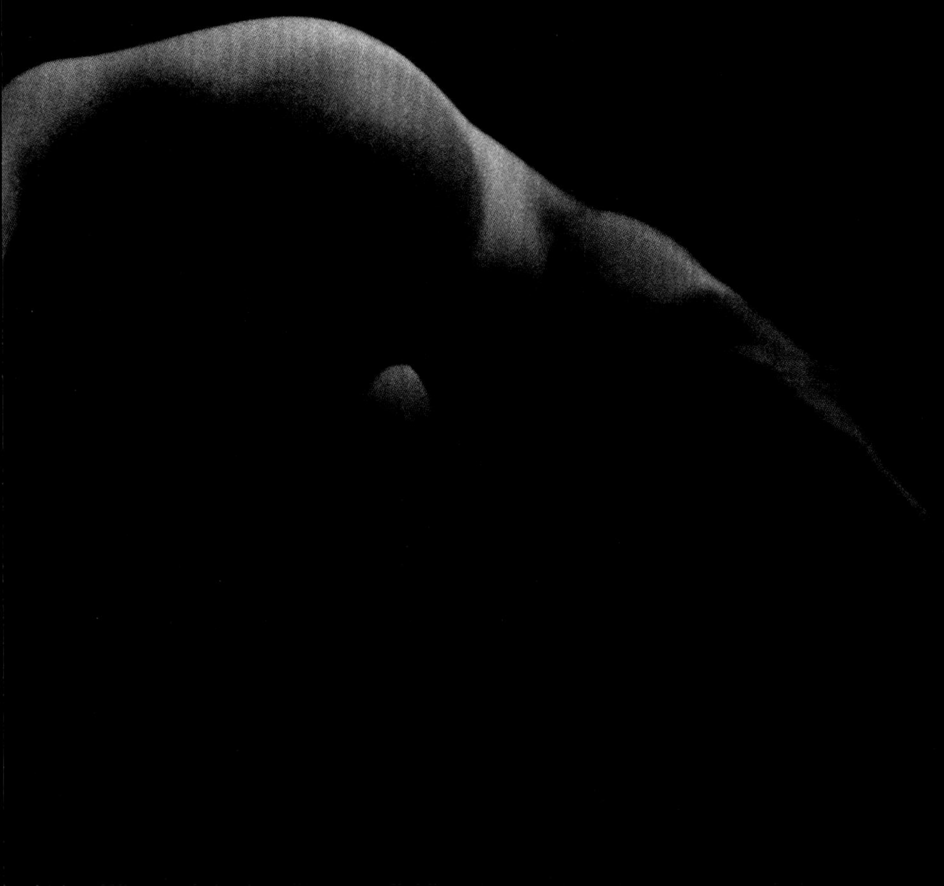

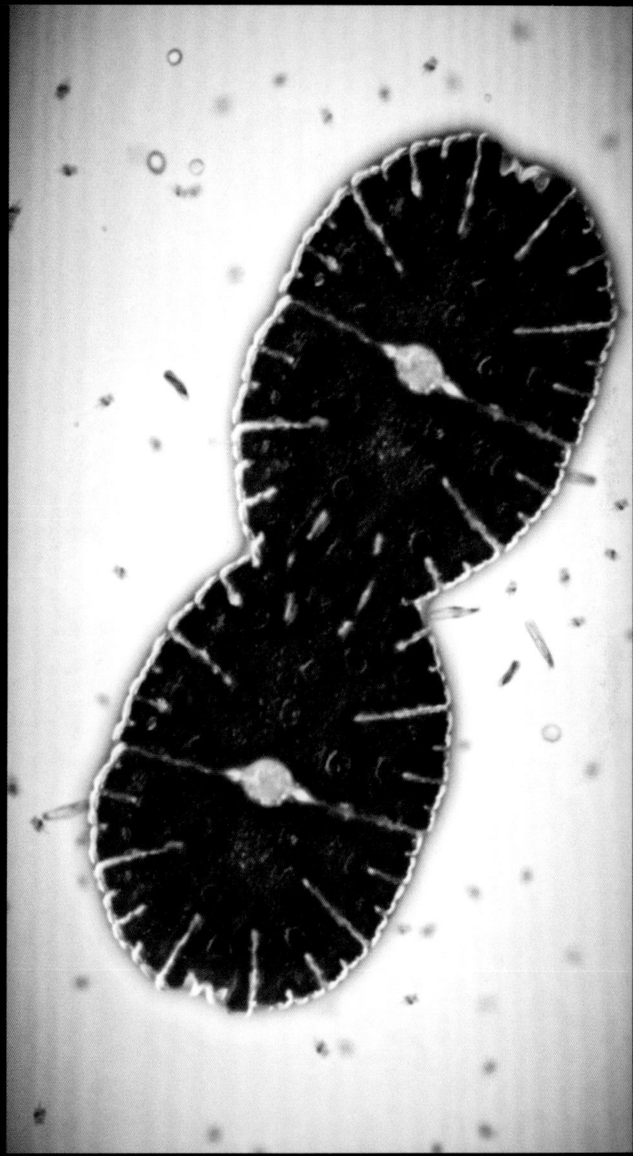

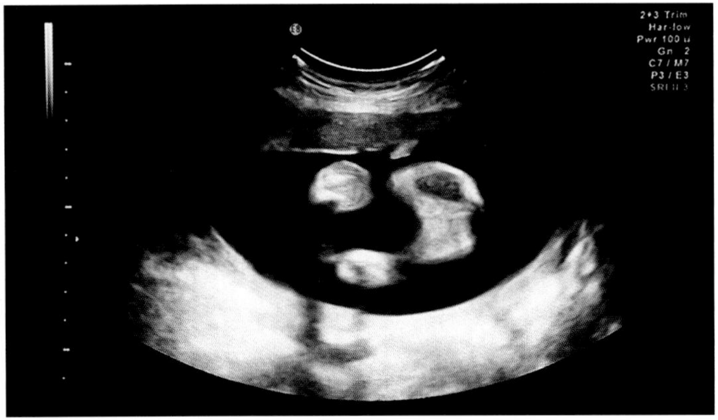
2+3 Trim
Har-low
Gn 2
C7 / M7
P3 / E3

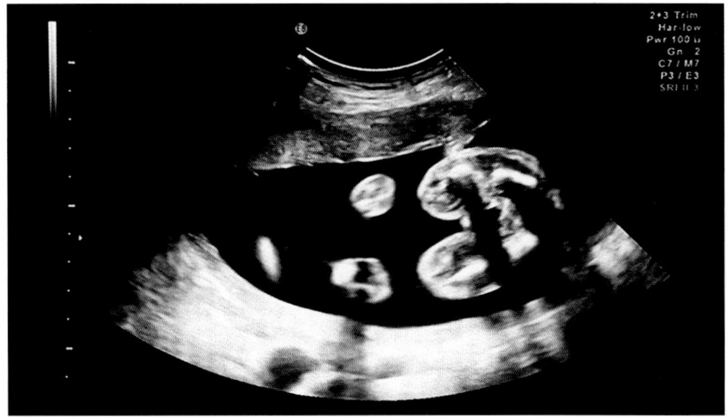
2+3 Trim
Har-low
Gn 2
C7 / M7
P3 / E3

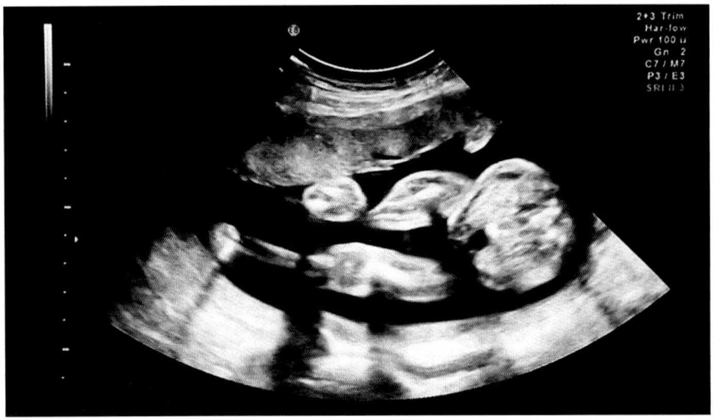
2+3 Trim
Har-low
Gn 2
C7 / M7
P3 / E3

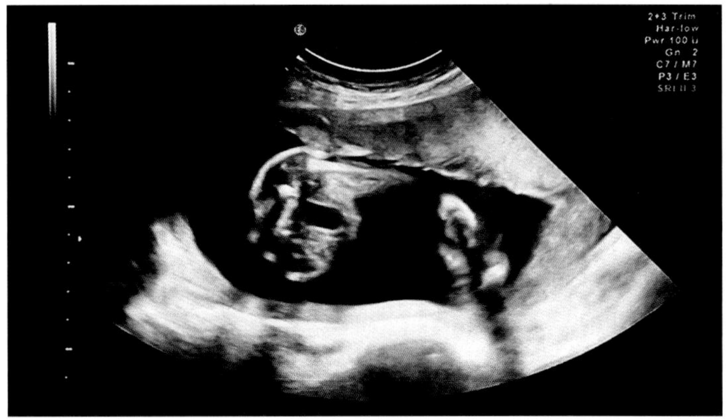
2+3 Trim
Har-low
Gn 2
C7 / M7
P3 / E3

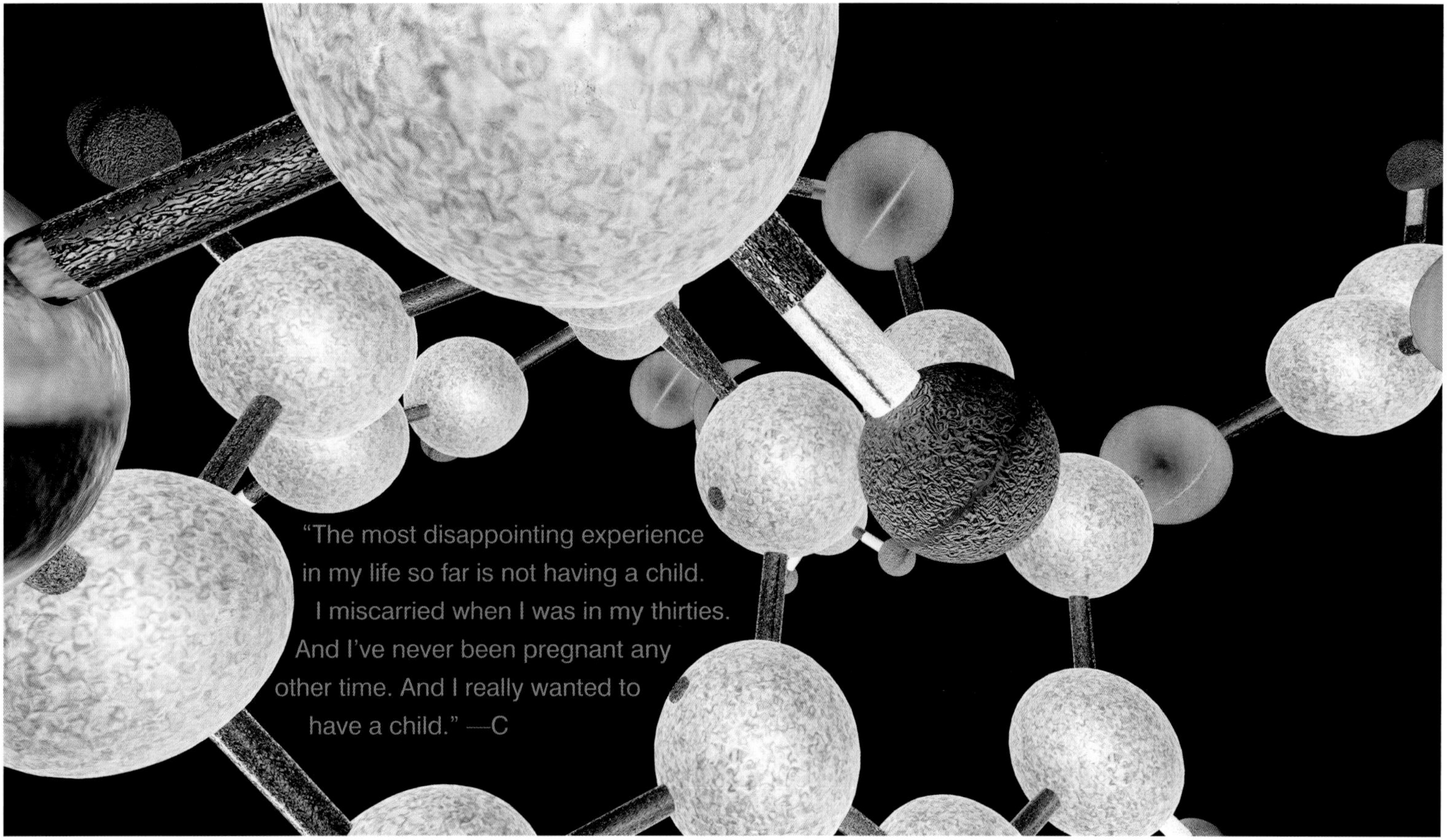

"The most disappointing experience in my life so far is not having a child. I miscarried when I was in my thirties. And I've never been pregnant any other time. And I really wanted to have a child." —C

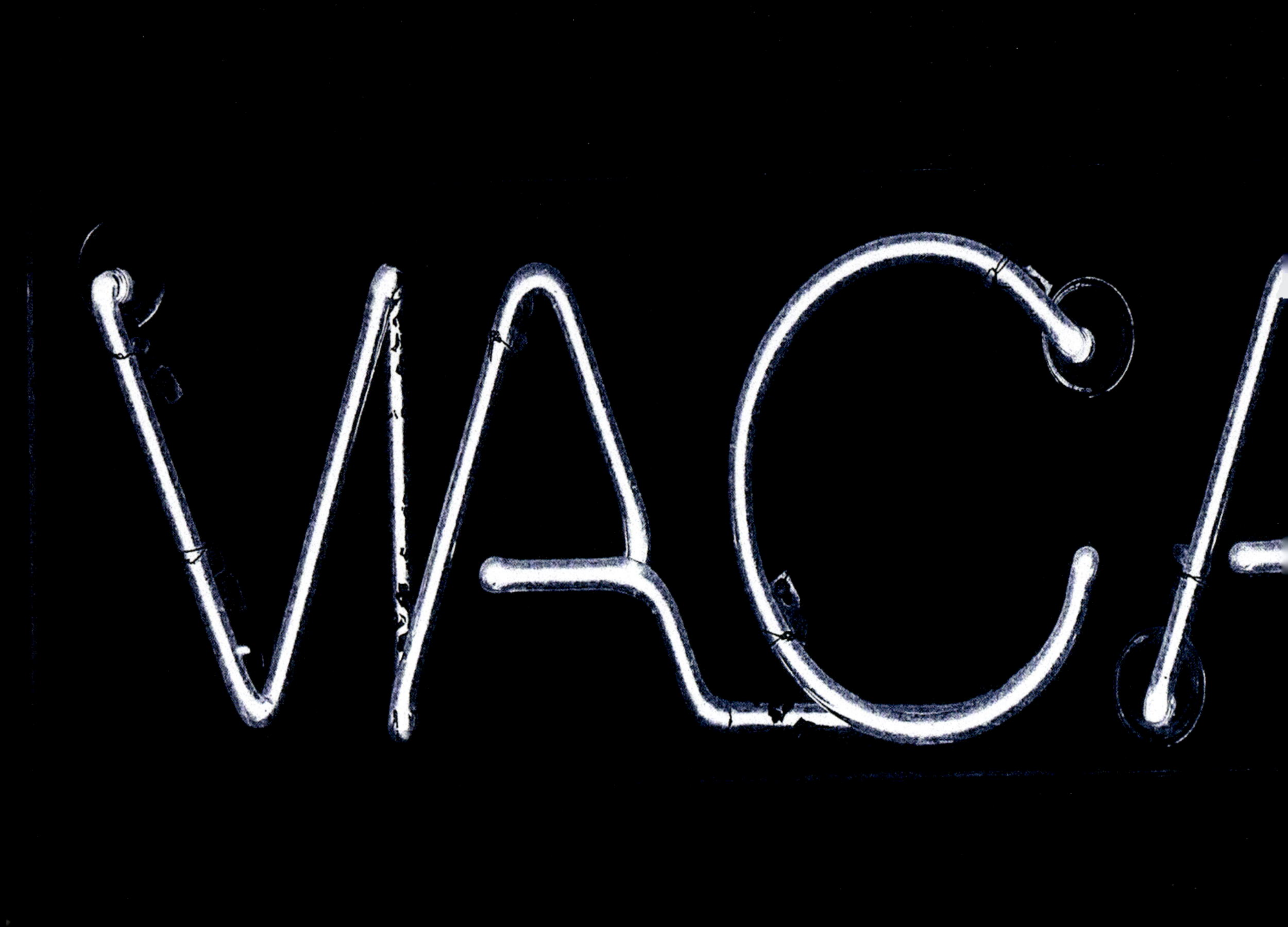
VAC

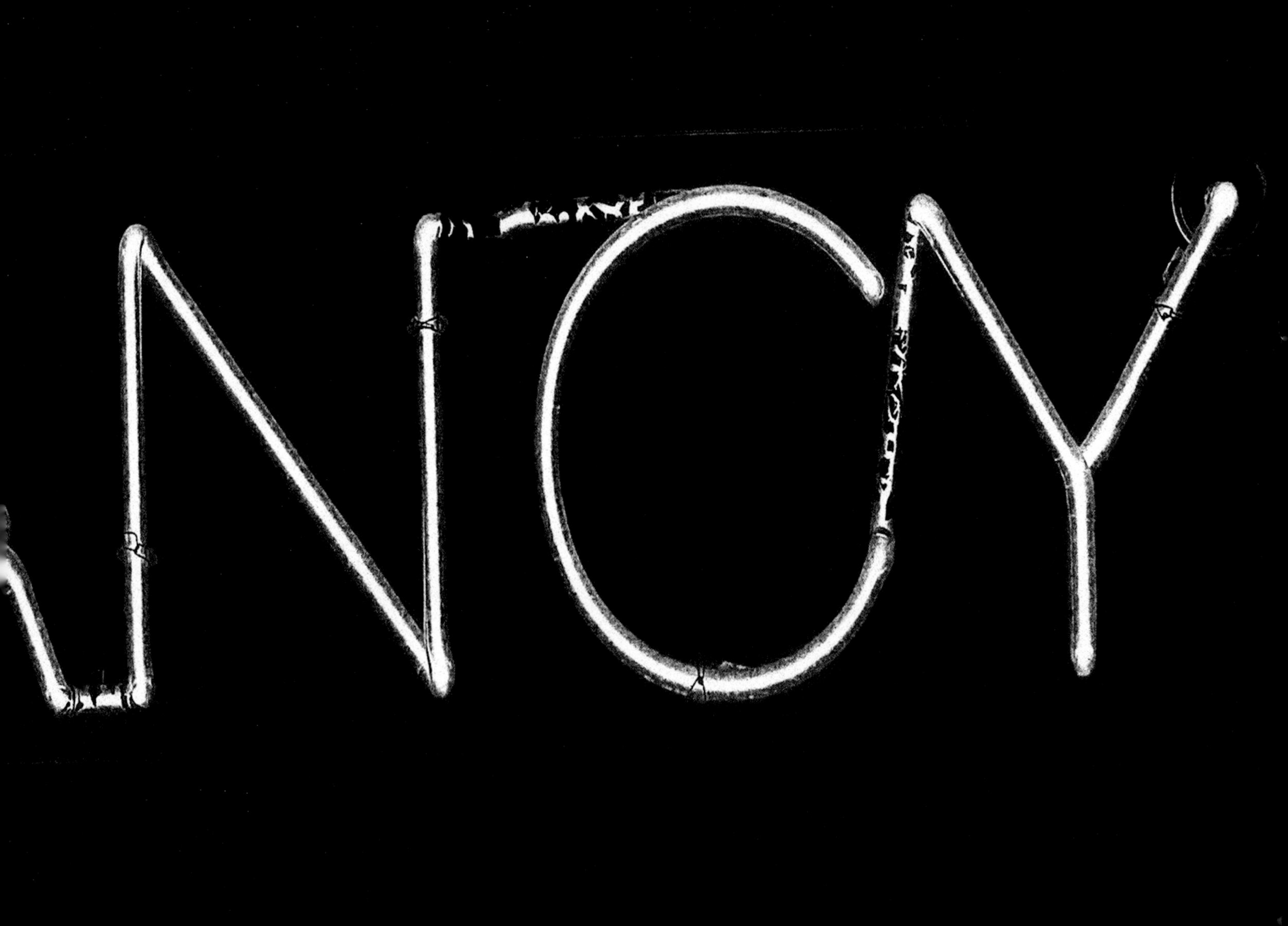
NOY

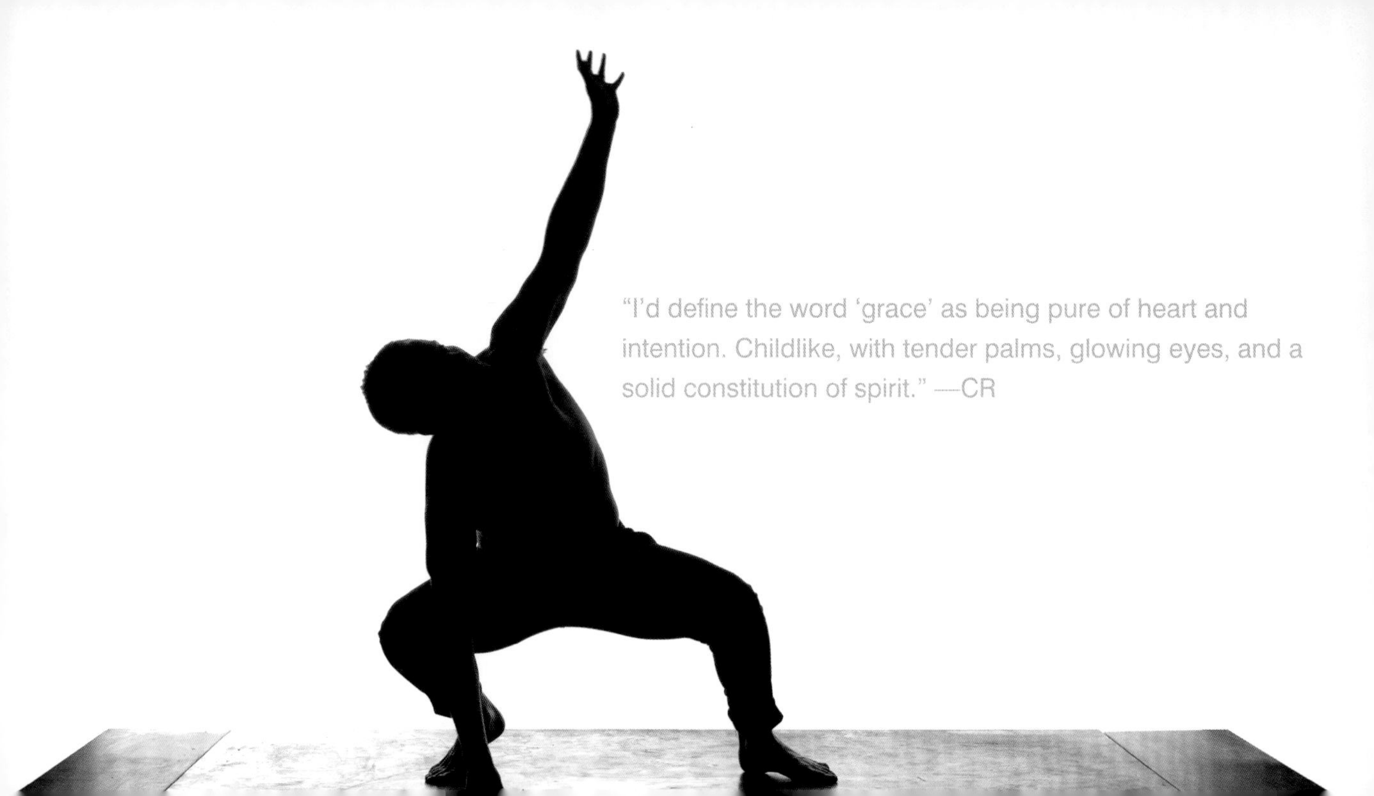

"I'd define the word 'grace' as being pure of heart and intention. Childlike, with tender palms, glowing eyes, and a solid constitution of spirit." —CR

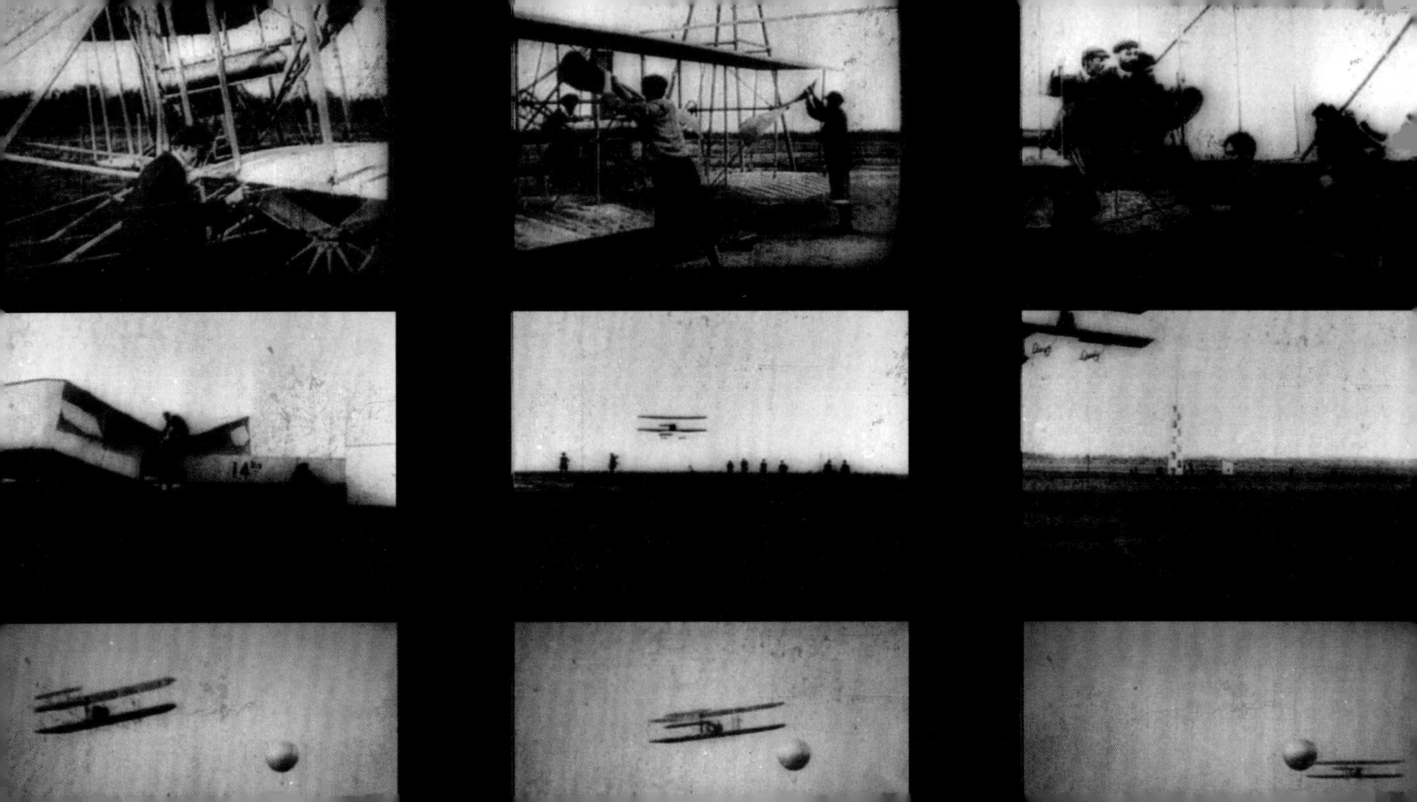

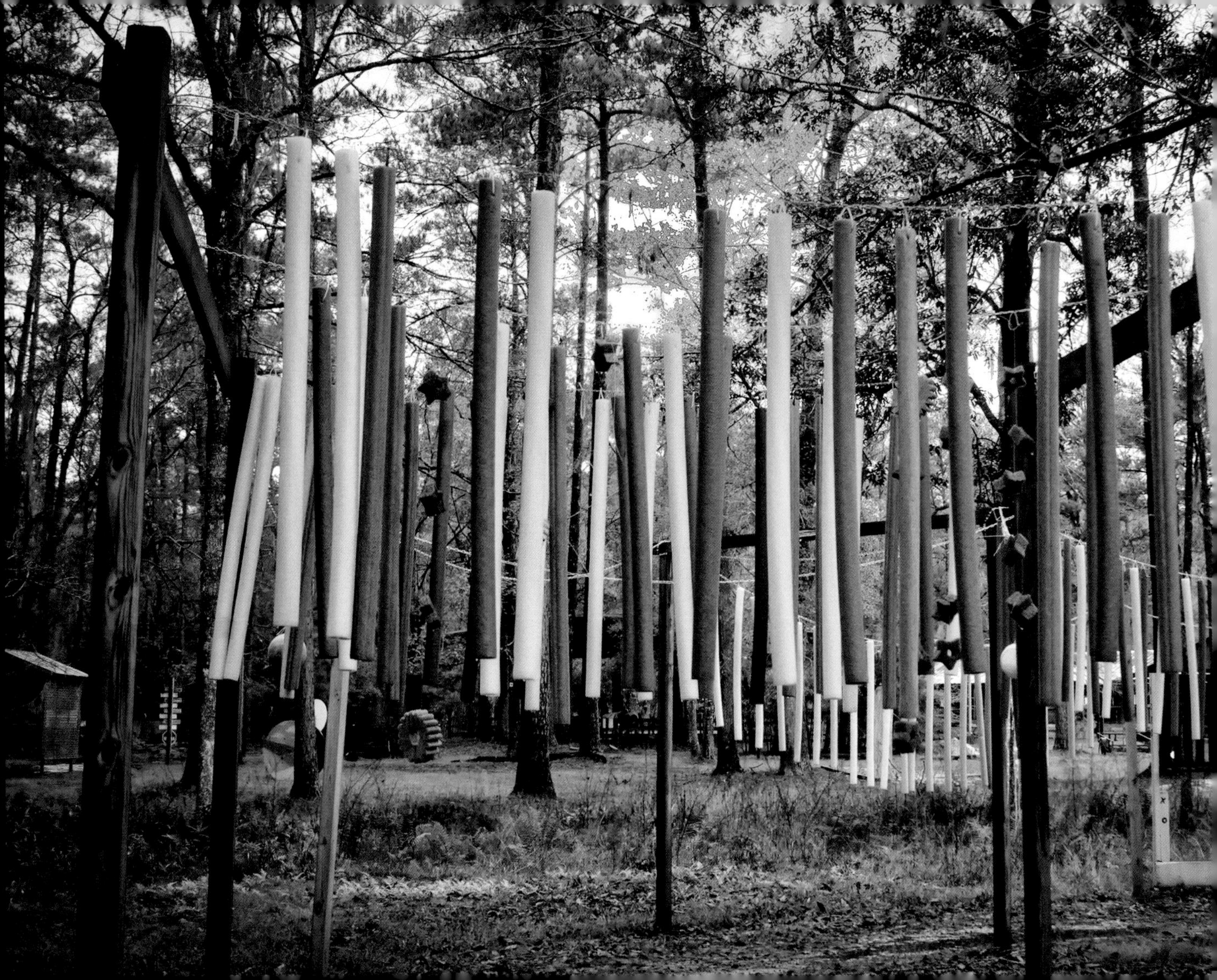

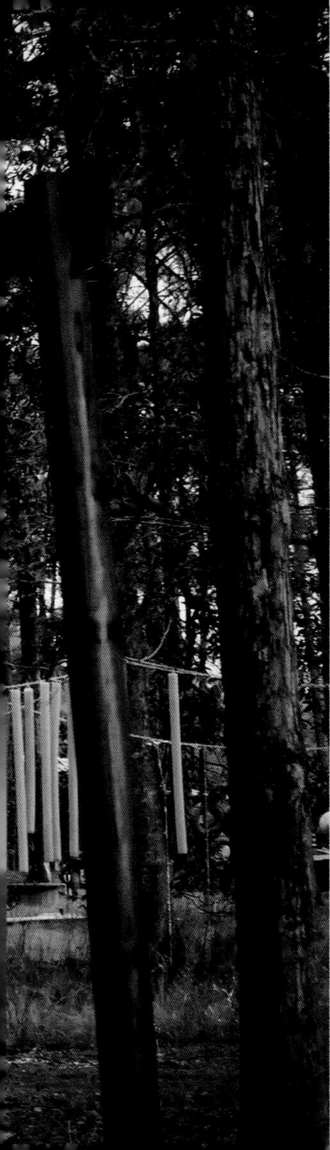

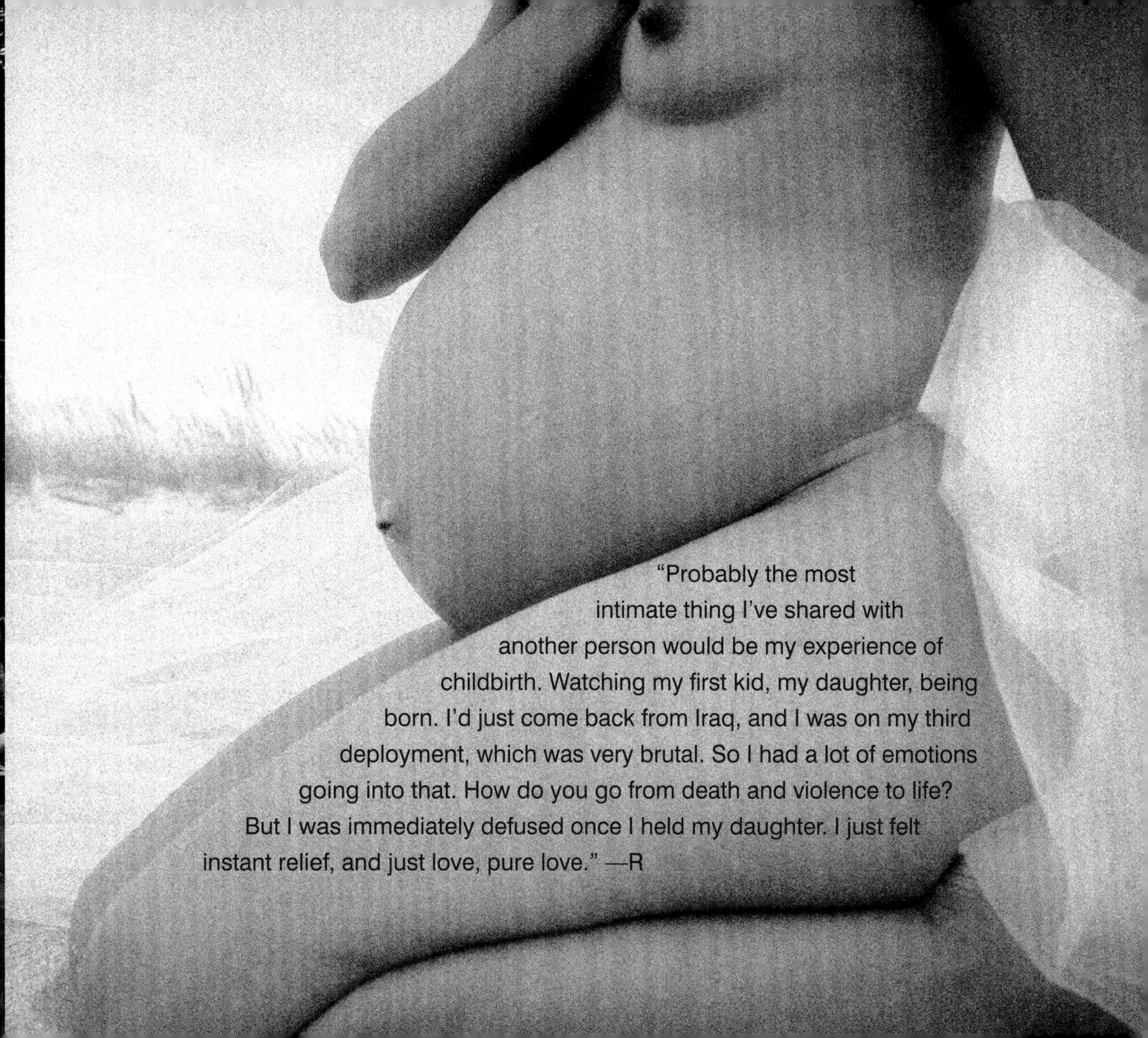

"Probably the most intimate thing I've shared with another person would be my experience of childbirth. Watching my first kid, my daughter, being born. I'd just come back from Iraq, and I was on my third deployment, which was very brutal. So I had a lot of emotions going into that. How do you go from death and violence to life? But I was immediately defused once I held my daughter. I just felt instant relief, and just love, pure love." —R

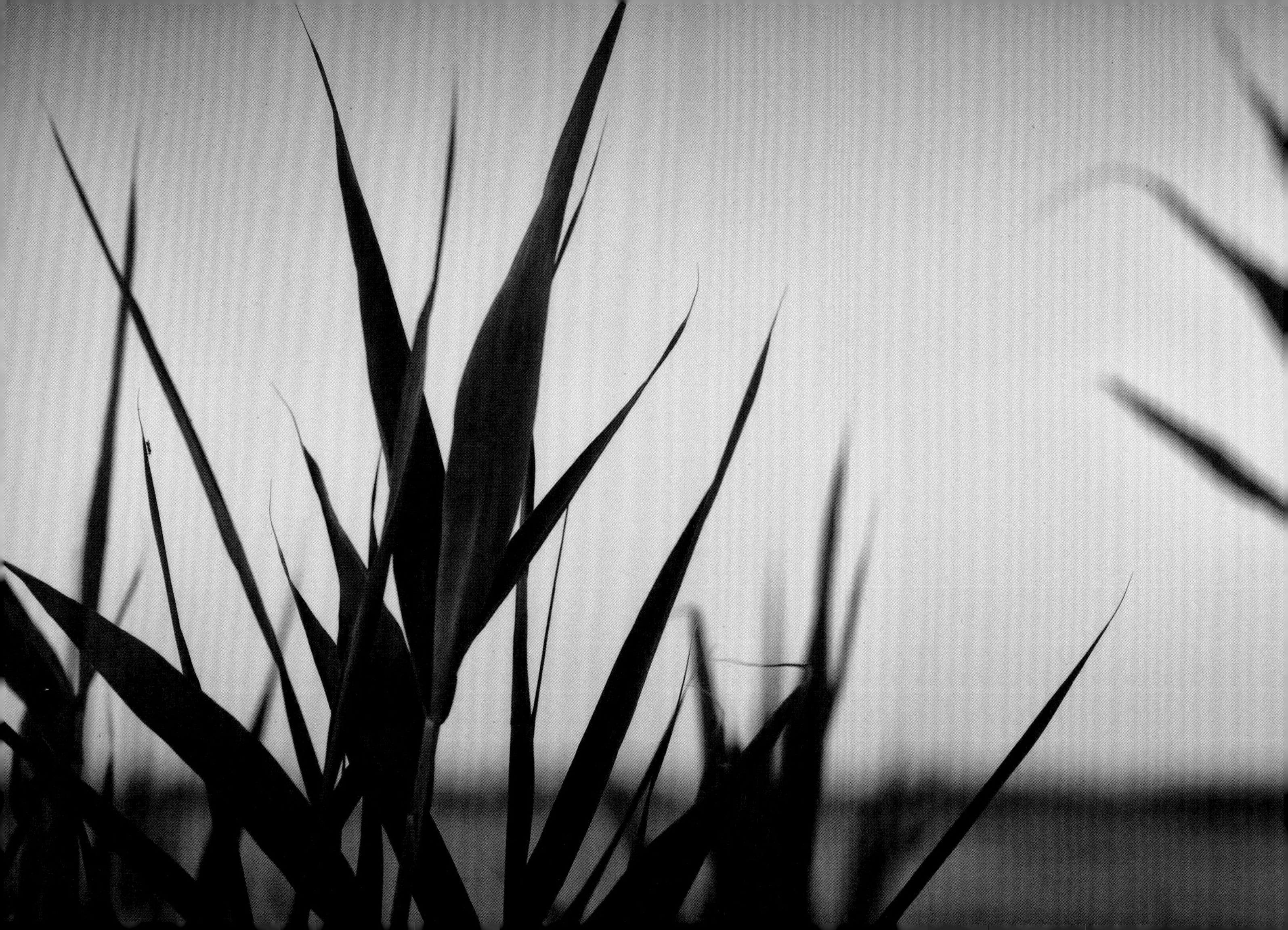

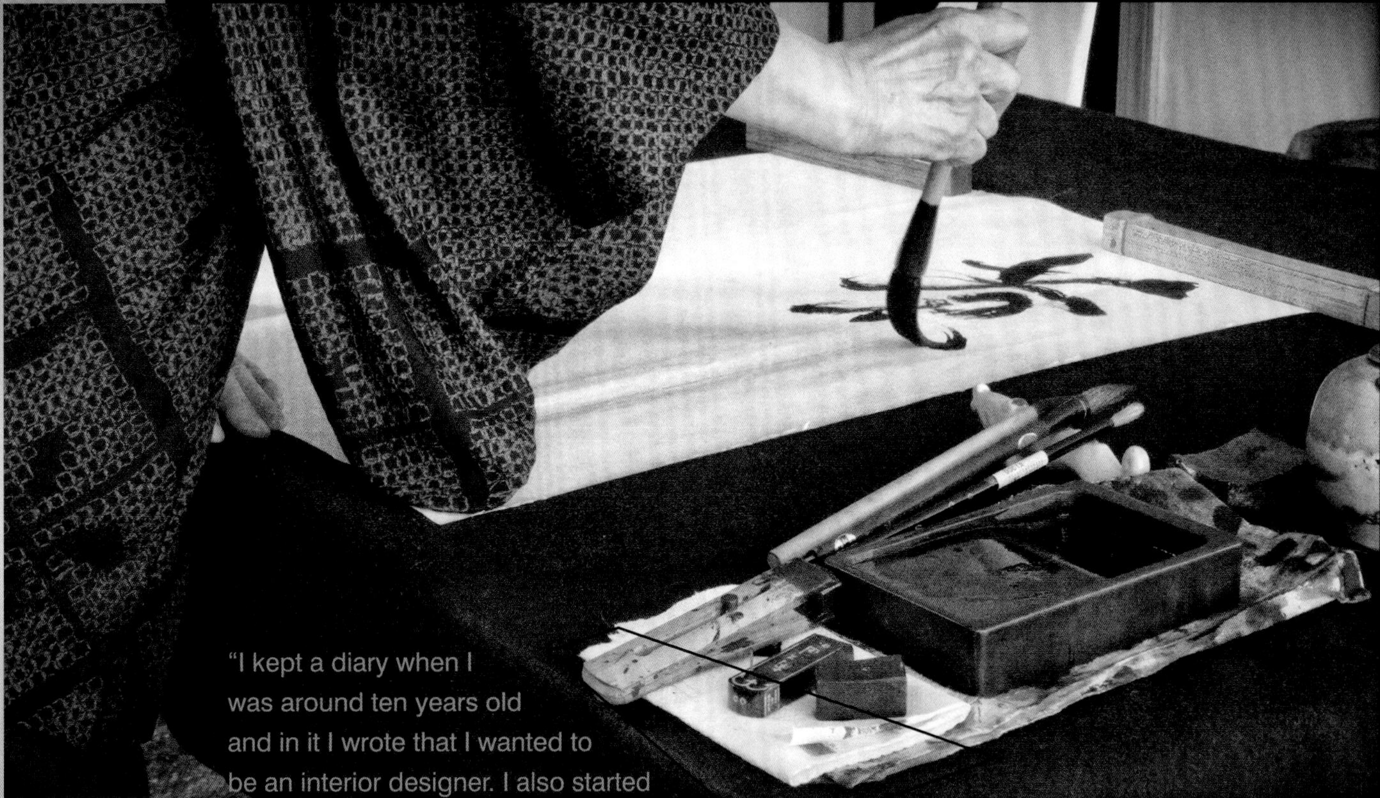

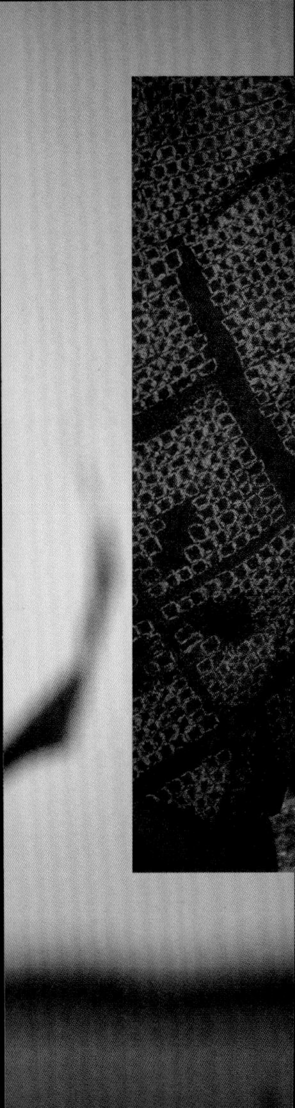

"I kept a diary when I was around ten years old and in it I wrote that I wanted to be an interior designer. I also started really liking boys around that time. So I was going to marry this guy called Andy and become an interior designer." —C

"My greatest sense of purpose in life comes from my children. I love being a mom and seeing my kids flourish and have them be vulnerable with me. Growing up, I could never talk to my mom about anything like my period. I'd steal my bras from the people I was babysitting for. But with my kids it's completely different. It's funny. And intimate. We can joke about things like that." —A

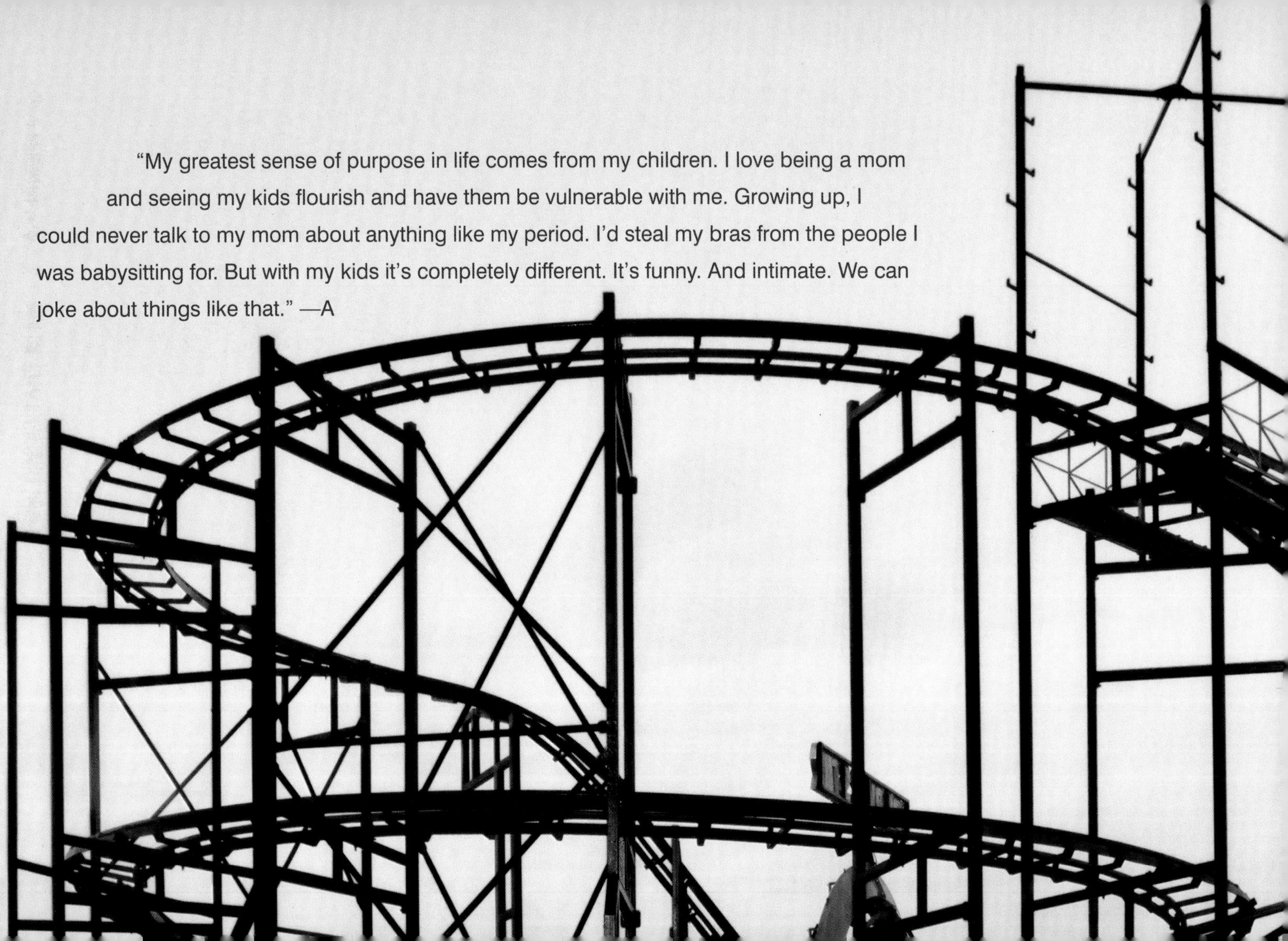

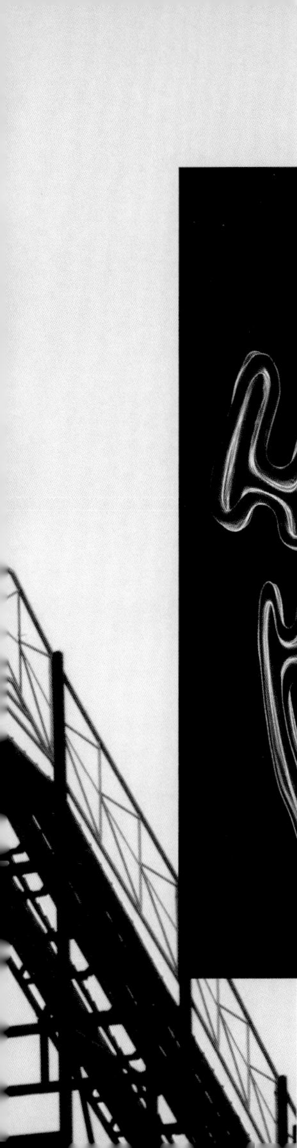

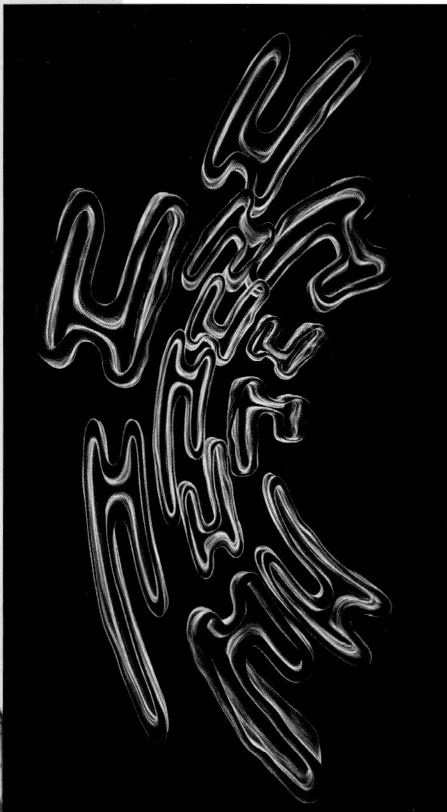

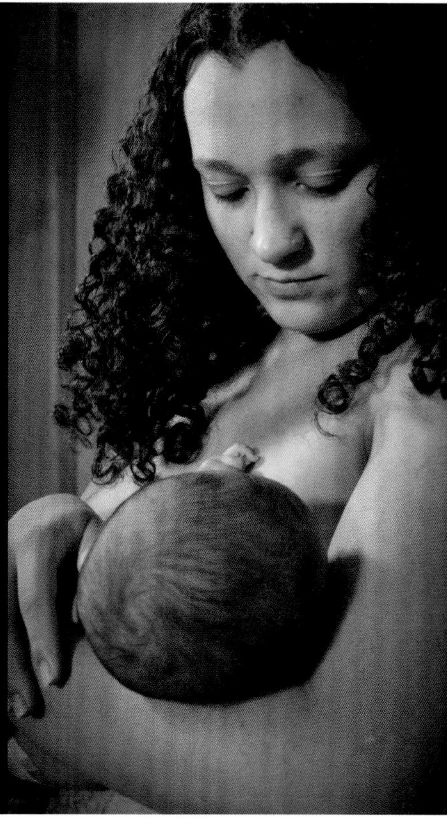

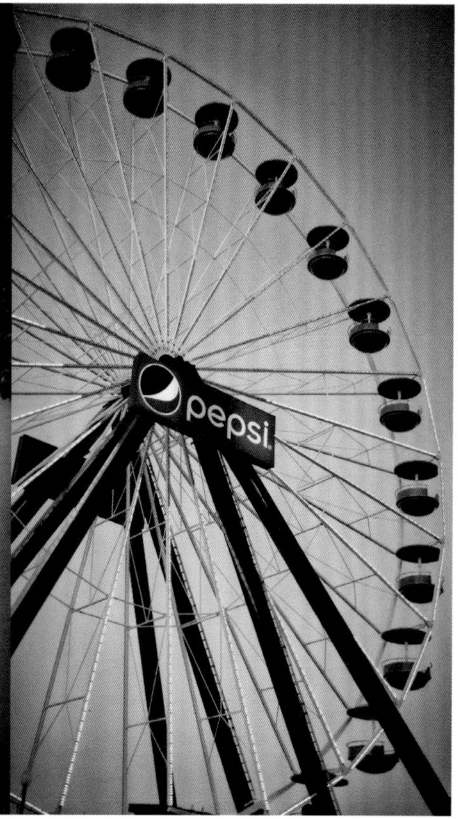
pepsi

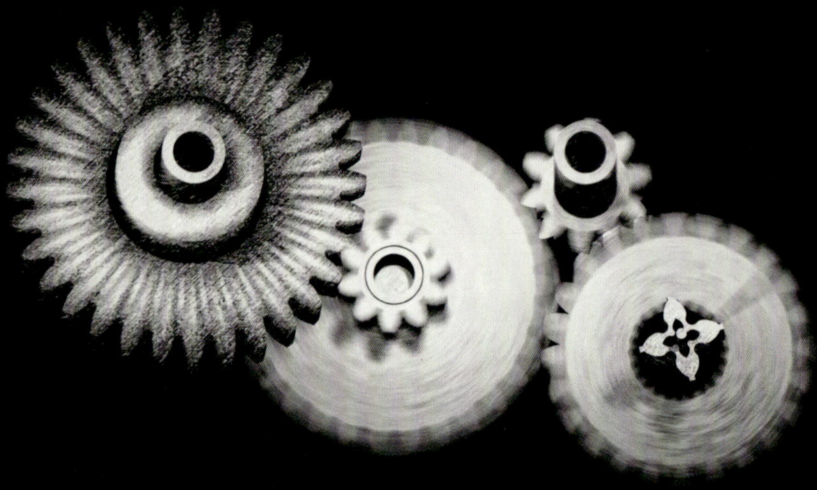

“When I was younger, my grandmother told me she’d had an out-of-body experience and that’s something that had a formative impact on the rest of my life. She told me about going into the light and hovering above the room and then hearing God’s voice, and that one story, that one experience she had gave me faith at times when I had none.” —CR

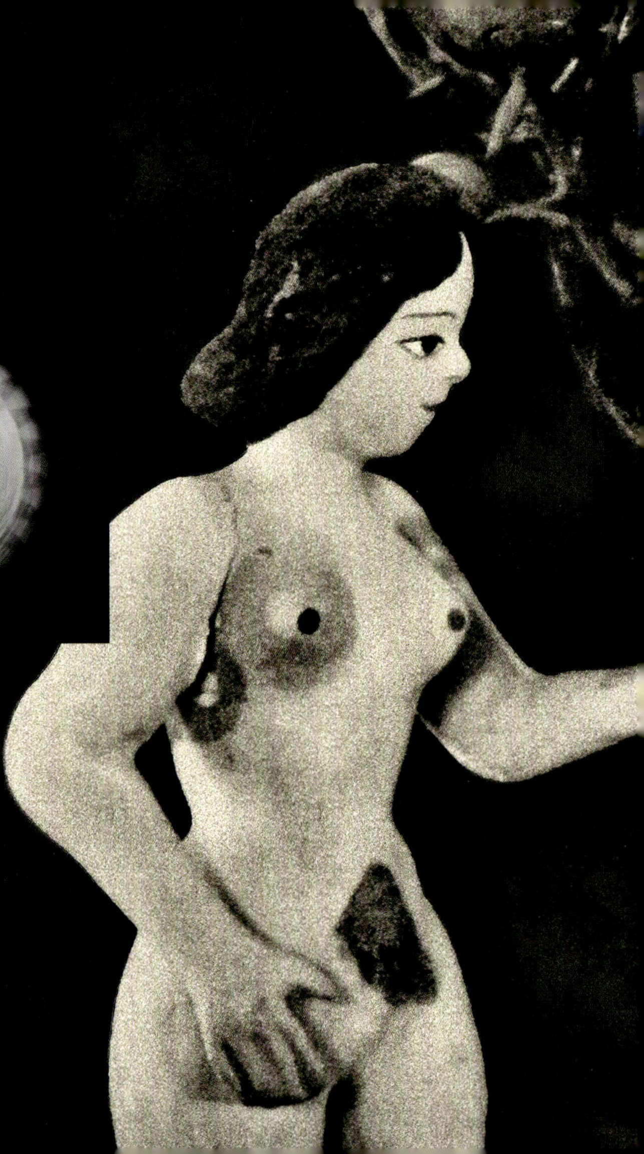

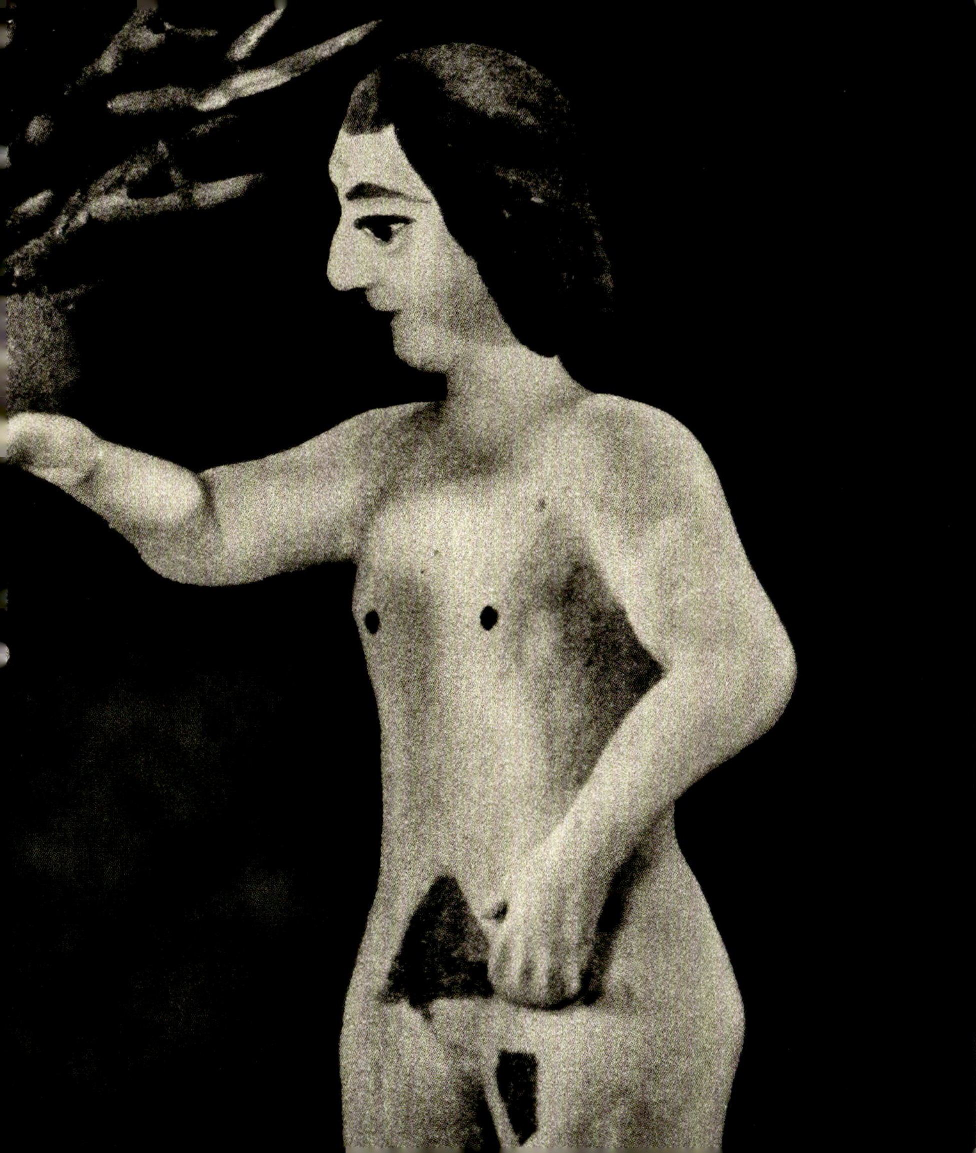
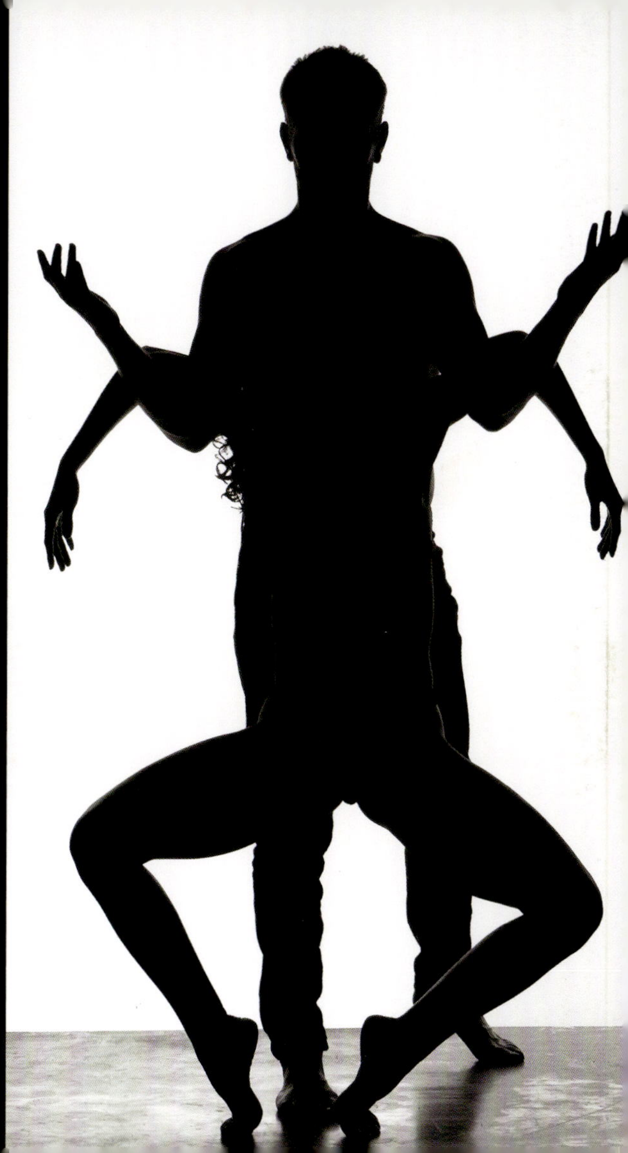

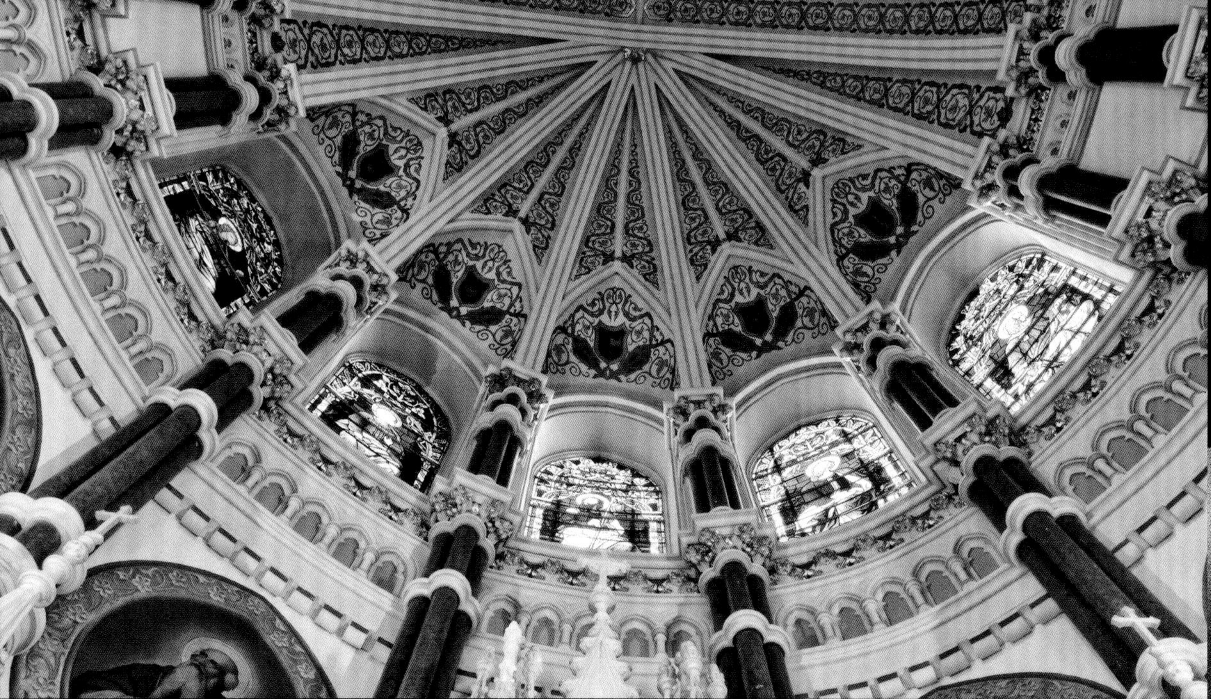

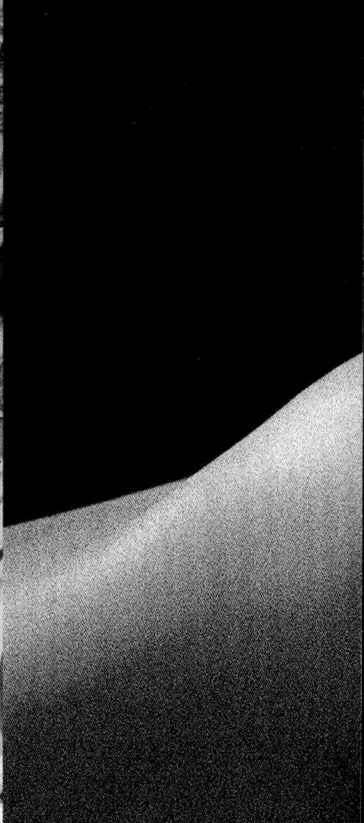

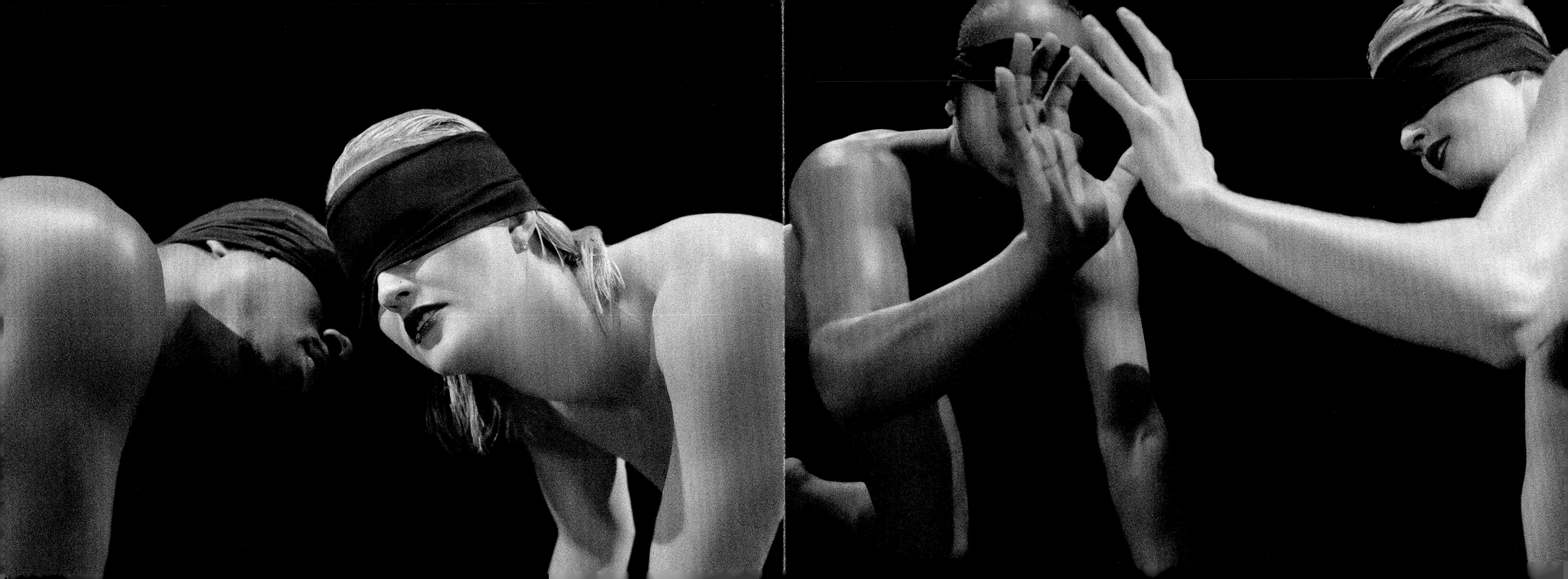

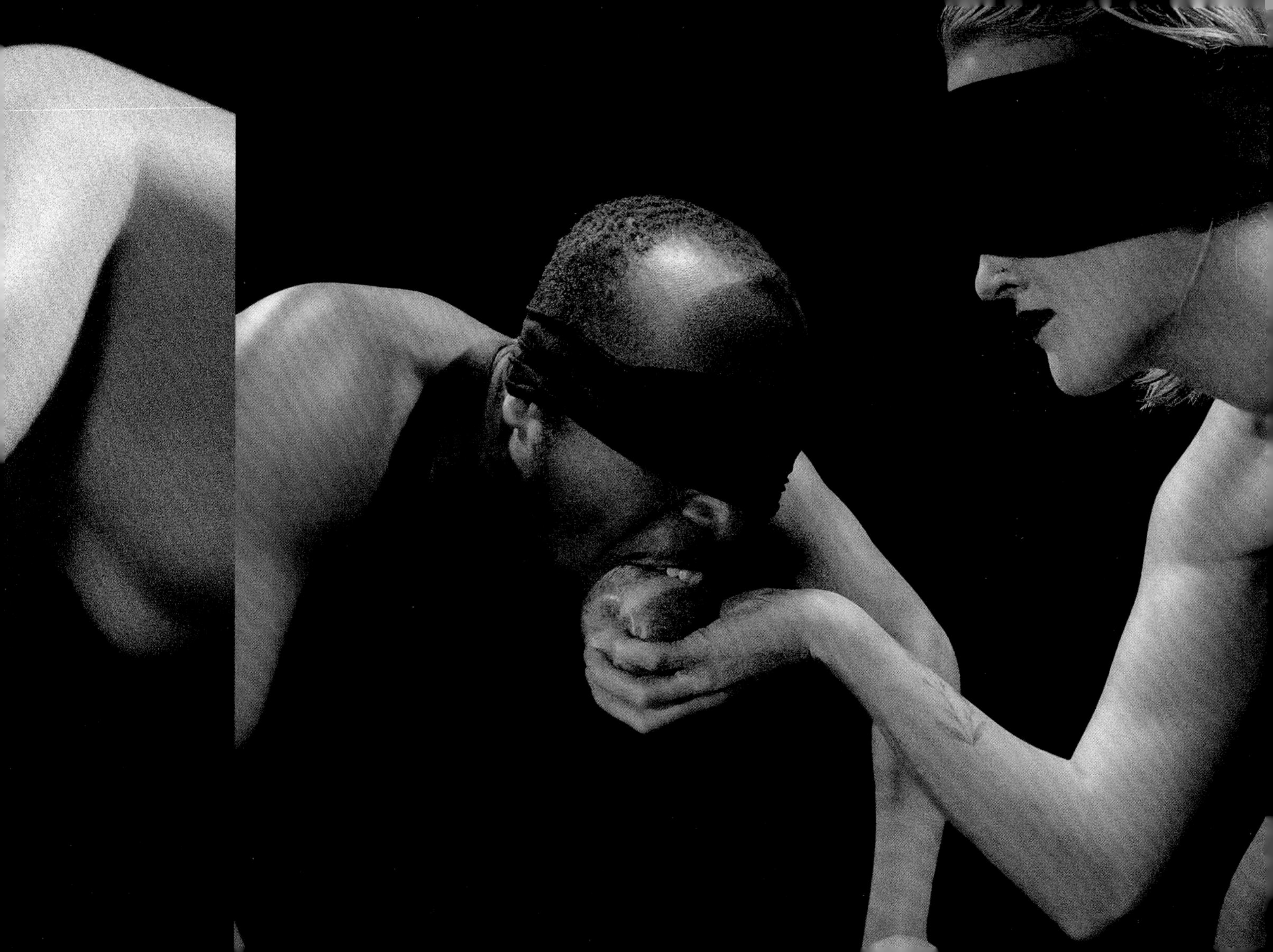

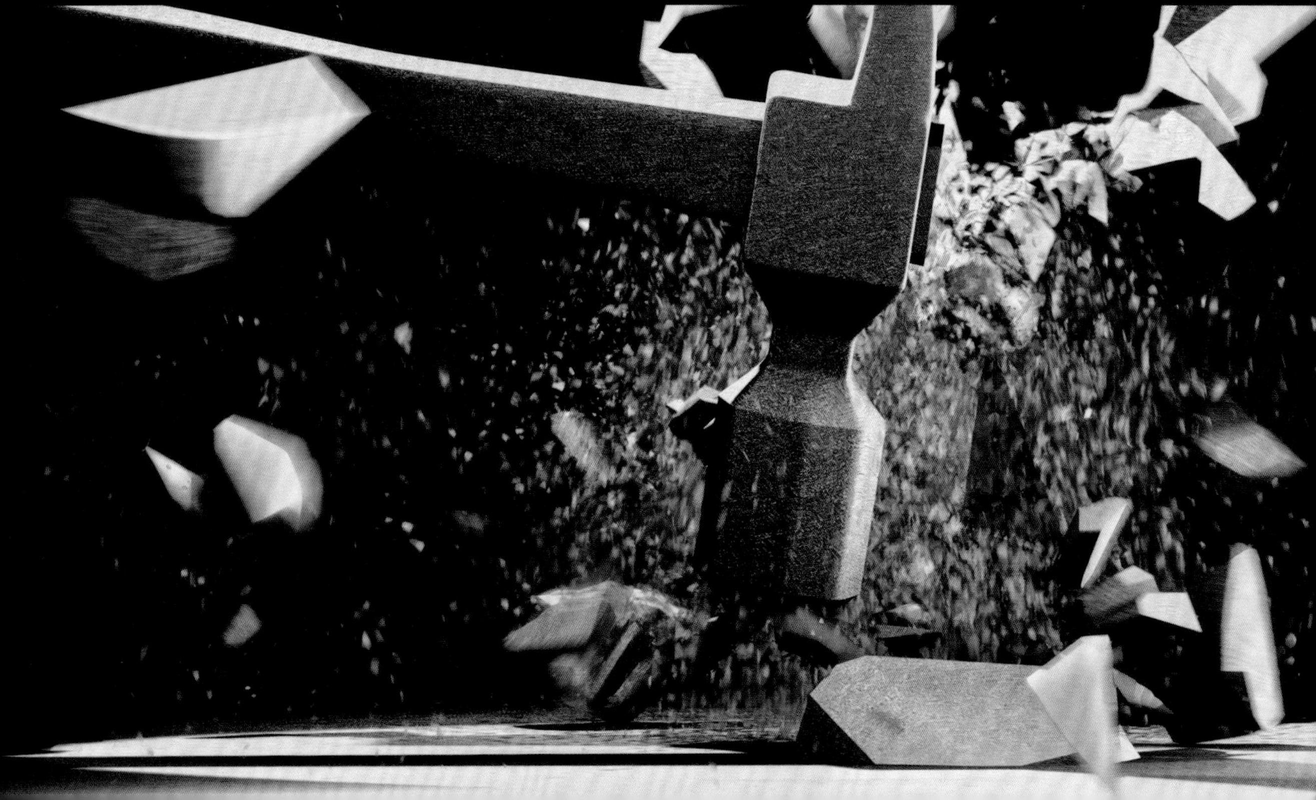

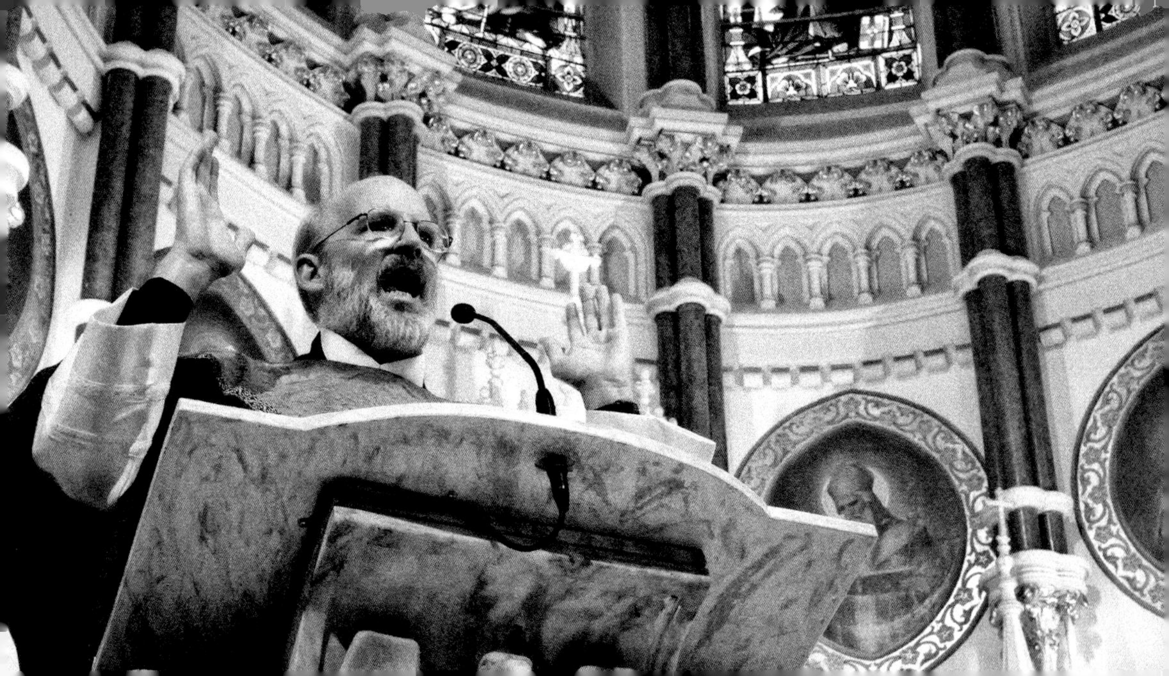

"My time in Iraq strongly shaped my thoughts about death. I was deployed to Kuwait in 2002 and a few months later the Iraq War kicked off. When I encountered my first dead body, I was terrified. You know that feeling when you get caught doing something wrong, that rush? It felt like everything got dark and that was all I saw. But he was still, his body hadn't hit rigor mortis yet. Seeing that body for the first time, I froze, you know, I couldn't move. That's the last time I felt that rush." —R

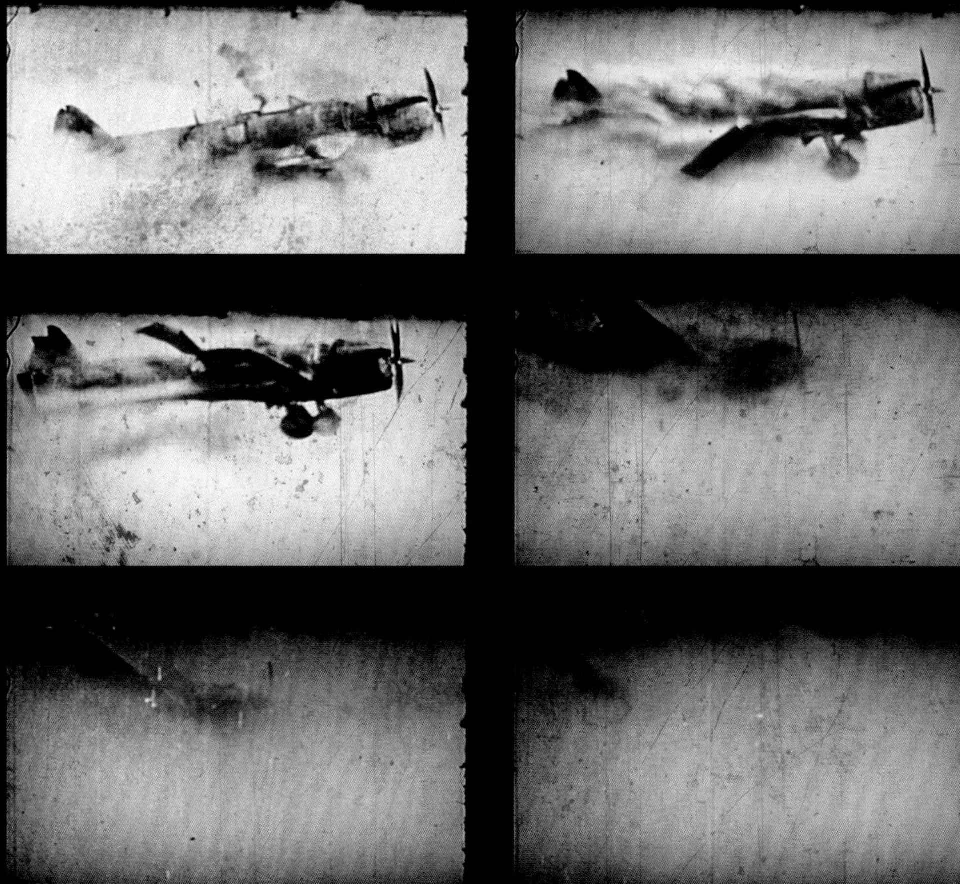

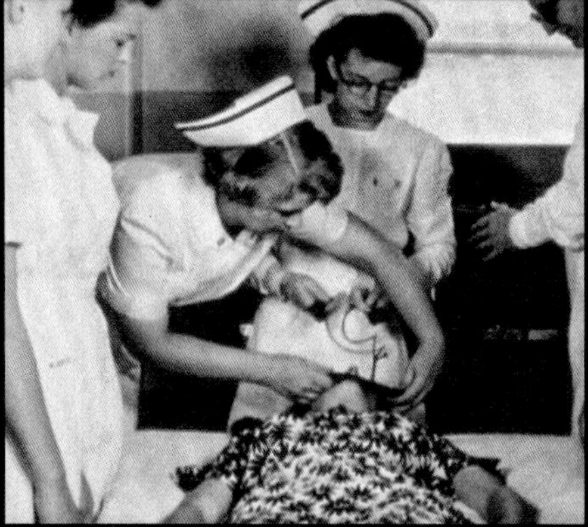

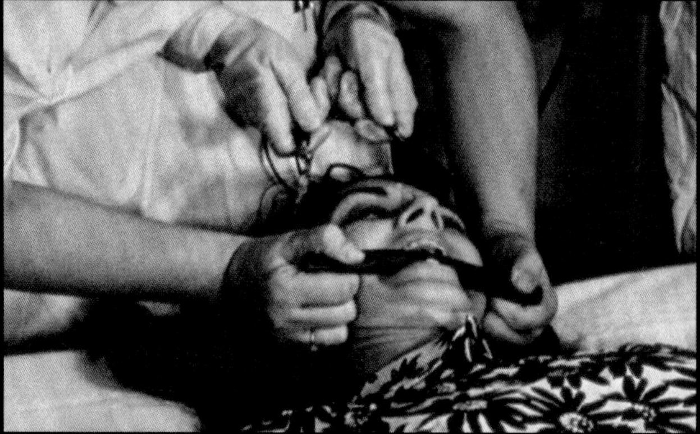

"The majority of experiences in my life I can't explain rationally. At the beginning of life, it all seemed so clear, but what happens when experiences just continue to accumulate and they stop representing anything cohesive? It's like I'm watching the manifestations of nature as it passes through, but I'm not really making the selections; I'm not qualified to do that." —G

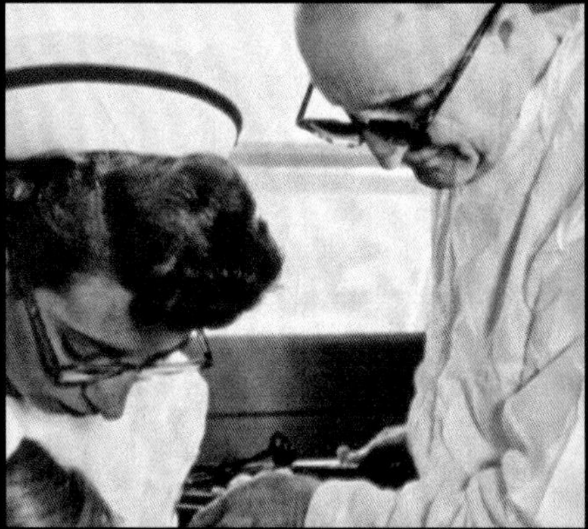

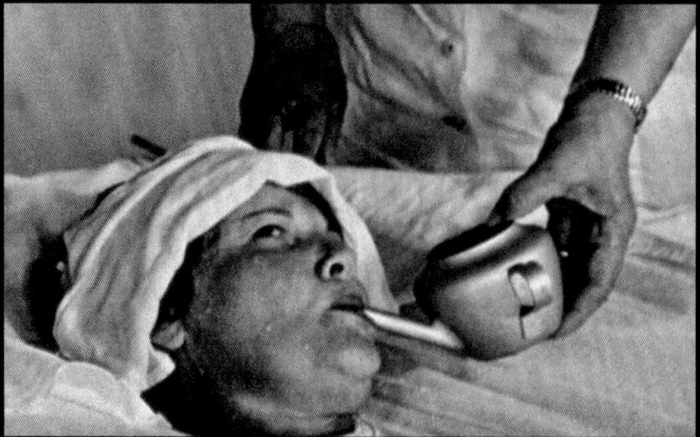

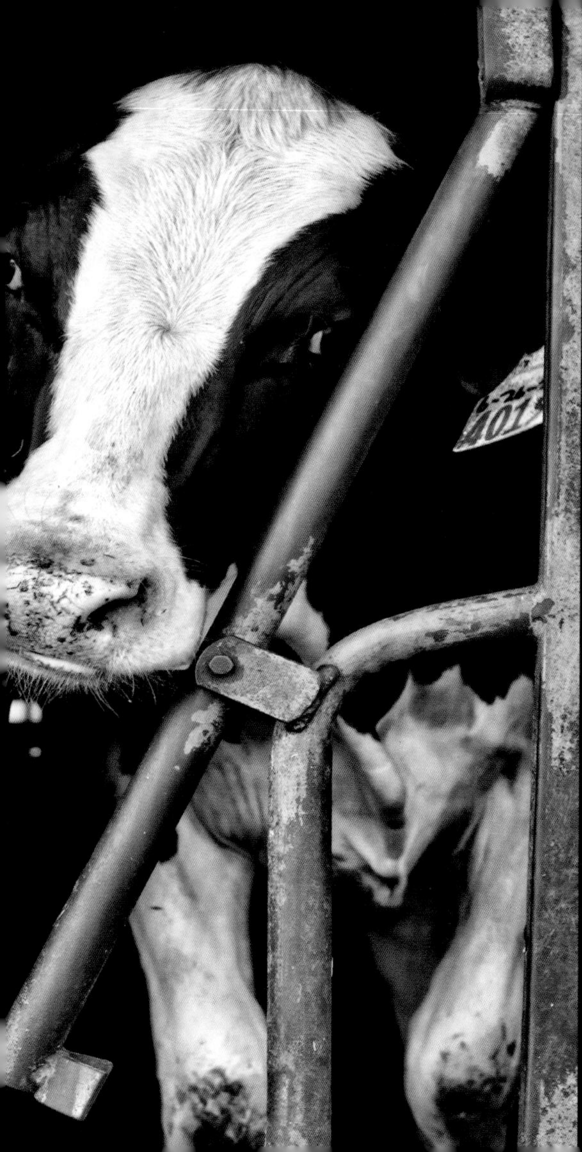

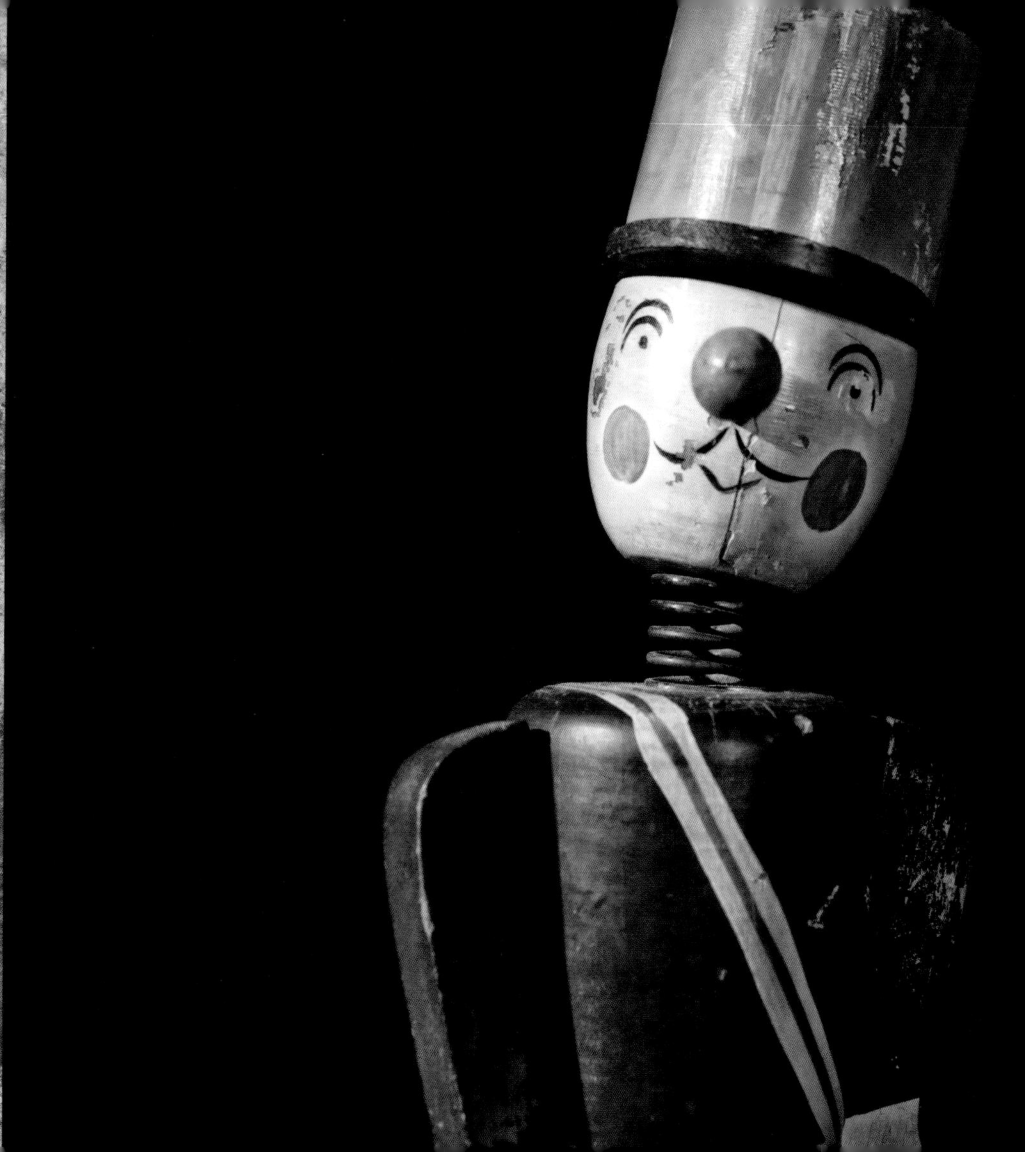

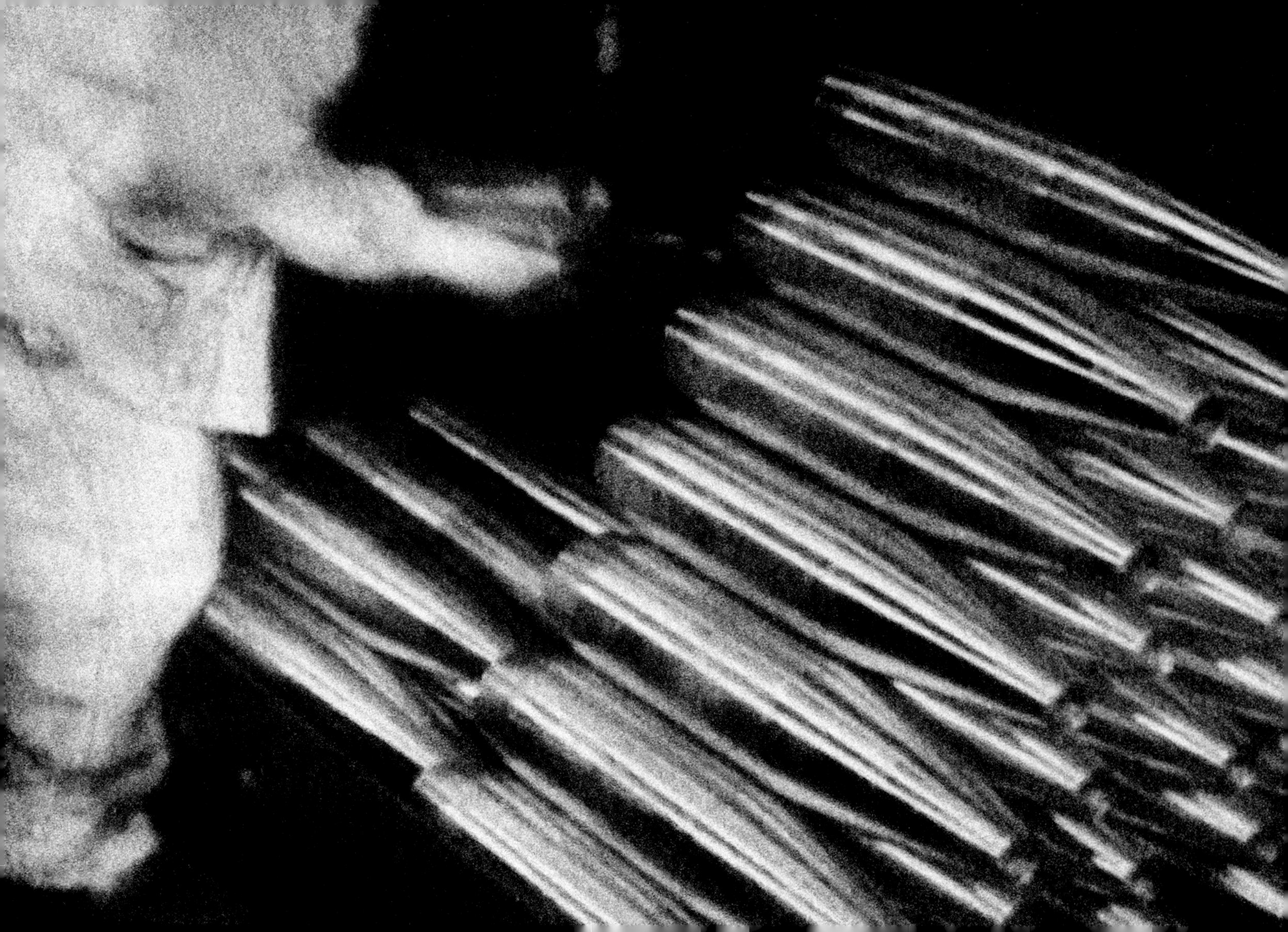

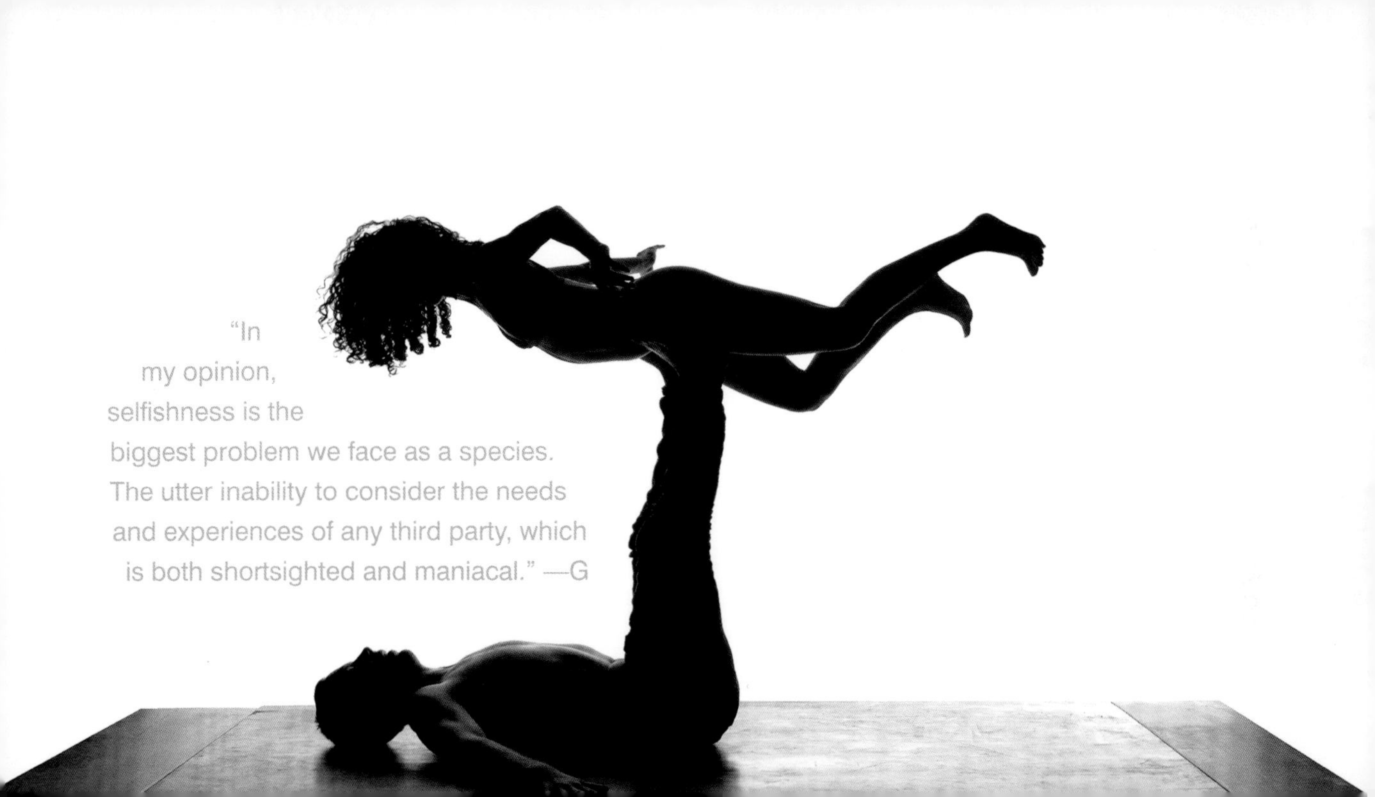

"In my opinion, selfishness is the biggest problem we face as a species. The utter inability to consider the needs and experiences of any third party, which is both shortsighted and maniacal." —G

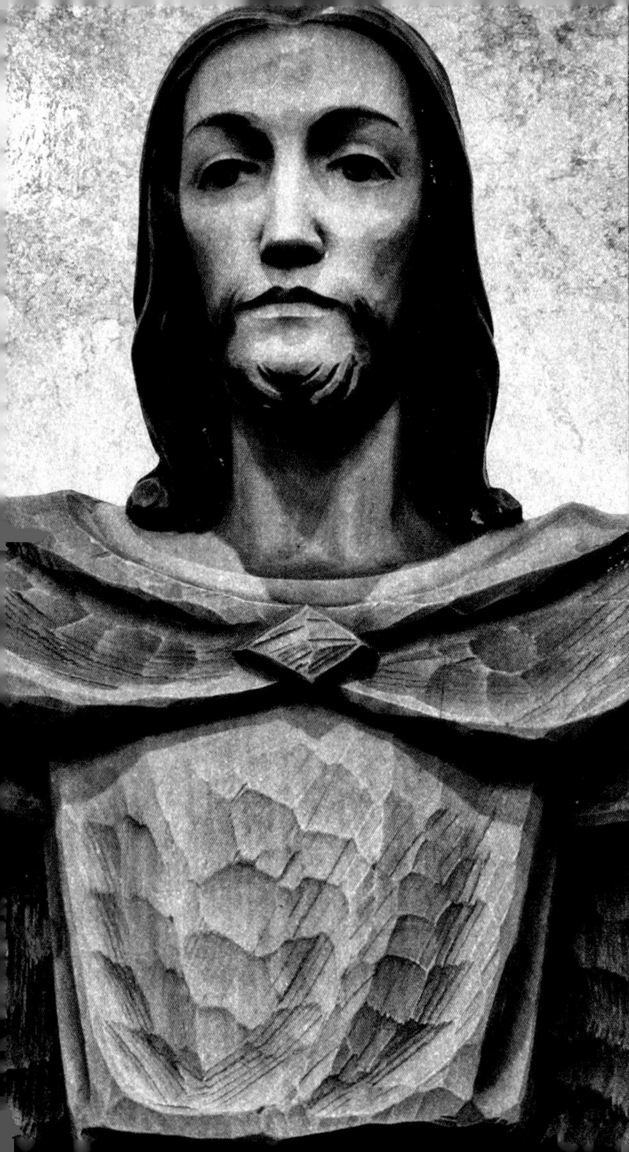

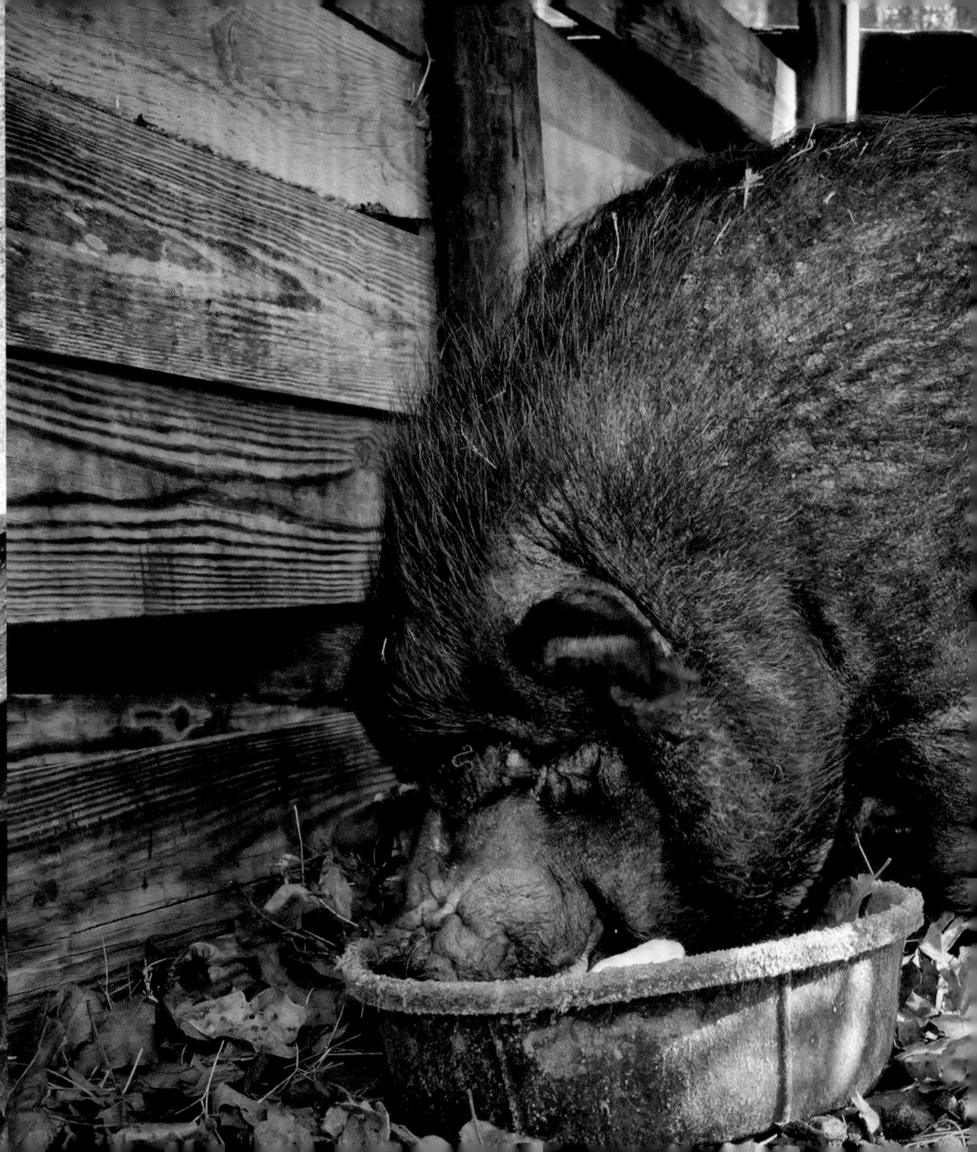

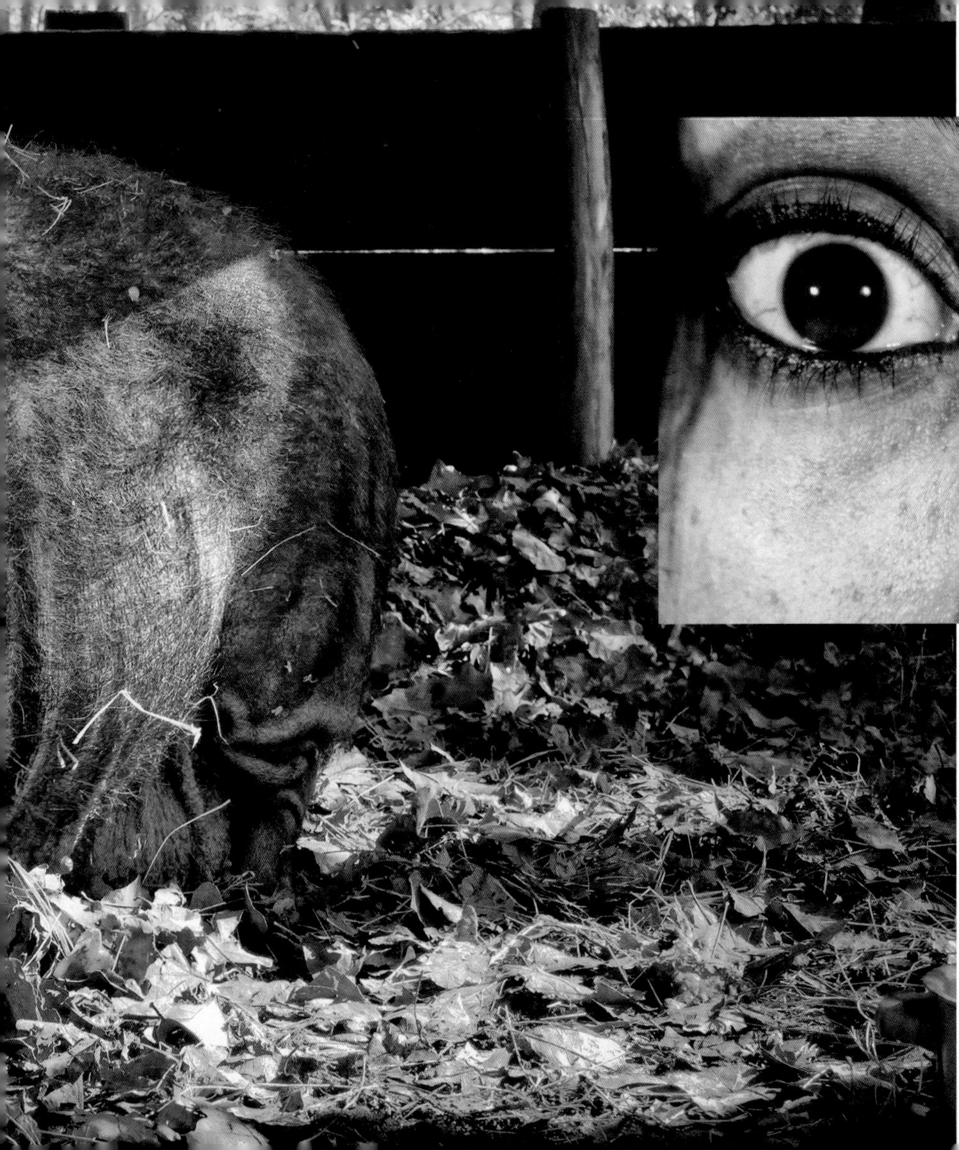

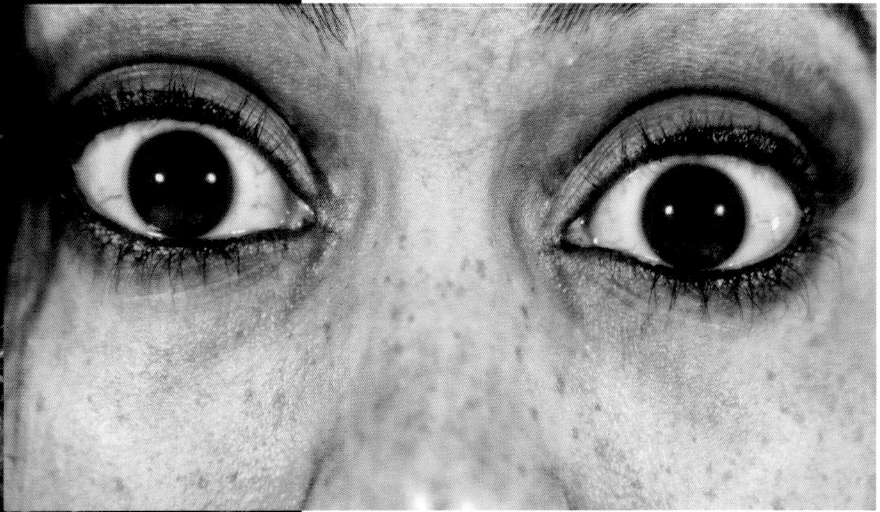

"I would define grace as giving somebody a second chance. Looking over their deficiencies, defects. Looking at them as who they are, not looking at their past, but giving them a second chance." —R

to avoid feelings of intimacy. Sexual relationships cause me so much physical discomfort. I don't like being touched and I would never want to subject someone to that. However, I can see my relationship with the needle as being very, very intimate."

—G

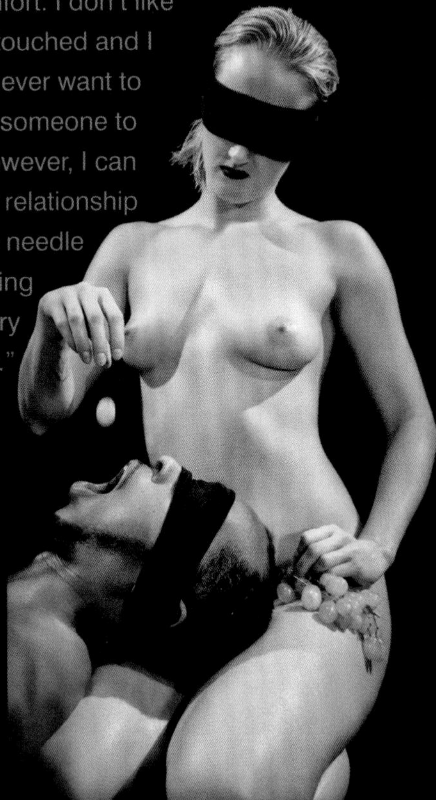

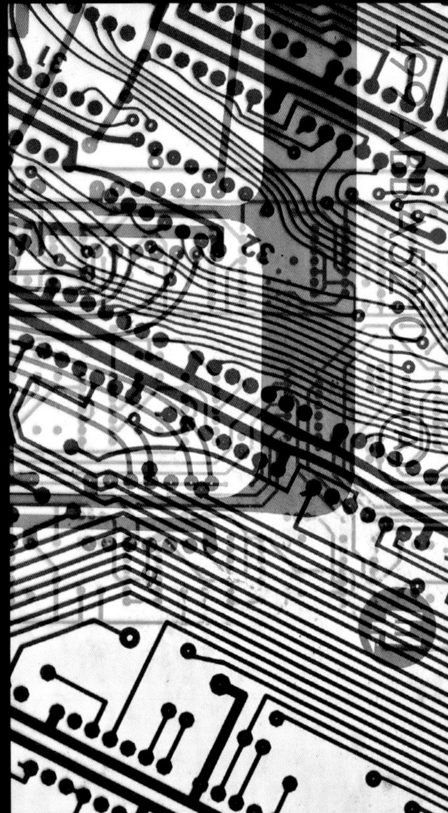

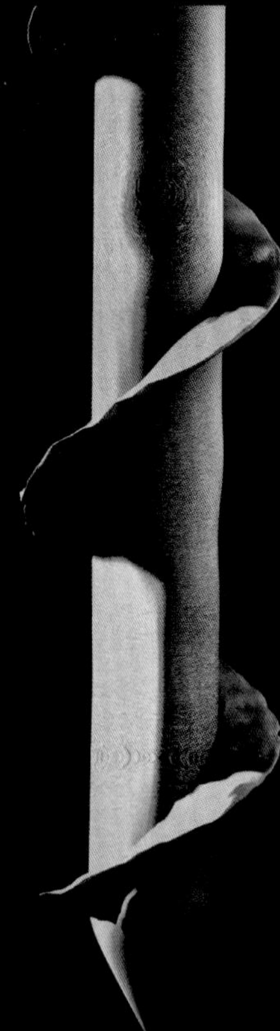

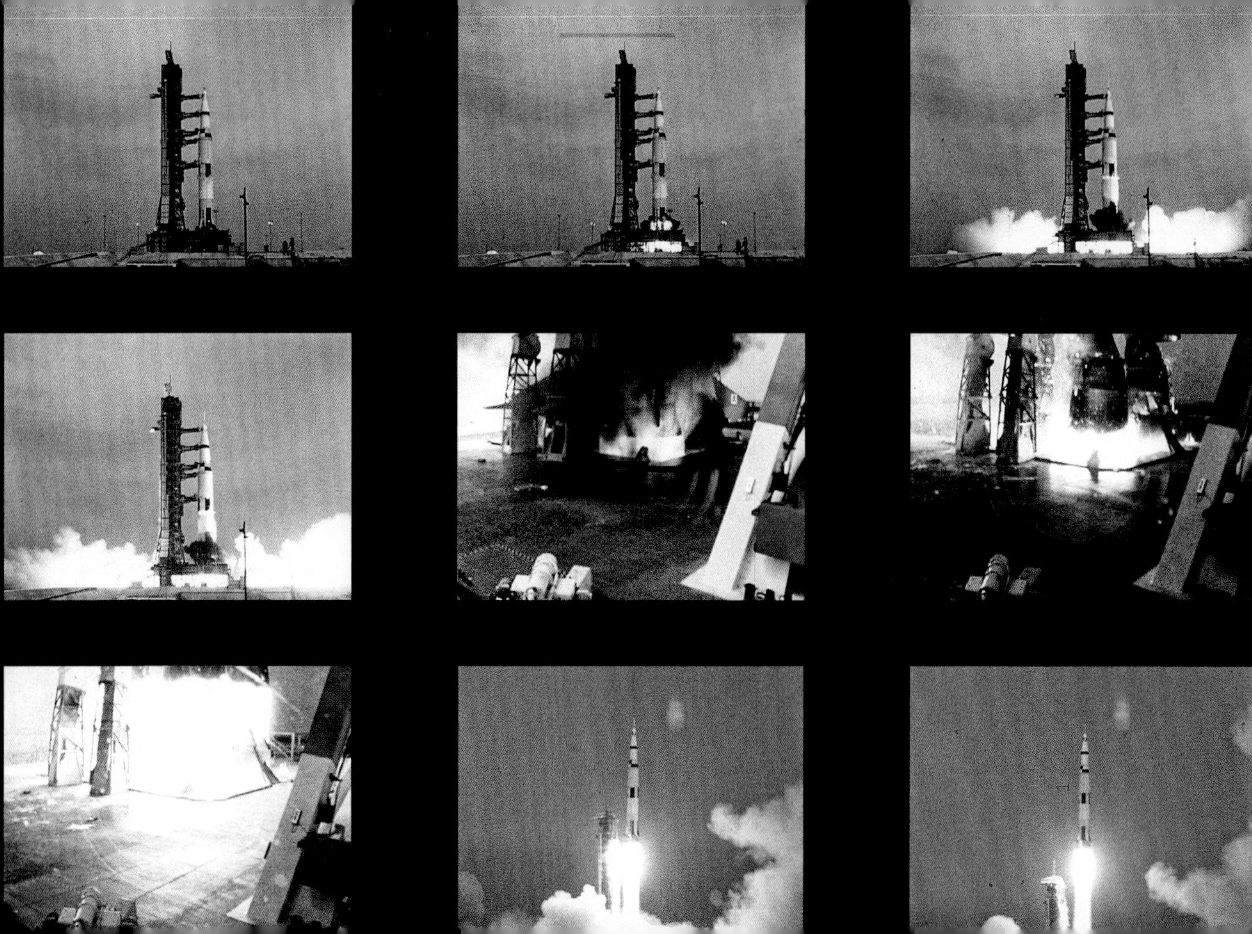

"My earliest memory is of my mother yelling at us to pay attention. Something was happening on the television—I think it was to do with the lunar landing and astronauts—and she was saying, 'This is important, pay attention, watch the television.'"

—A

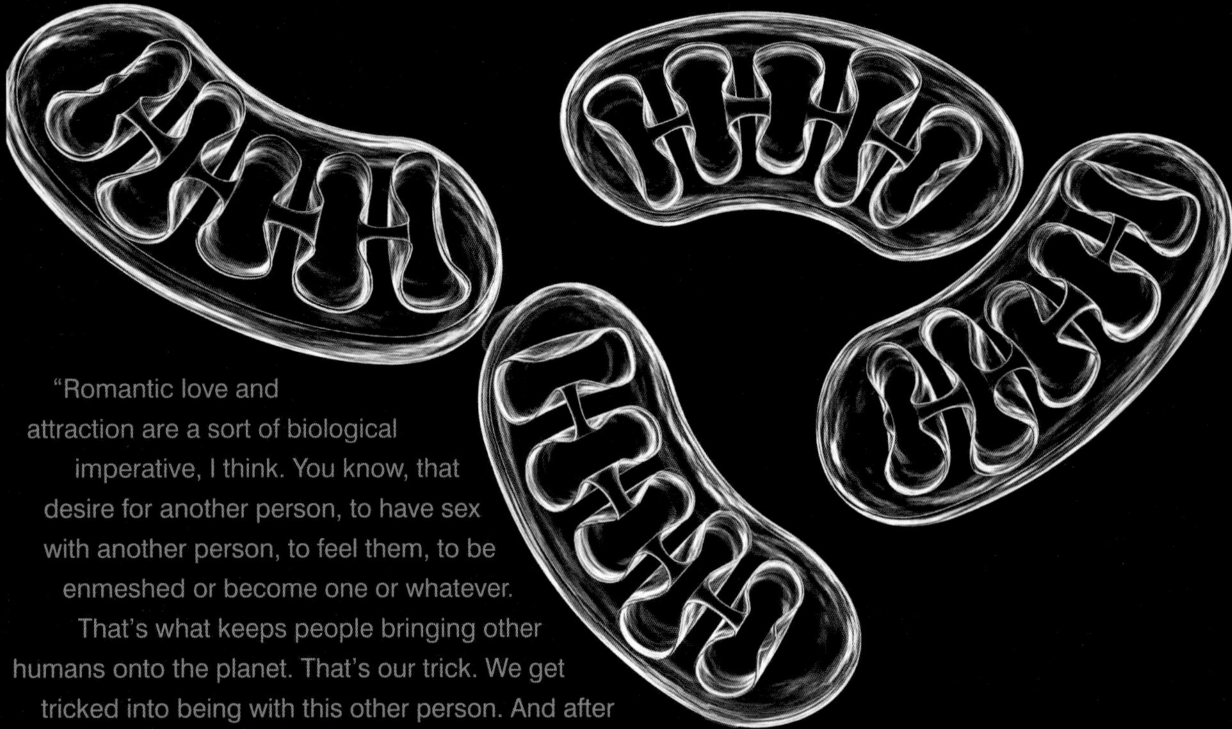

"Romantic love and attraction are a sort of biological imperative, I think. You know, that desire for another person, to have sex with another person, to feel them, to be enmeshed or become one or whatever. That's what keeps people bringing other humans onto the planet. That's our trick. We get tricked into being with this other person. And after that you learn how to love them." —C

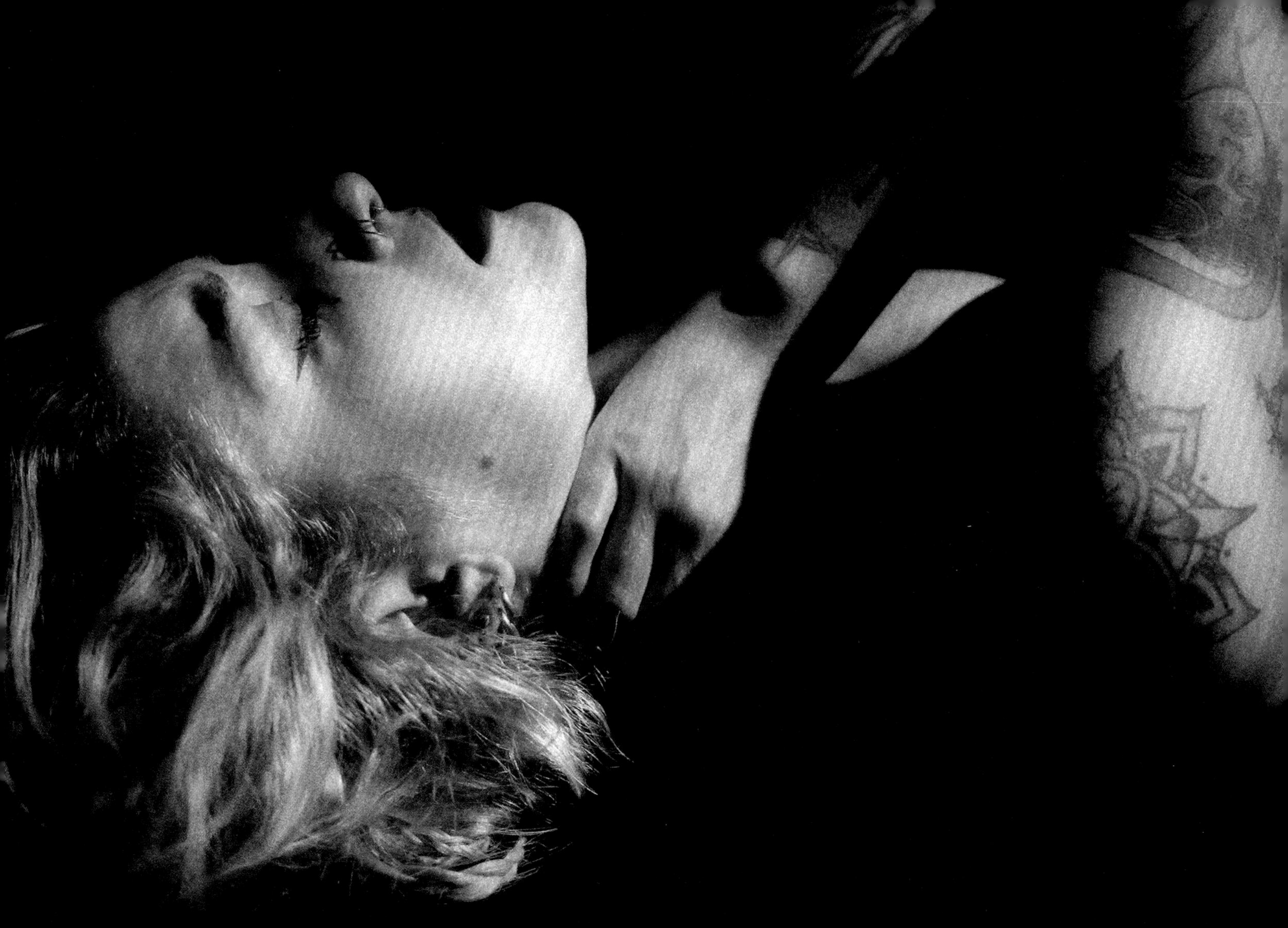

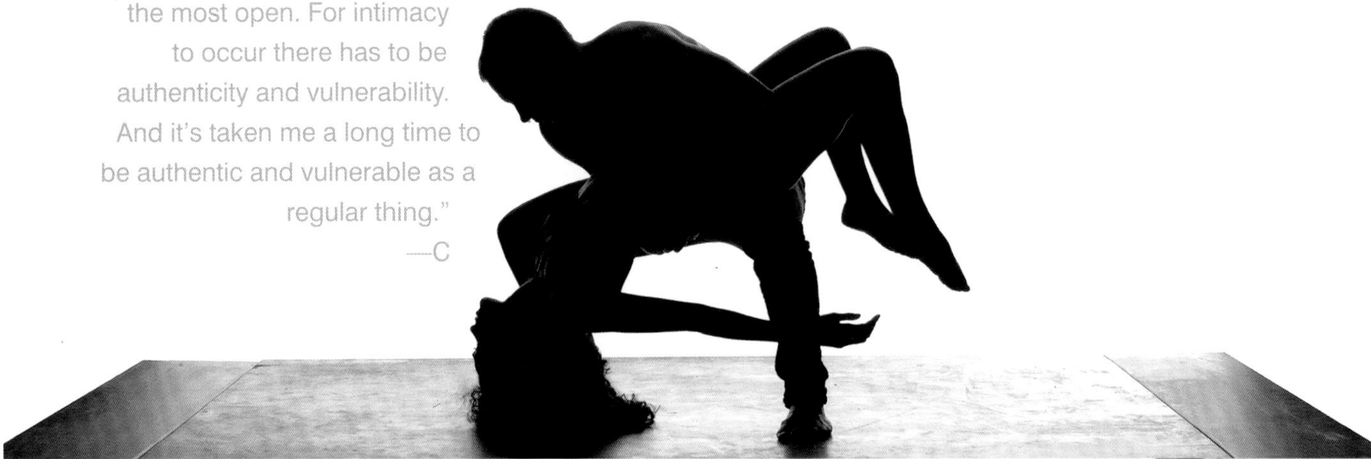

"I think the most intimate experience has been with my husband. I've been the most vulnerable with him; I've been the most open. For intimacy to occur there has to be authenticity and vulnerability. And it's taken me a long time to be authentic and vulnerable as a regular thing."

—C

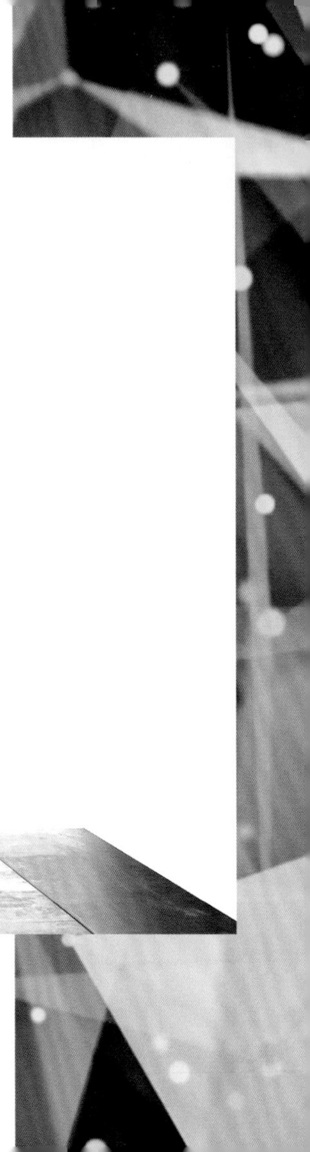

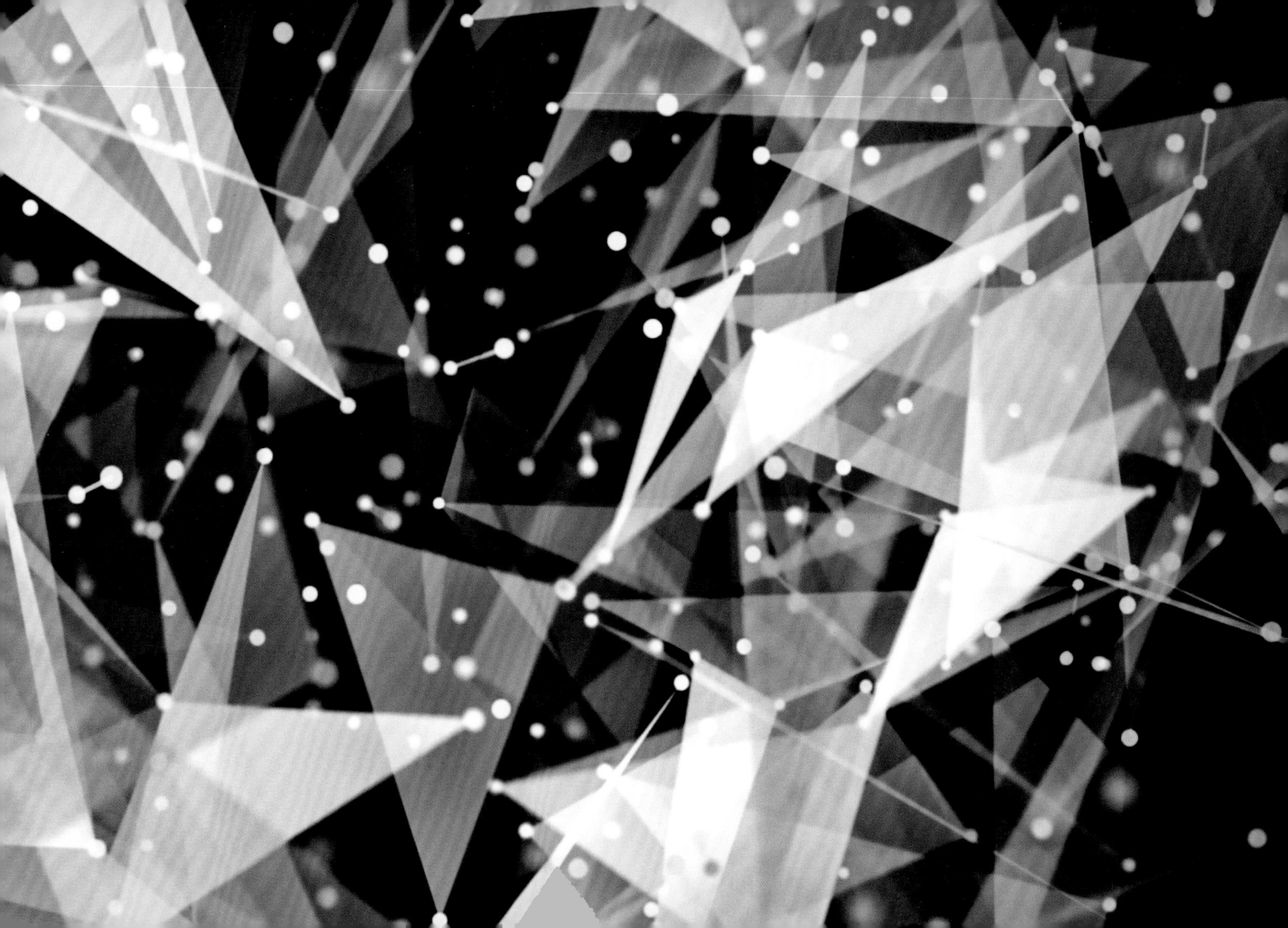

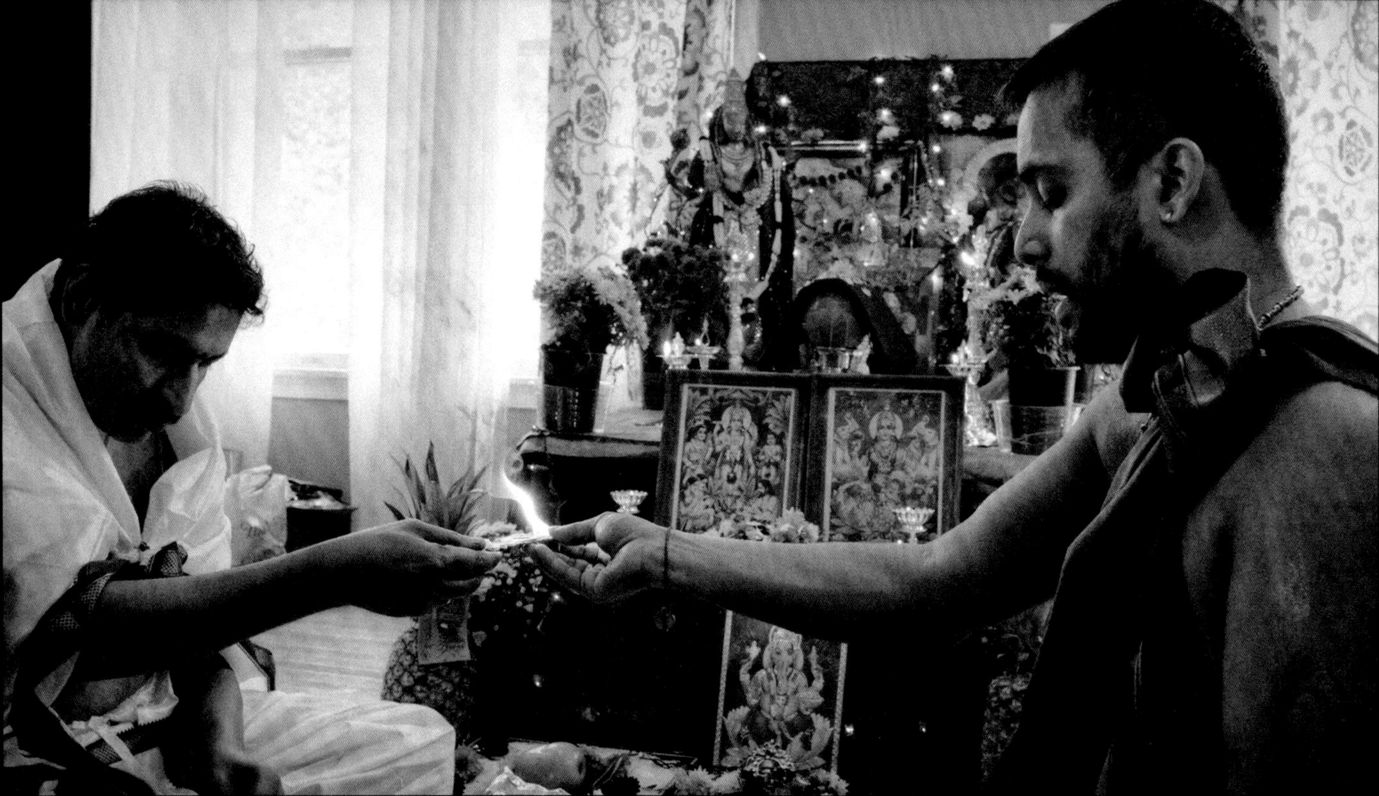

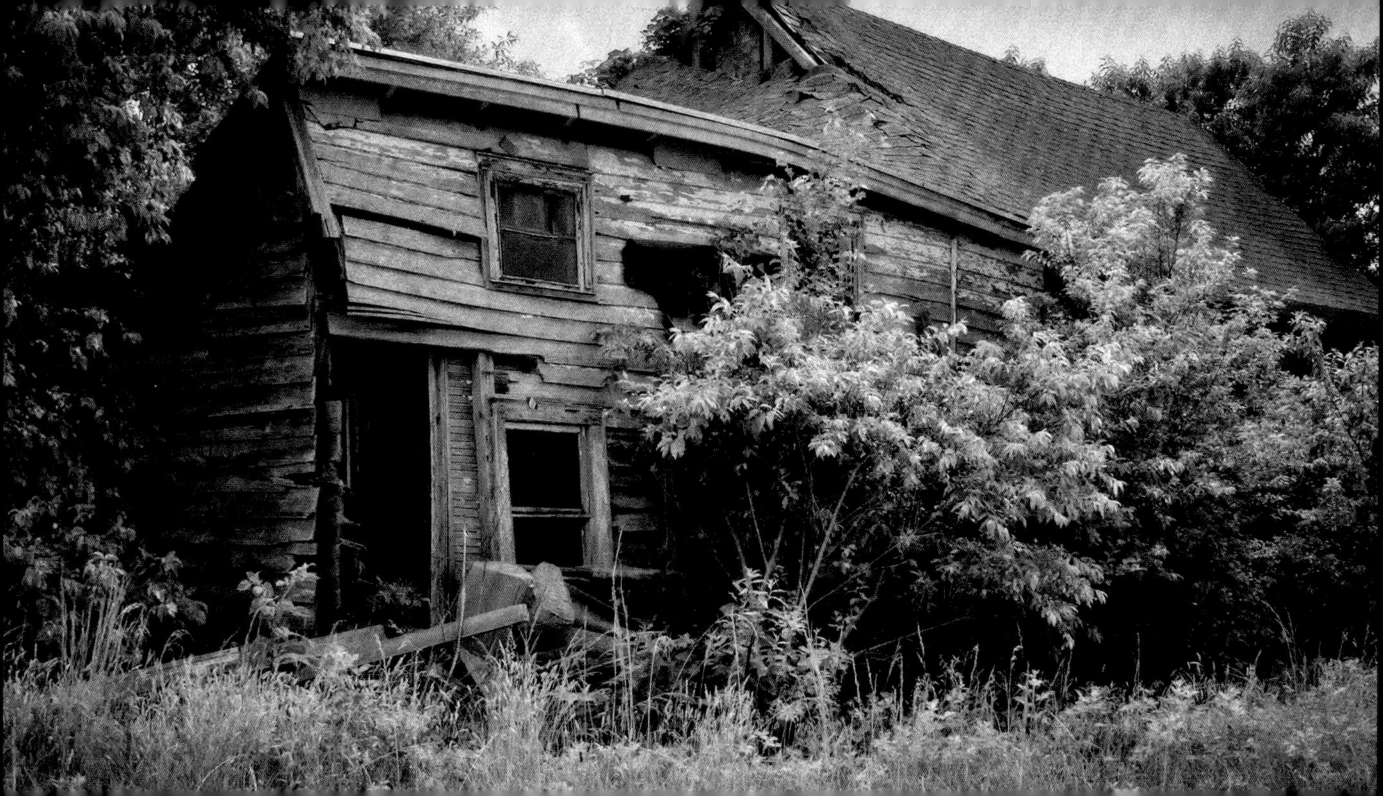

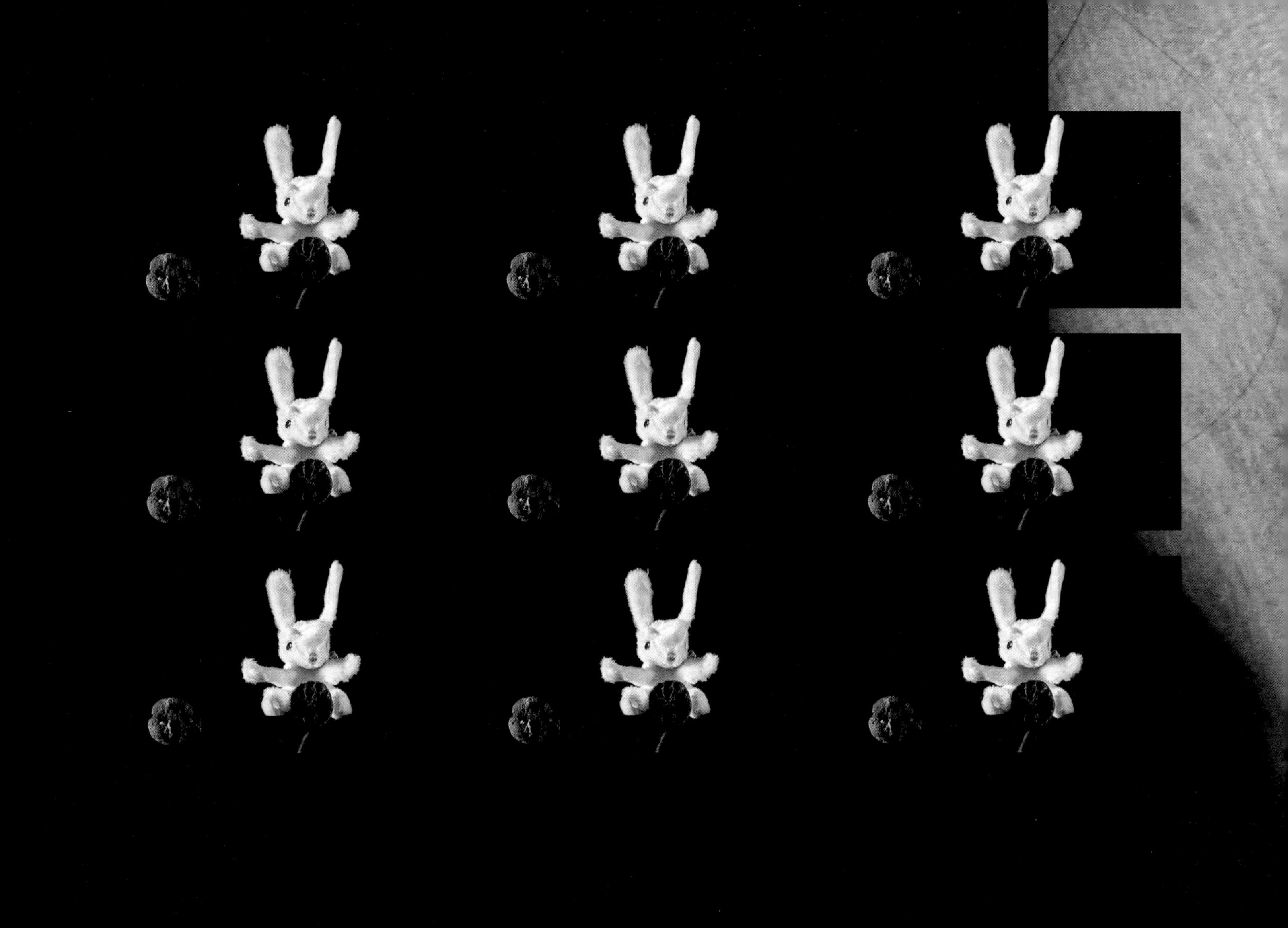

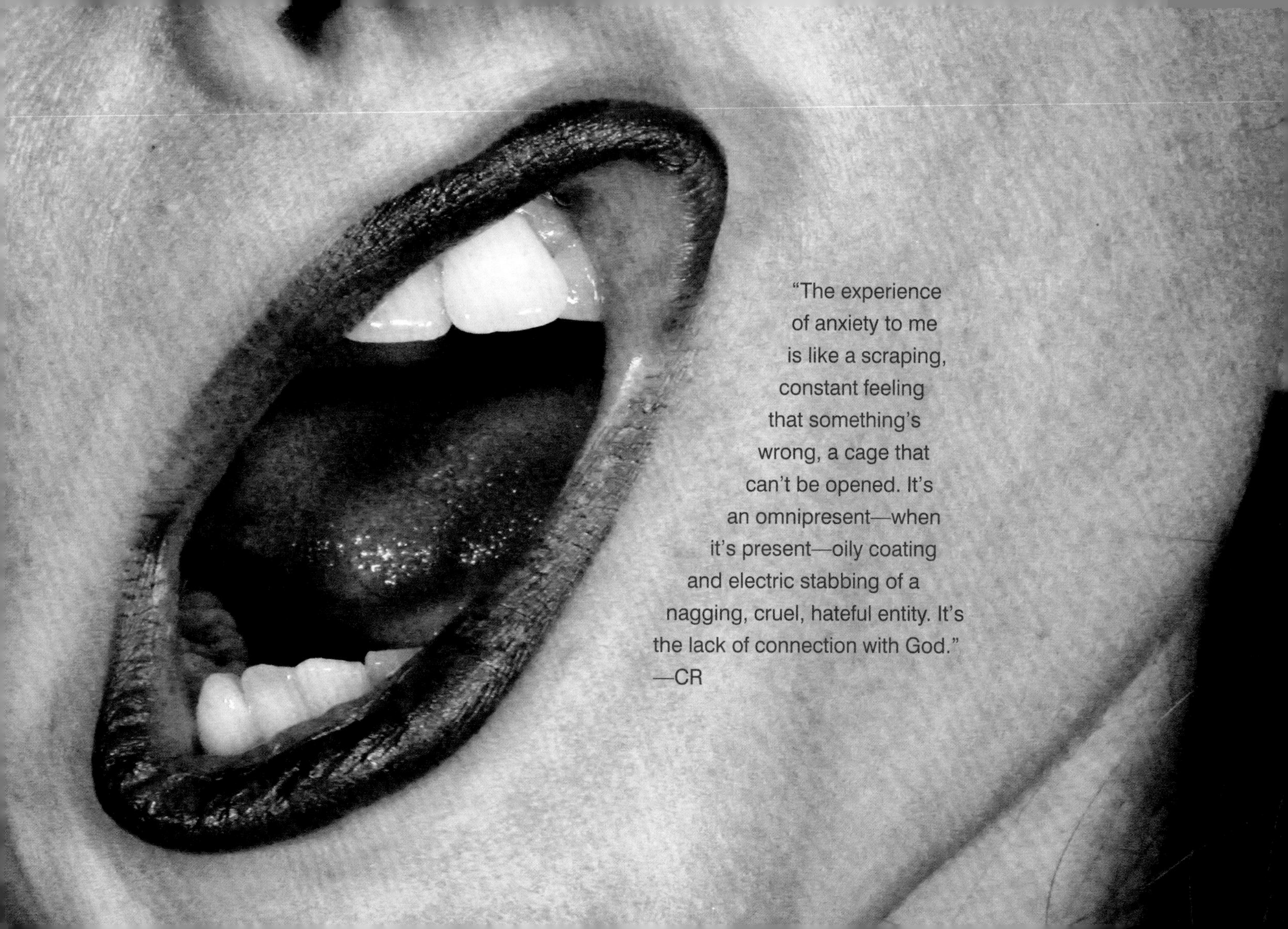

"The experience
of anxiety to me
is like a scraping,
constant feeling
that something's
wrong, a cage that
can't be opened. It's
an omnipresent—when
it's present—oily coating
and electric stabbing of a
nagging, cruel, hateful entity. It's
the lack of connection with God."
—CR

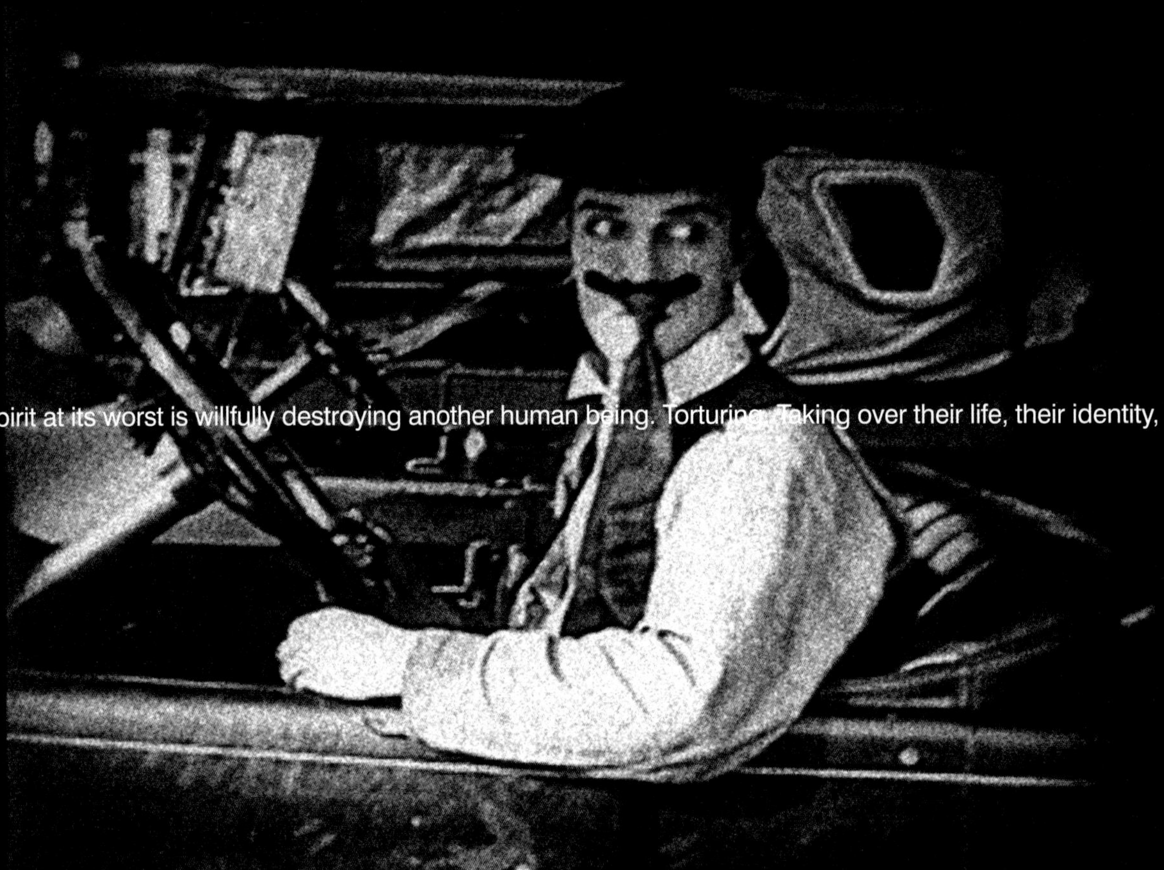

“The human spirit at its worst is willfully destroying another human being. Torturing. Taking over their life, their identity, or their body.” —C

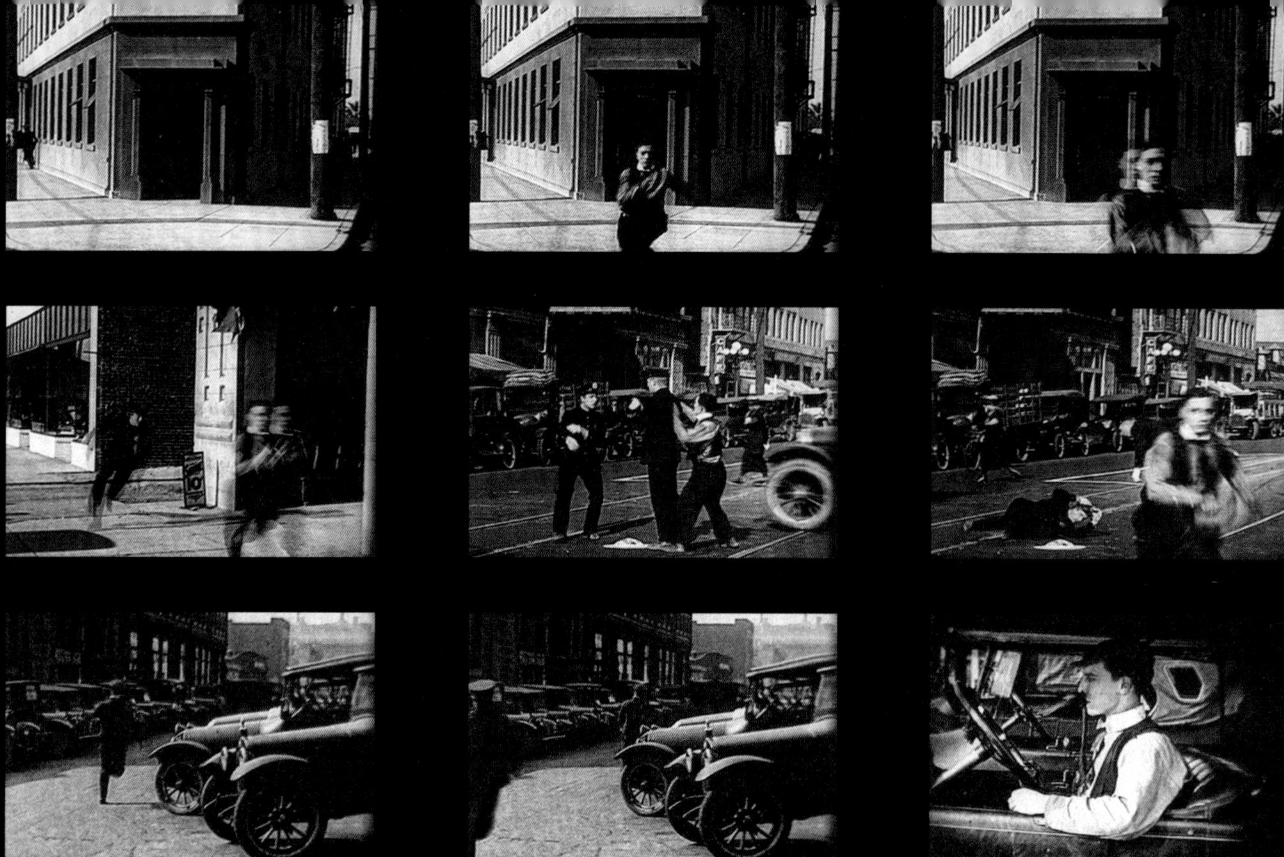

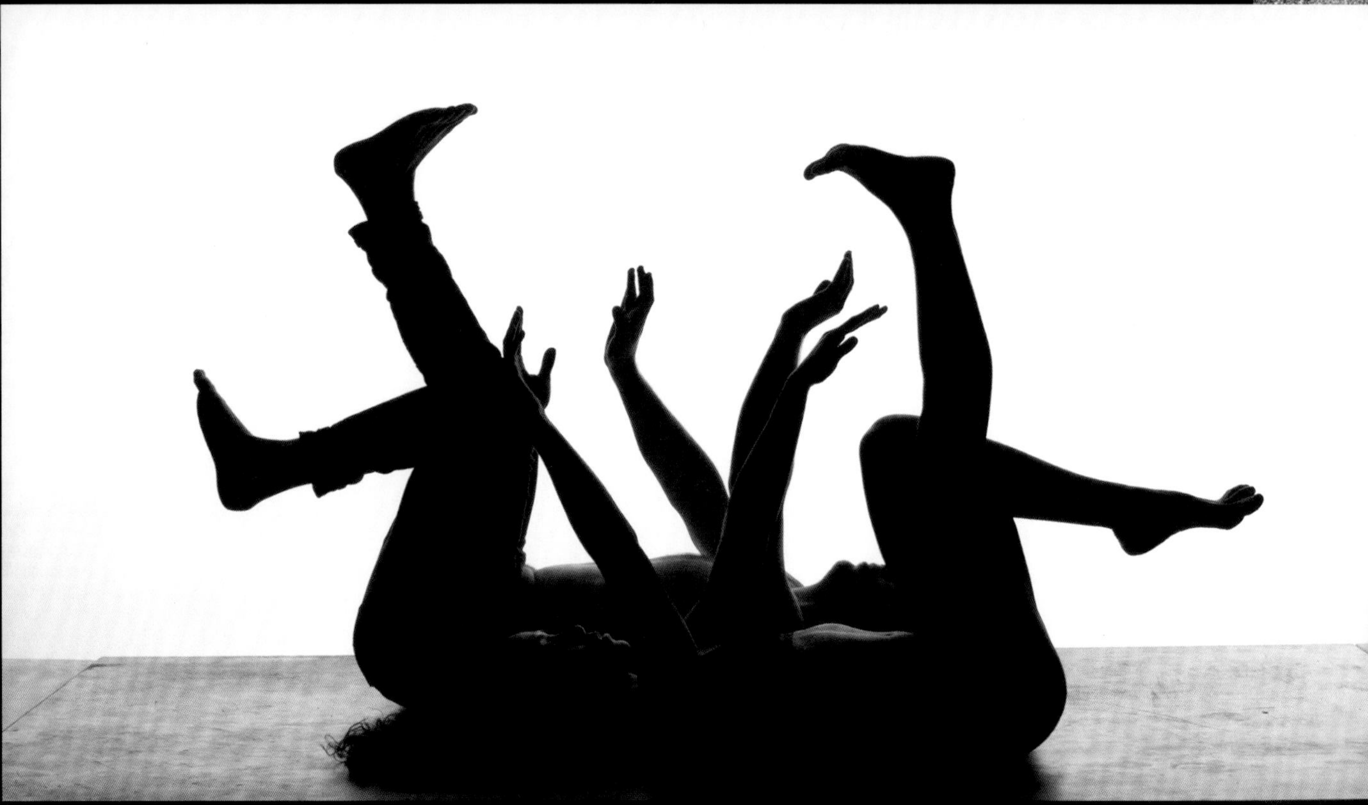

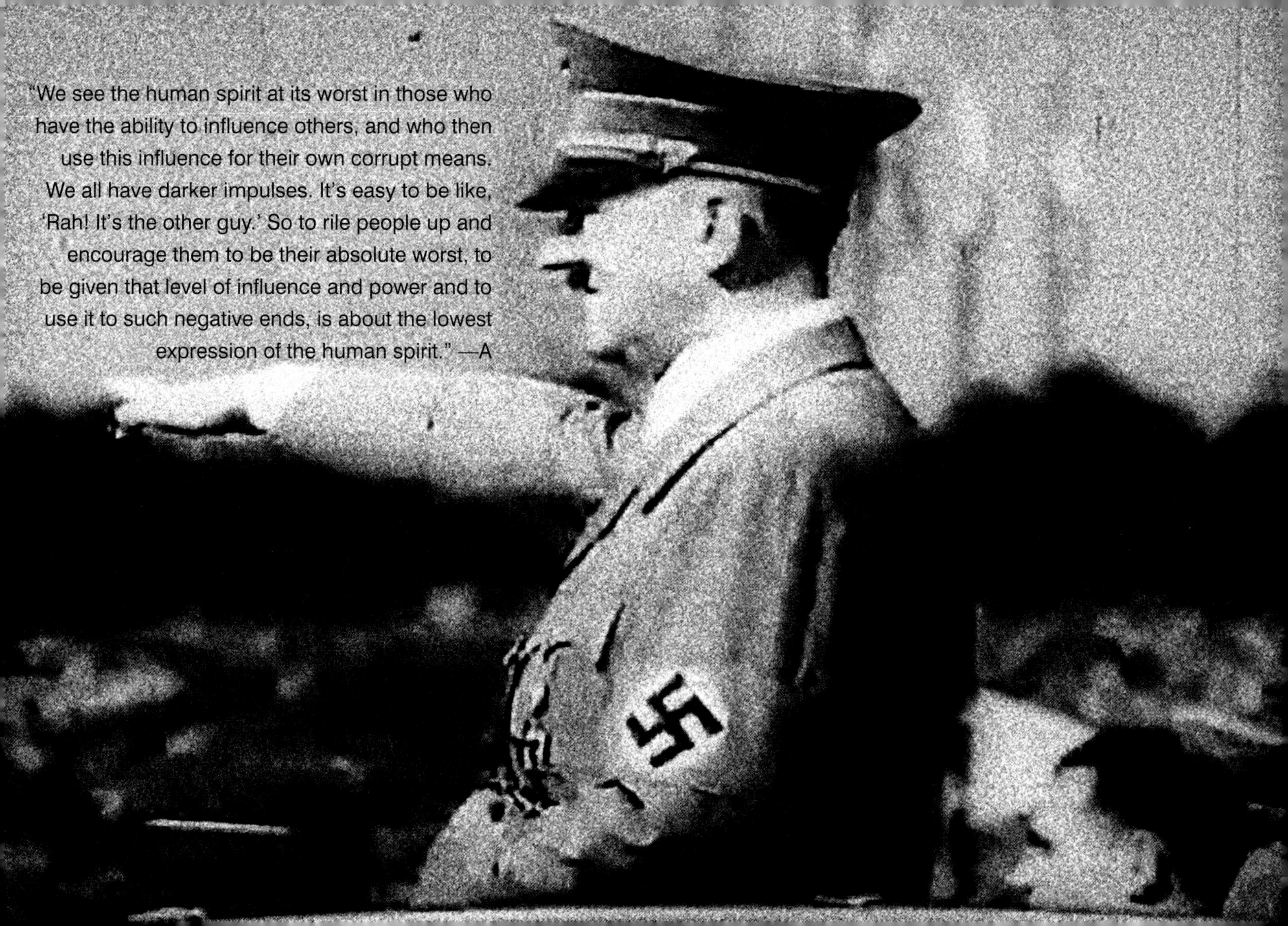

"We see the human spirit at its worst in those who have the ability to influence others, and who then use this influence for their own corrupt means. We all have darker impulses. It's easy to be like, 'Rah! It's the other guy.' So to rile people up and encourage them to be their absolute worst, to be given that level of influence and power and to use it to such negative ends, is about the lowest expression of the human spirit." —A

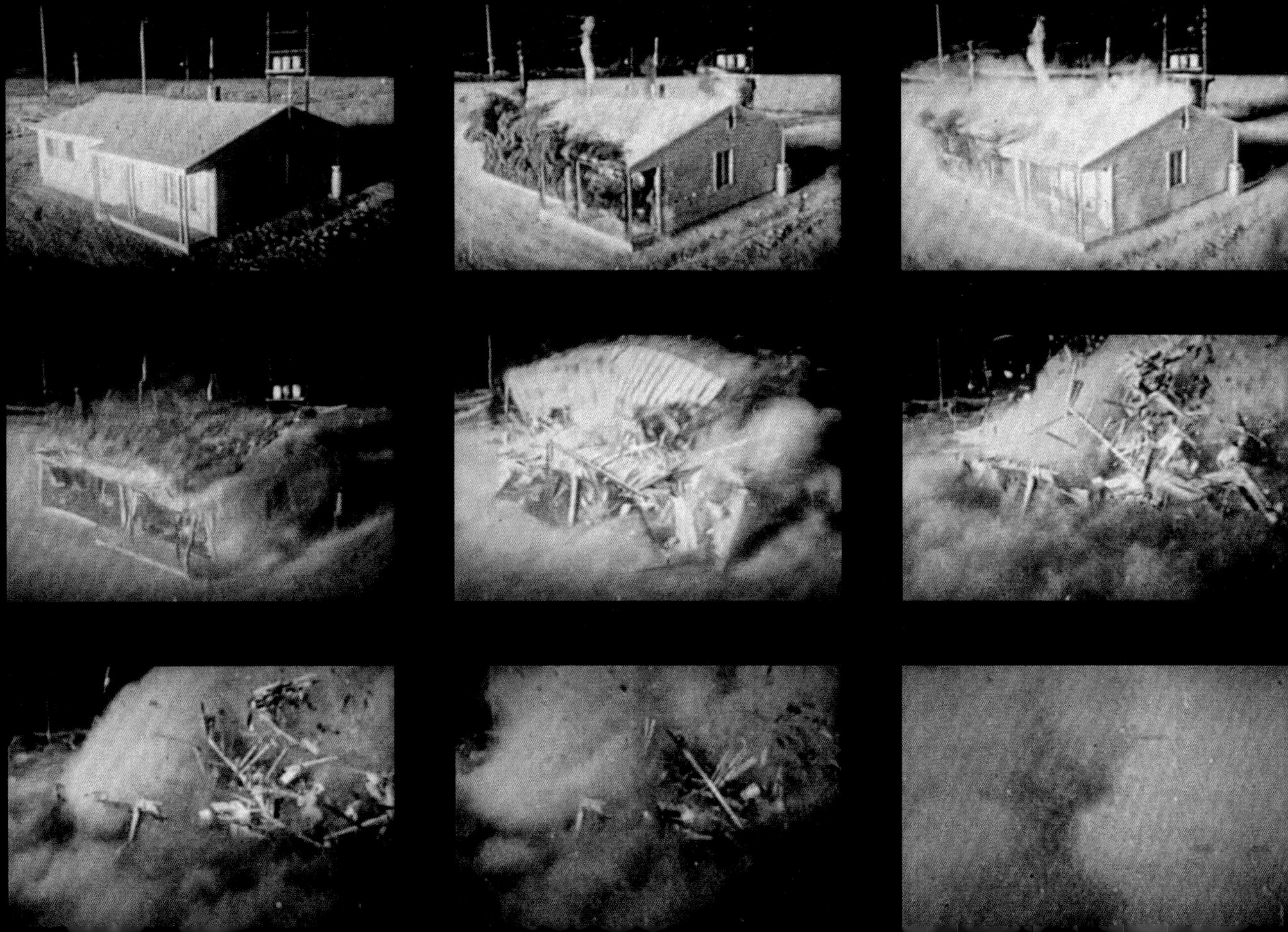

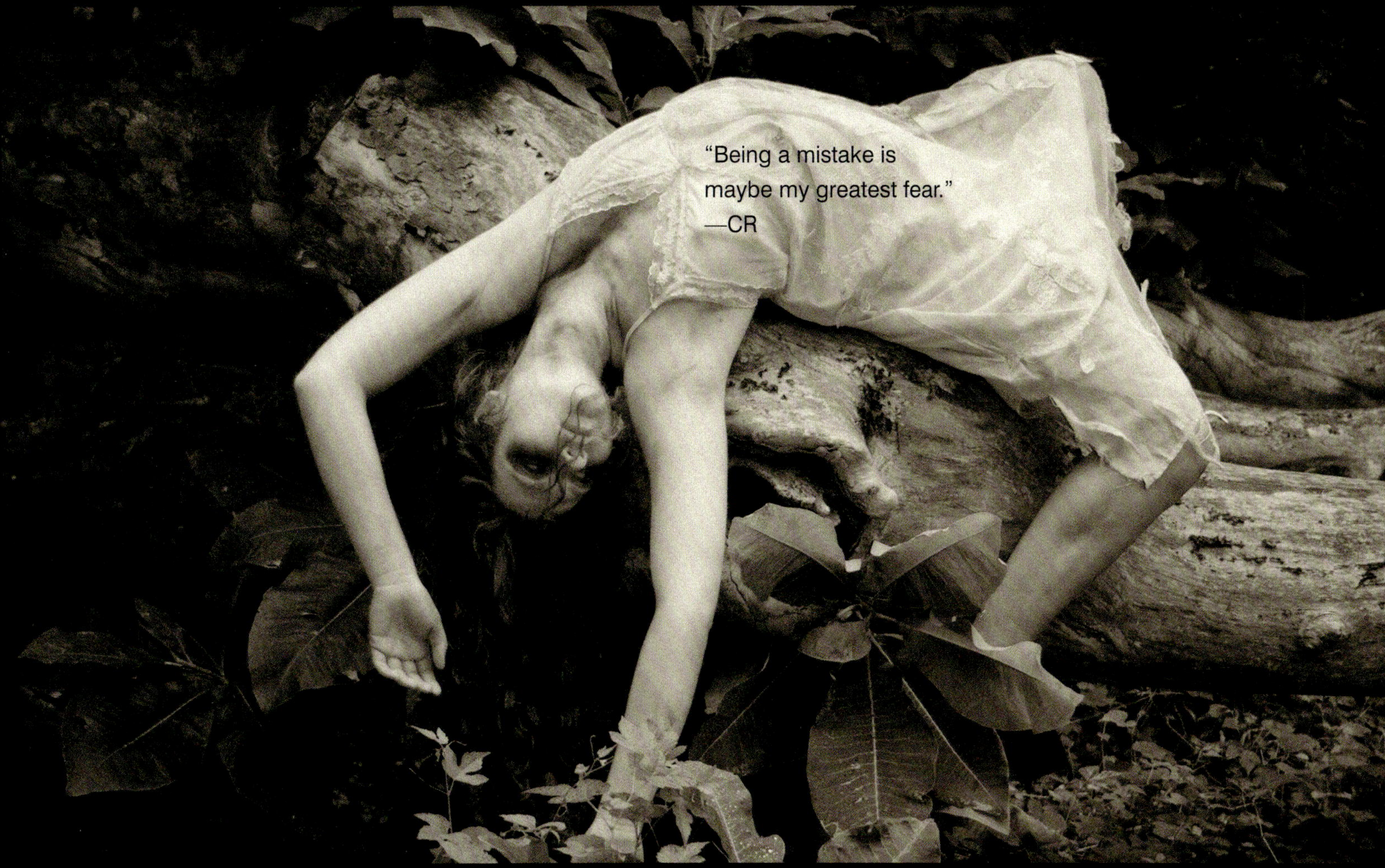

“Being a mistake is
maybe my greatest fear.”
—CR

"My inability to make the decision to step forward and father my daughter has been the most disappointing thing for me. It's lifelong; there's no escape." —G

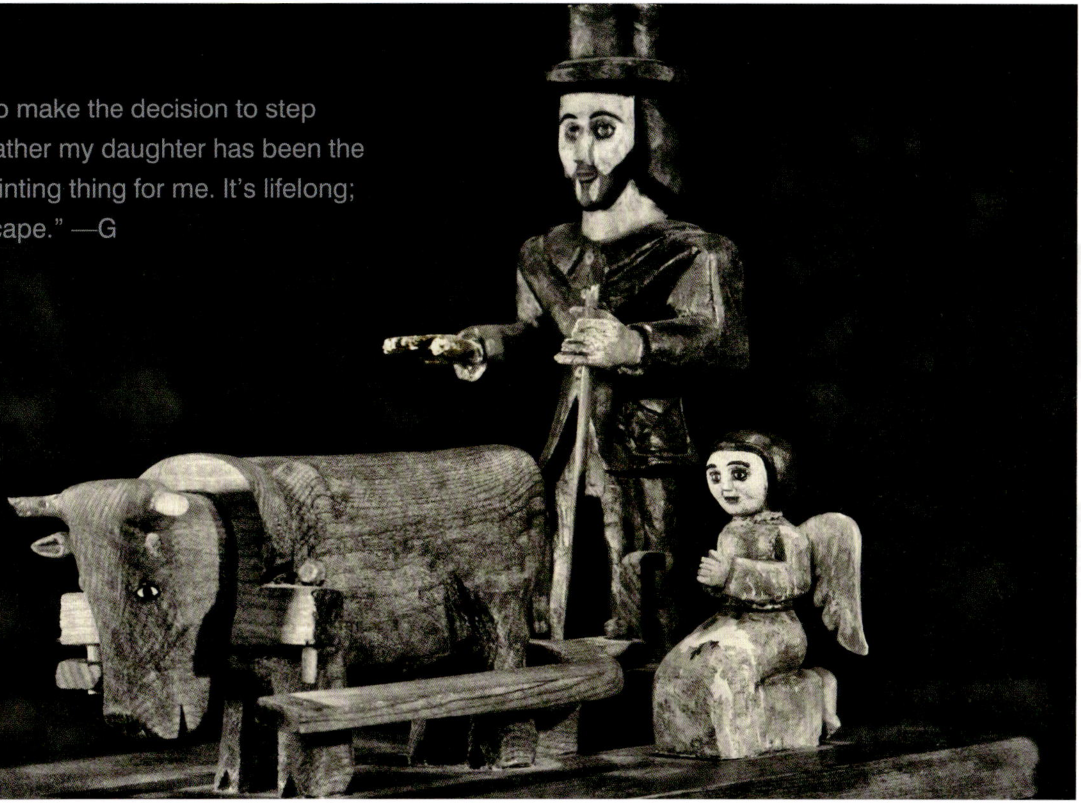

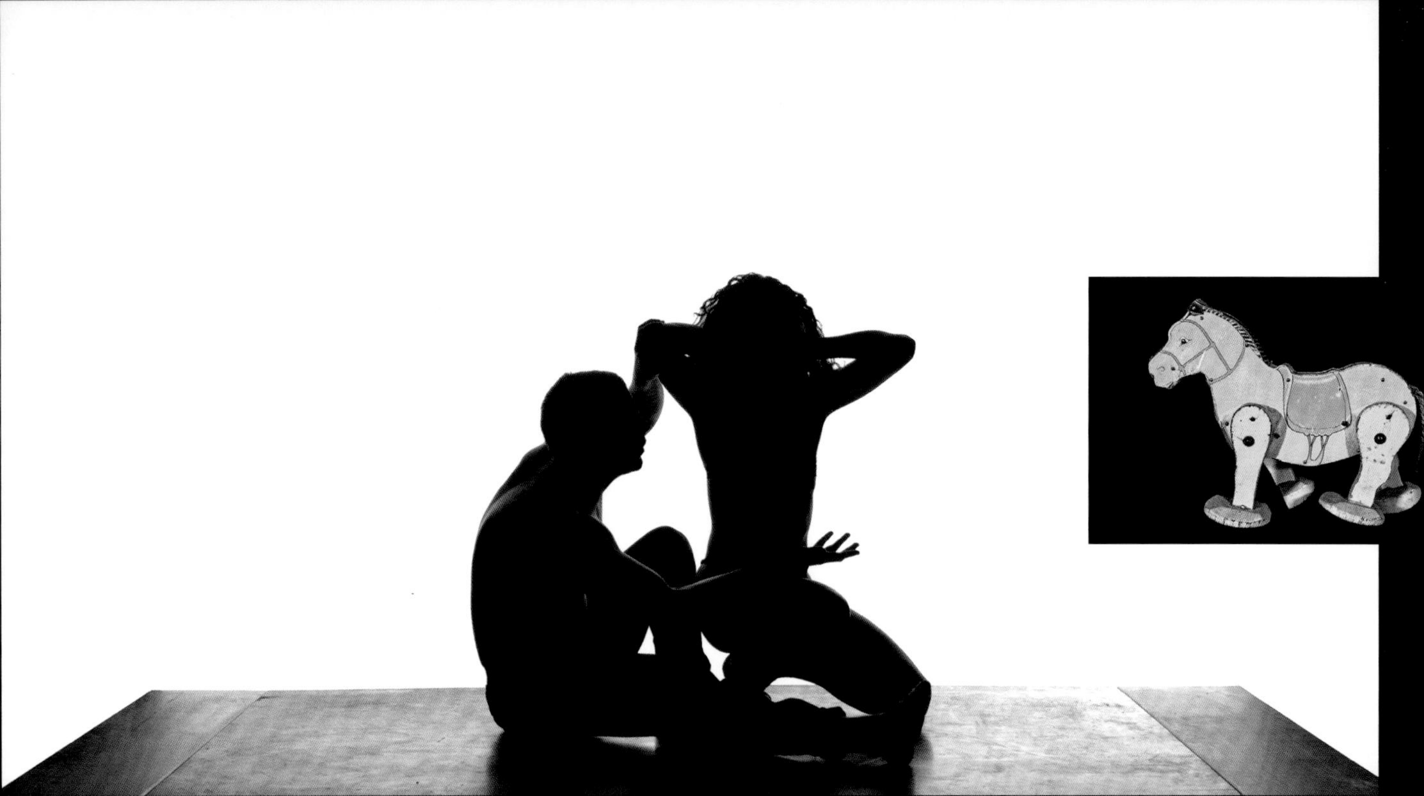

The concept of romantic love is a necessity from evolution's point of view. I think love is one of the highest forms of expression. We're here in a physical body and we exist on these multiple different planes. There's sex, and the

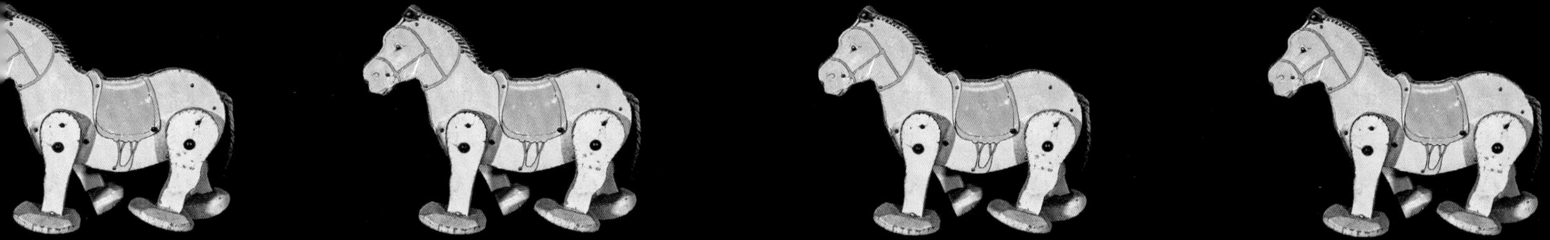

physical plane. But when you meet two individuals who are communicating and fitting together on that really subtle plane … the Sufi poet Rumi channels it in this beautiful phase, which is, 'My heart and your heart are very, very old friends.'" —A

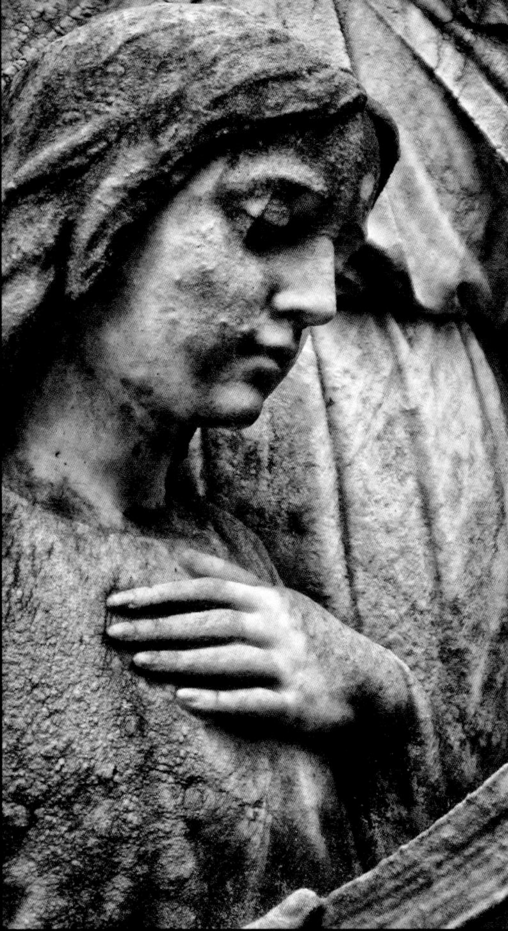

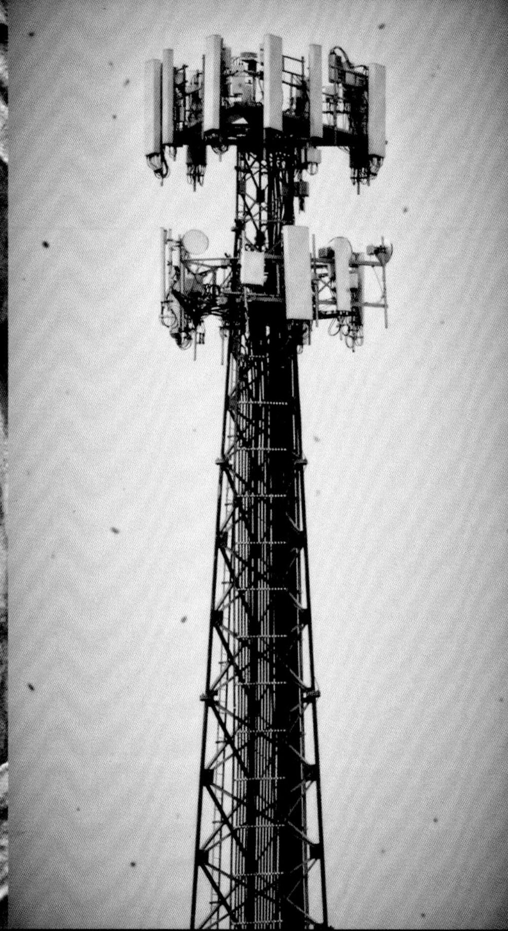

“There are
some things
about the
spirit

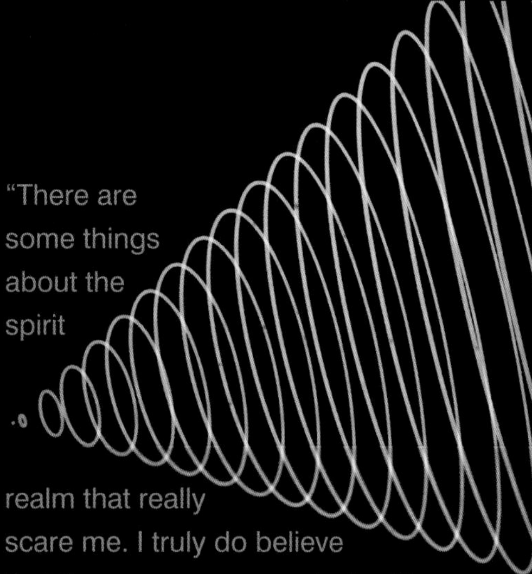

realm that really
scare me. I truly do believe
that there are powers, principalities,
rulers of darkness. And early on, when I wa
eighteen, nineteen, I had an experience livi
in New York City that was really wild. I felt li
there was a clear ‘Make your
choice now, light or da
decision to be made.” —C

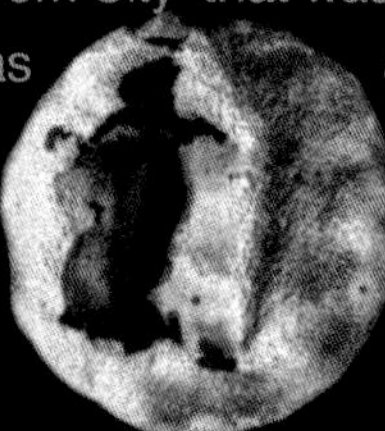

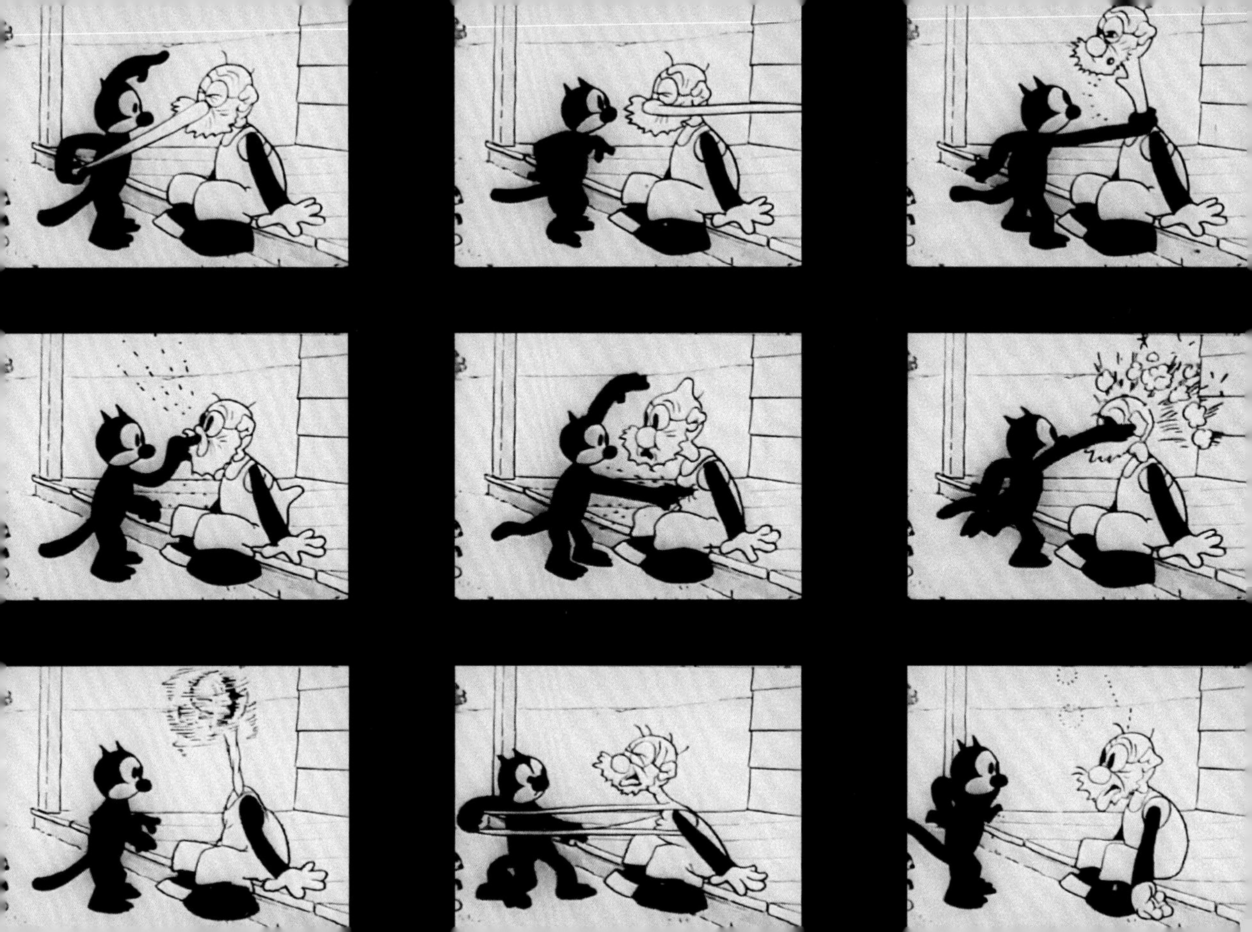

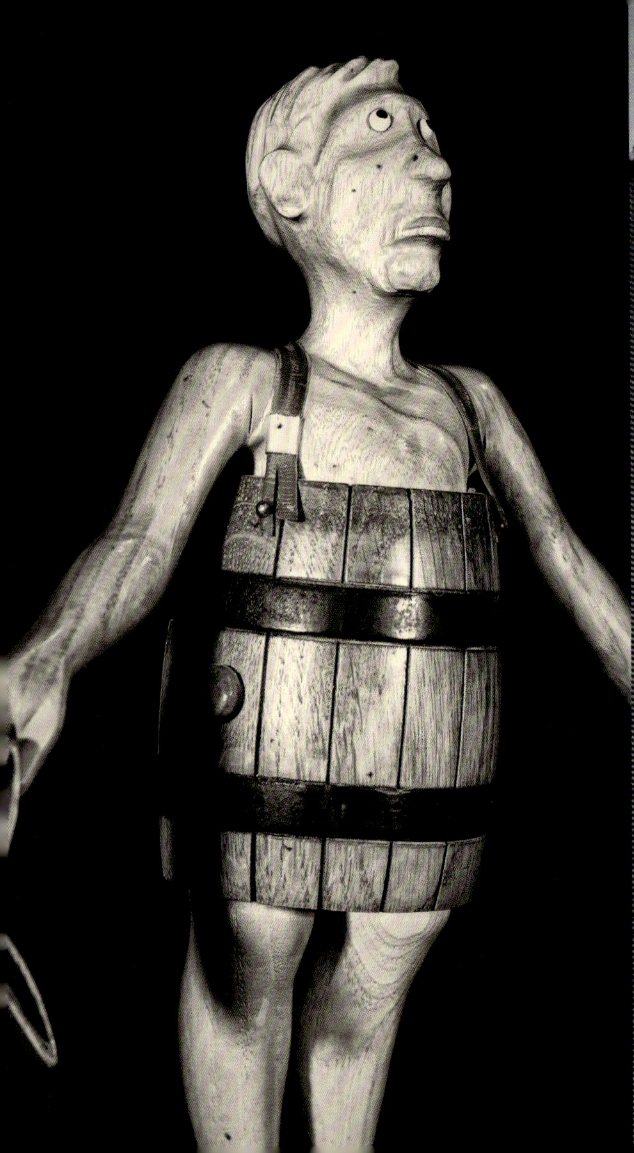

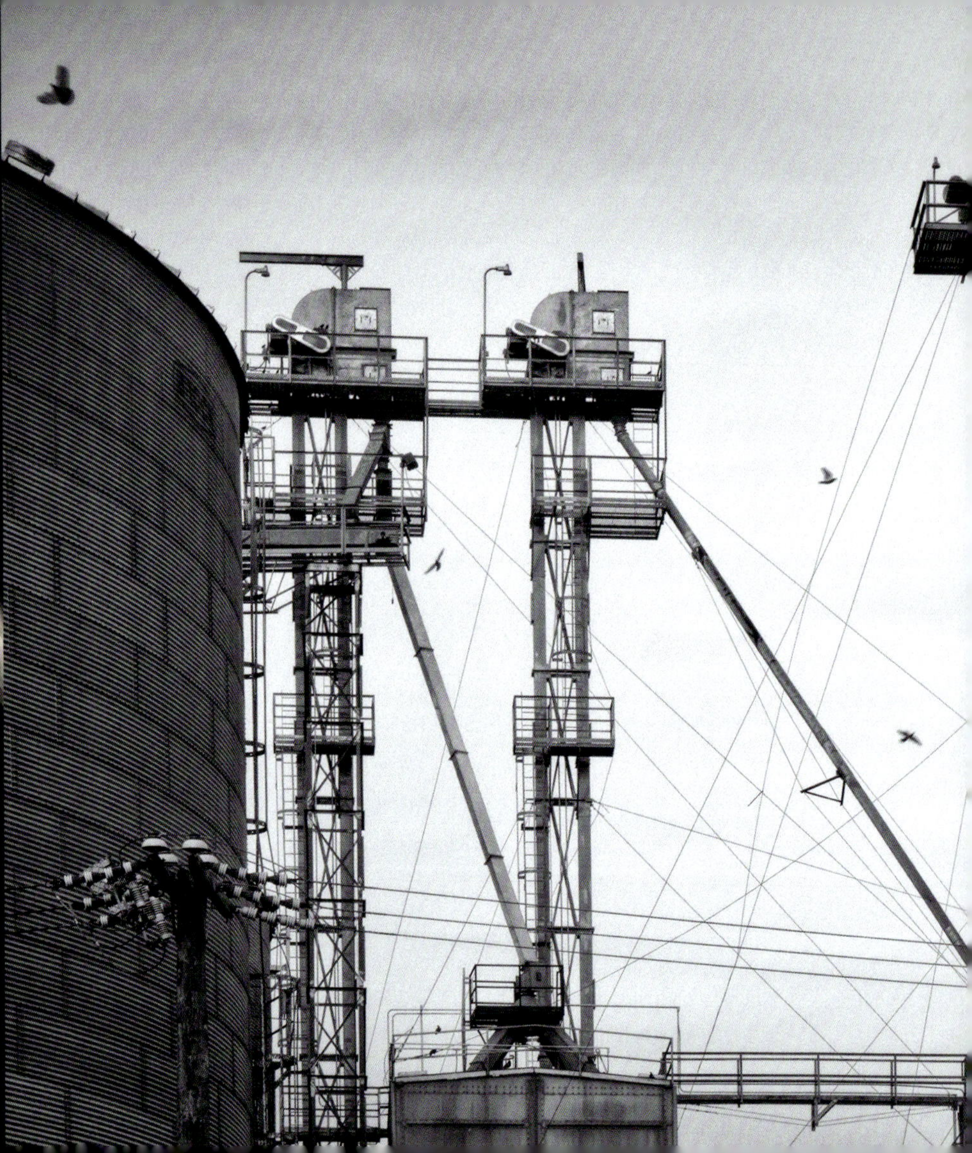

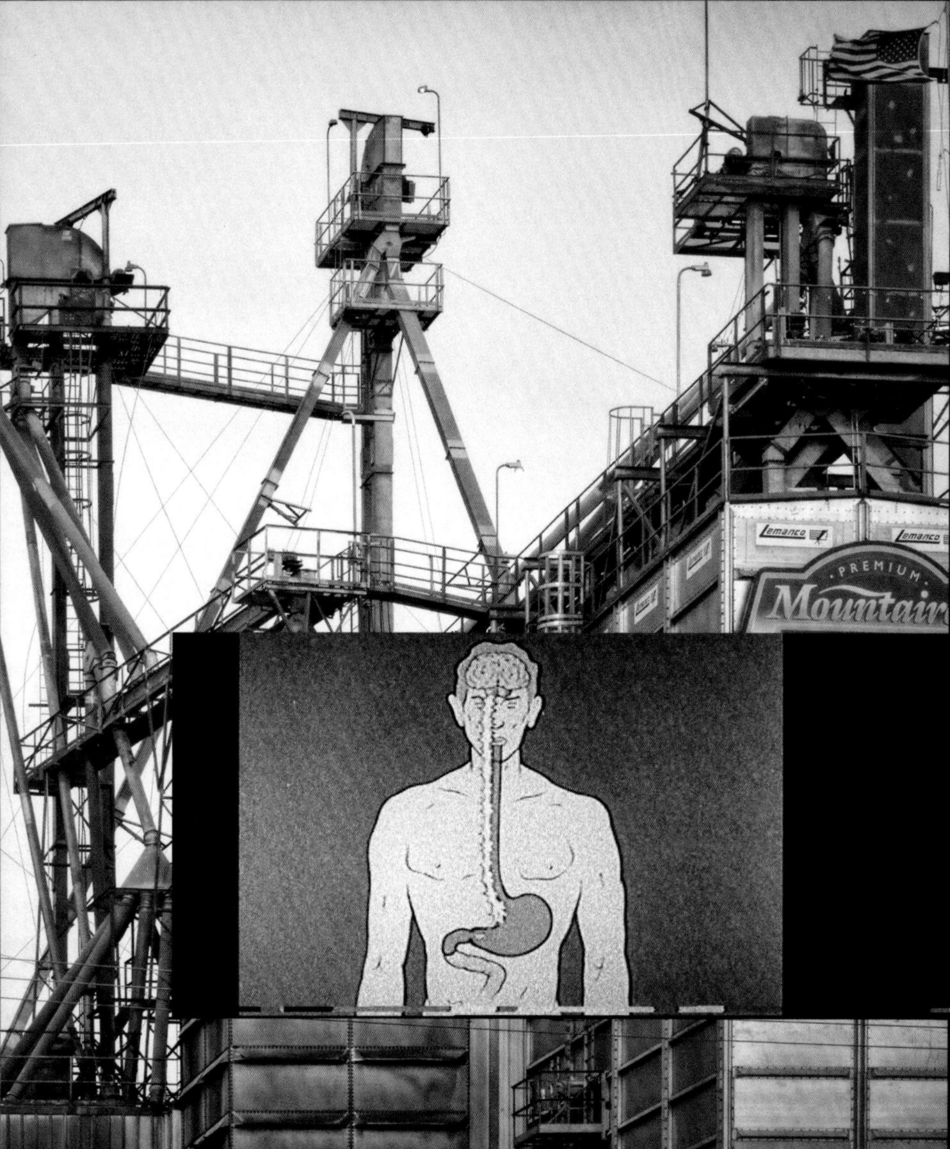

"Foster children came into my parents' home when I was about ten years old. That was a pretty unique aspect of my childhood. There were already six of us before my parents started to do foster care for kids who'd had the worst start in life. Kids who'd either almost been killed, or were starved, tortured." —C

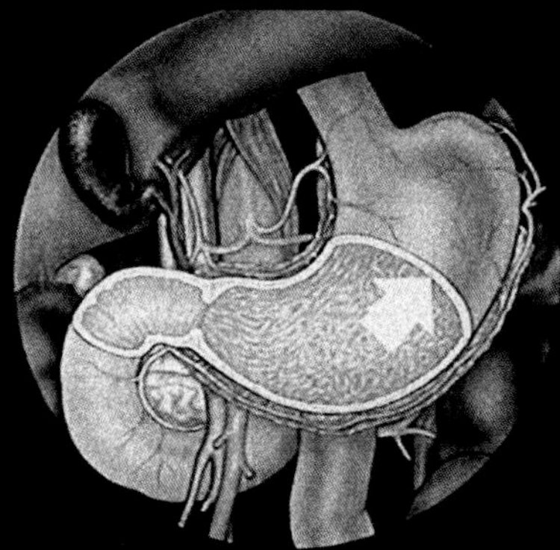

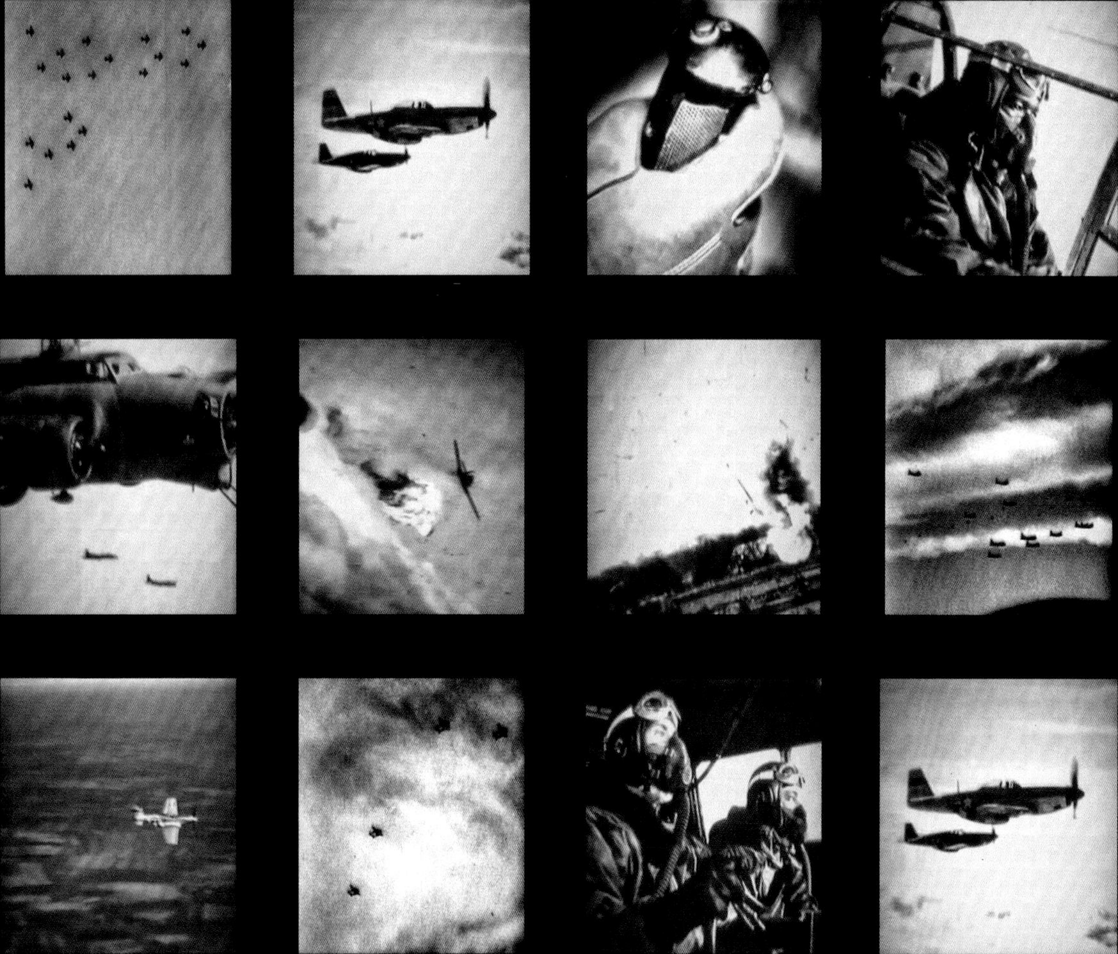

"I've felt despair. I've been in a dark space and not known how I'm going to get out of it. But I've never considered suicide or felt that active desire to end things. But I can understand how people get there. It's very easy to make a rash decision nowadays, and we live in a very isolated world." —A

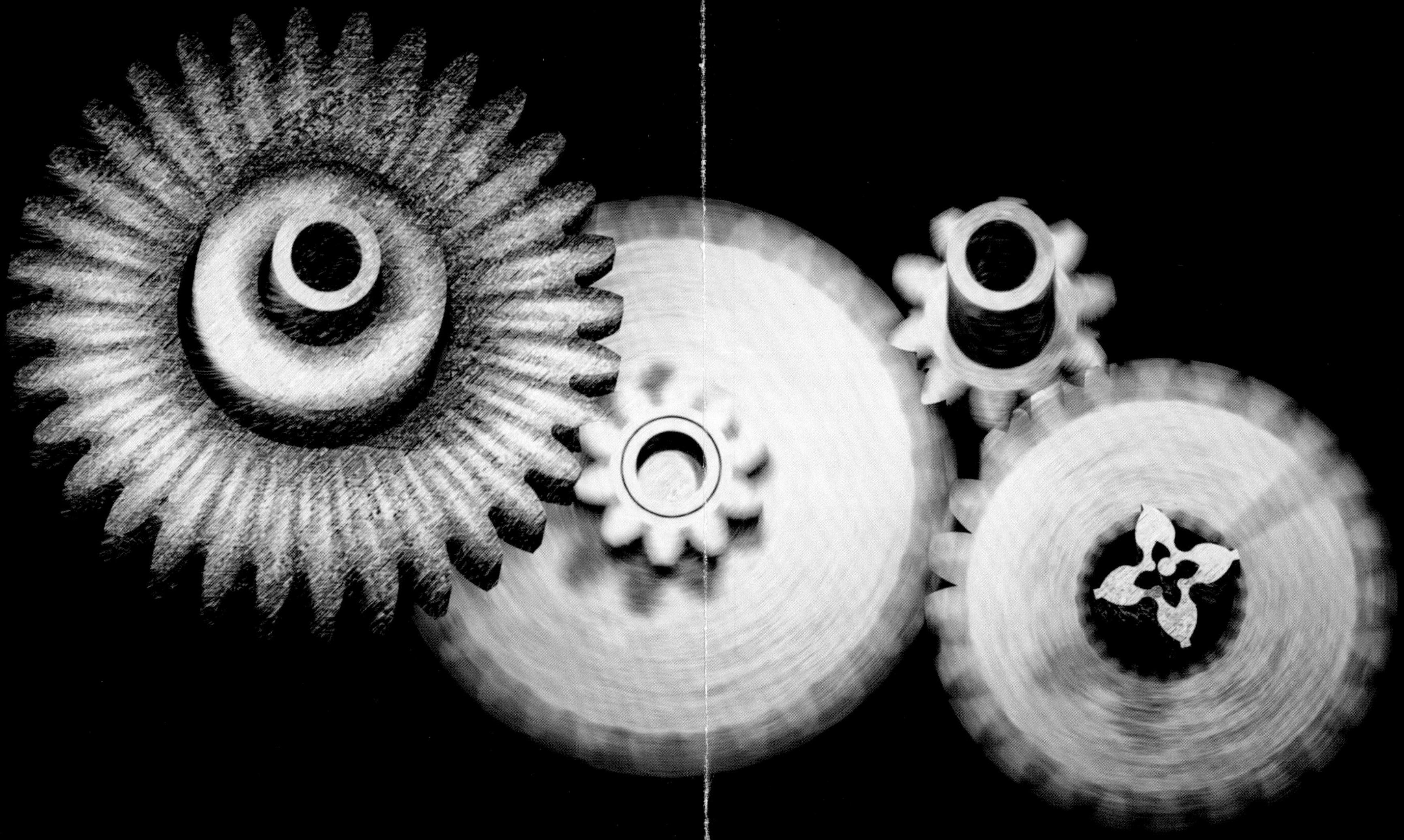

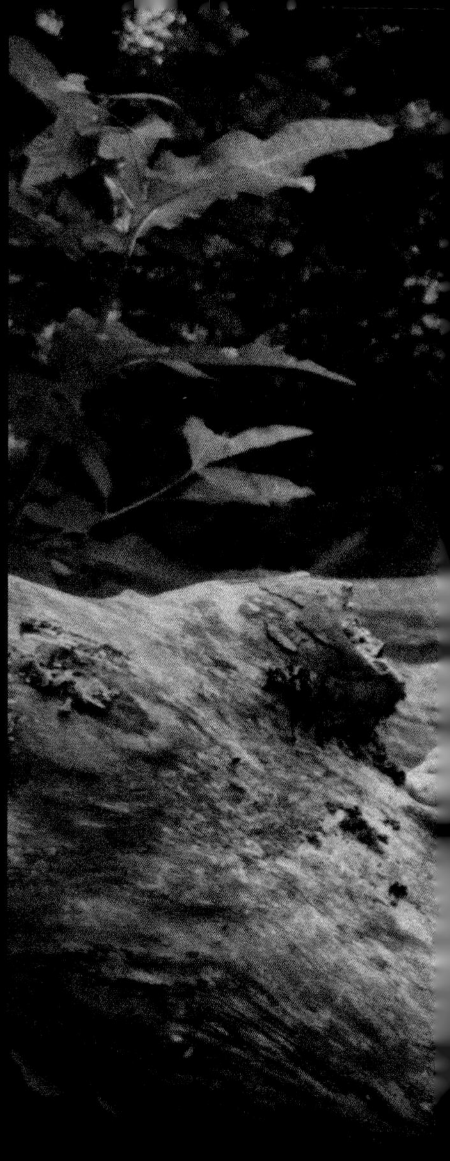

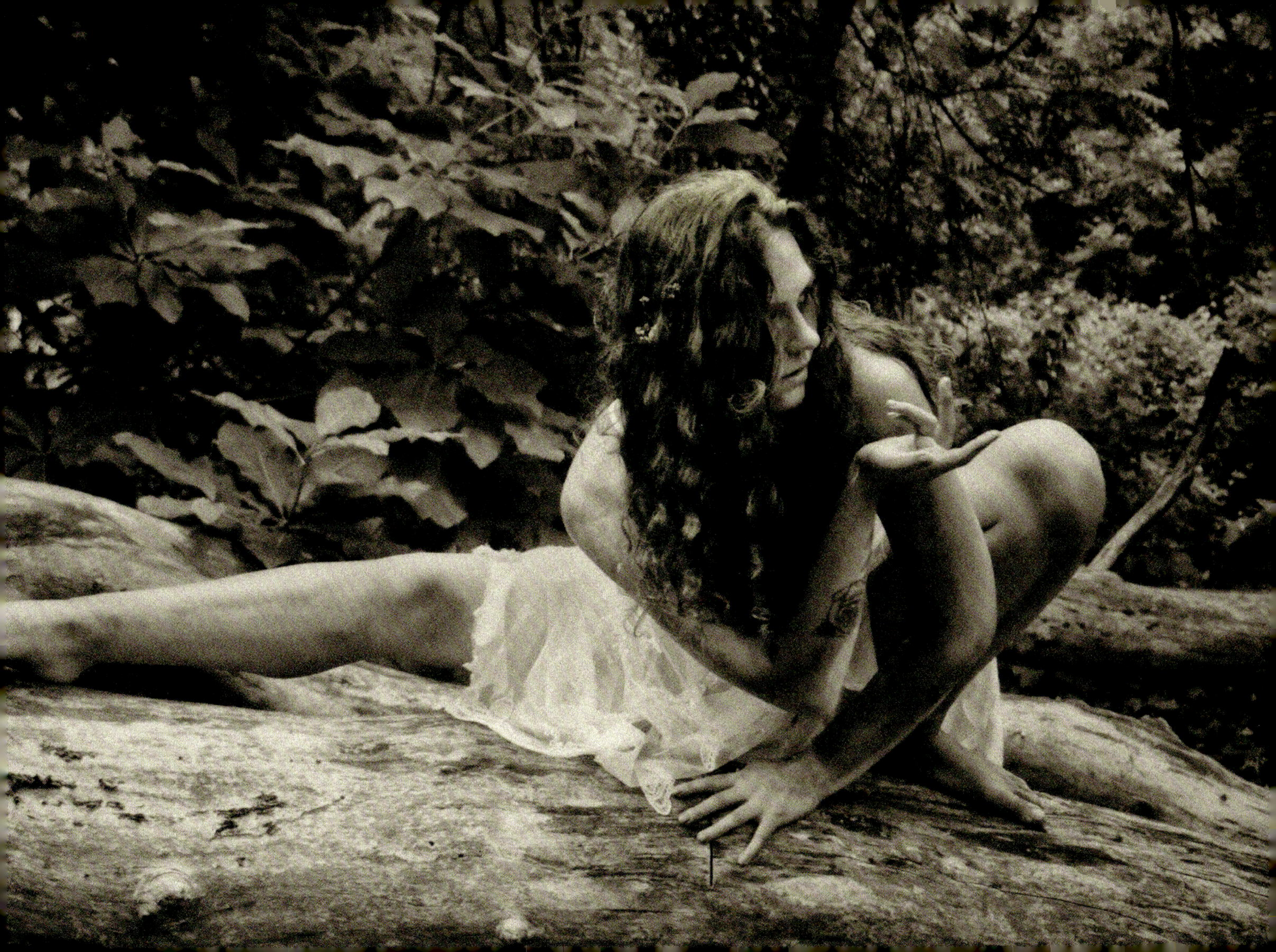

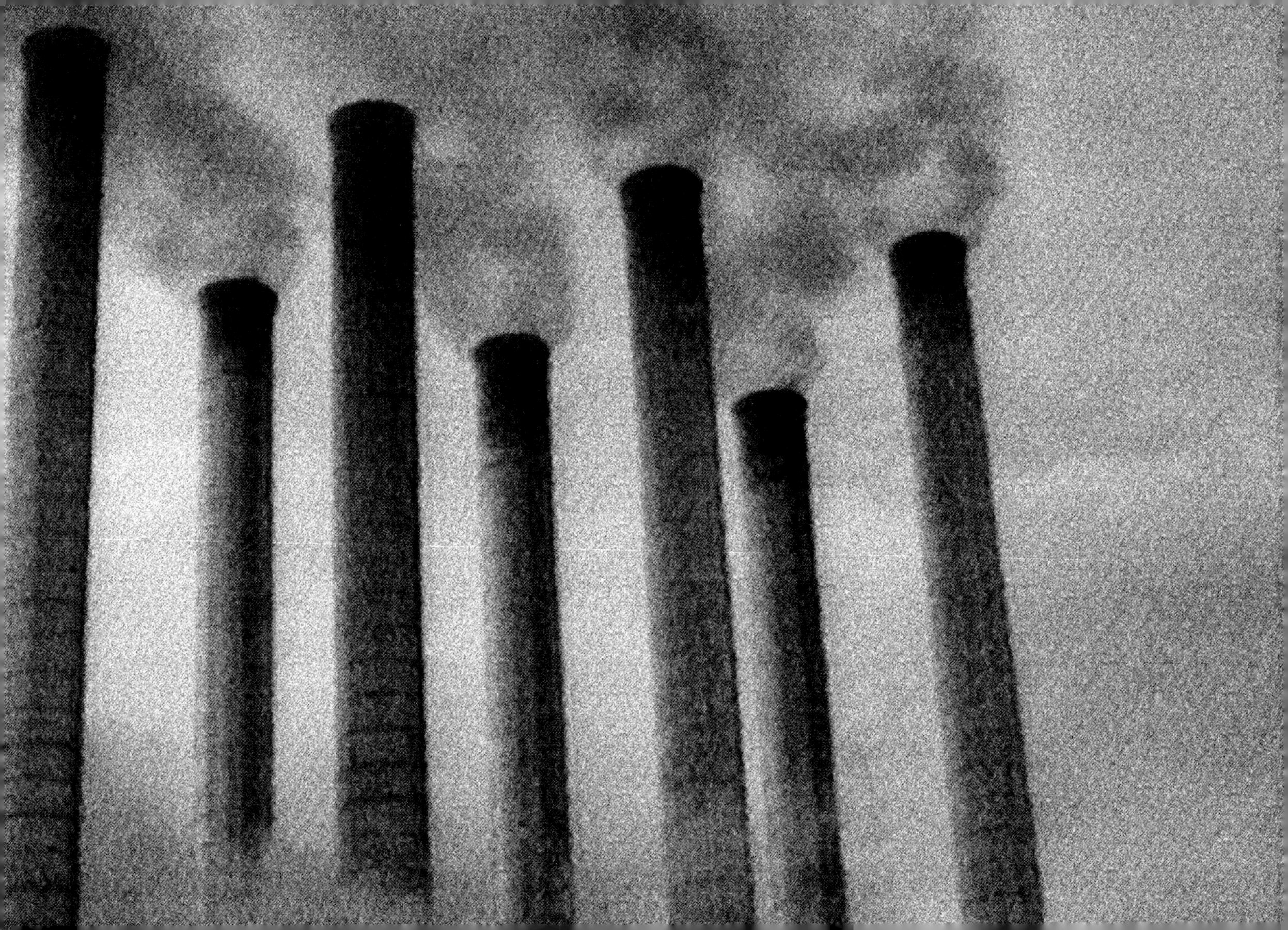

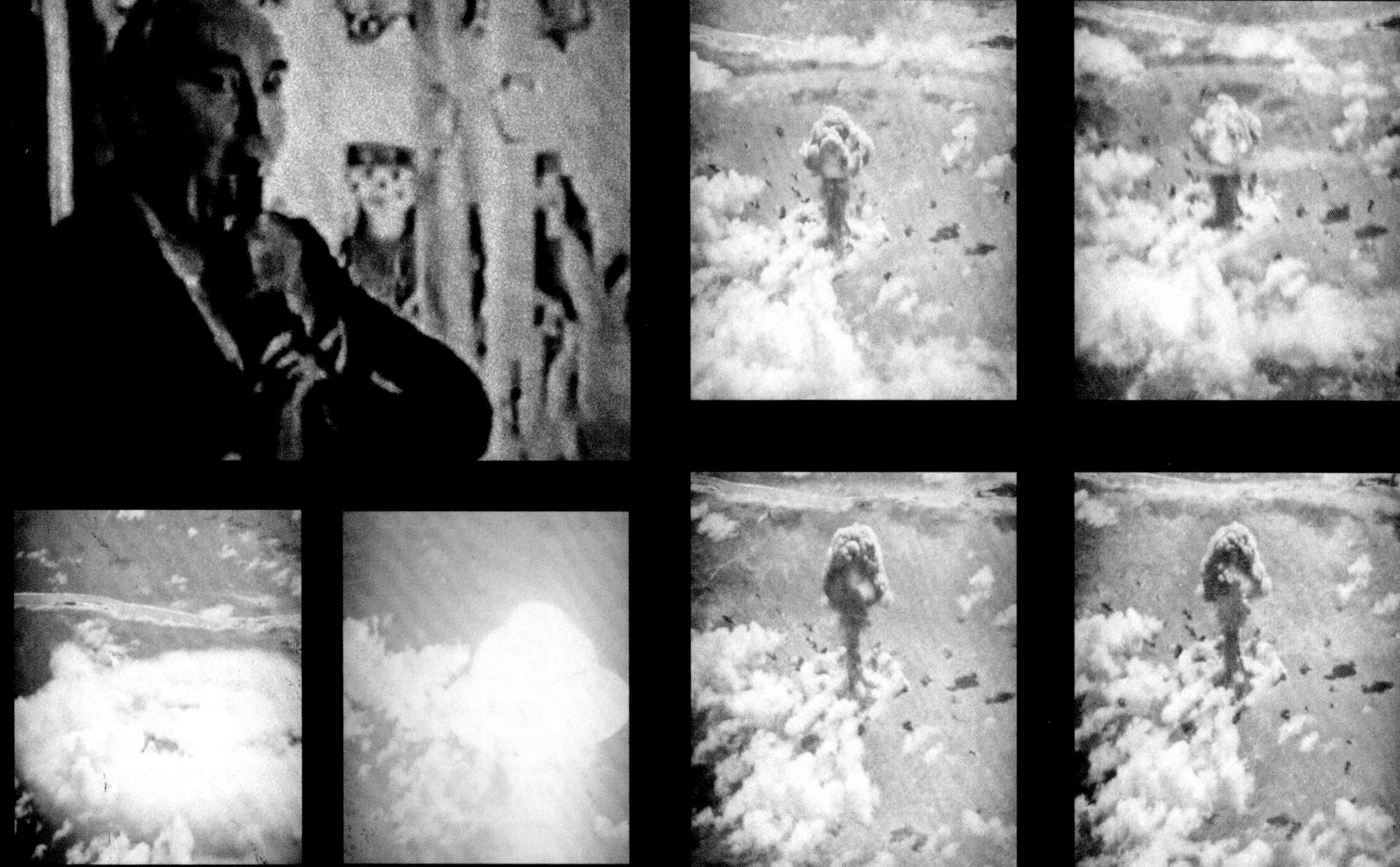

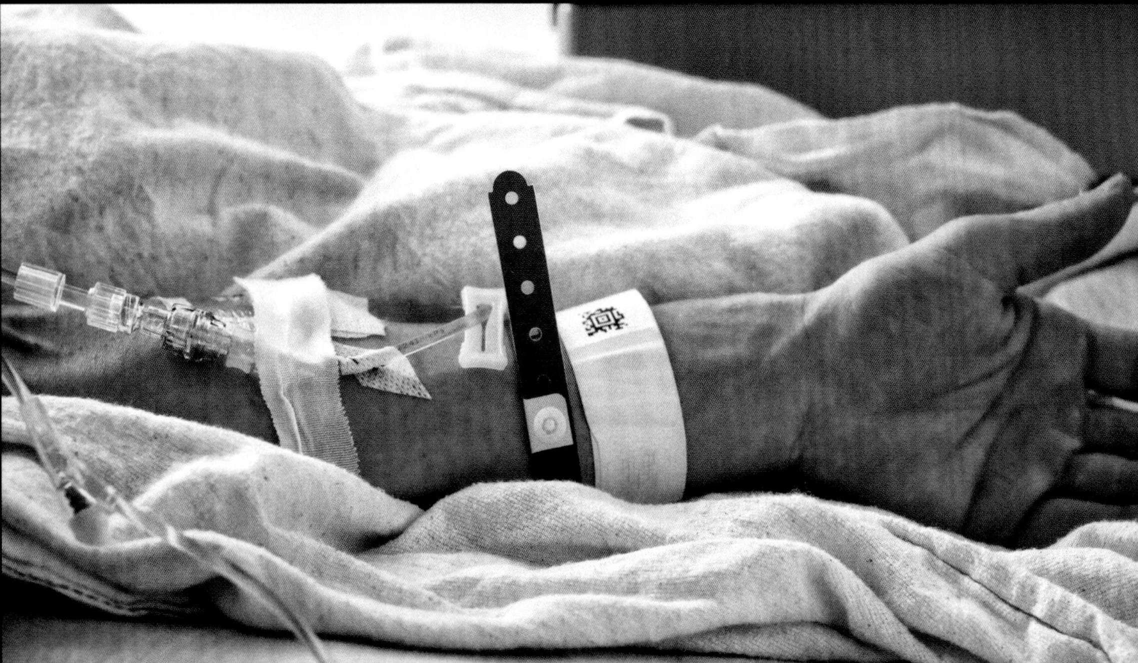

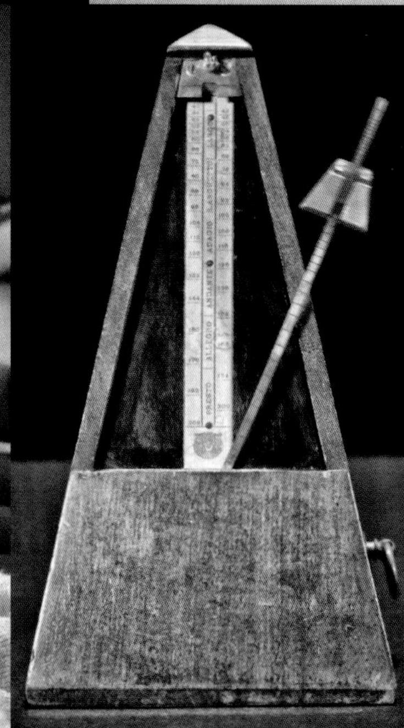

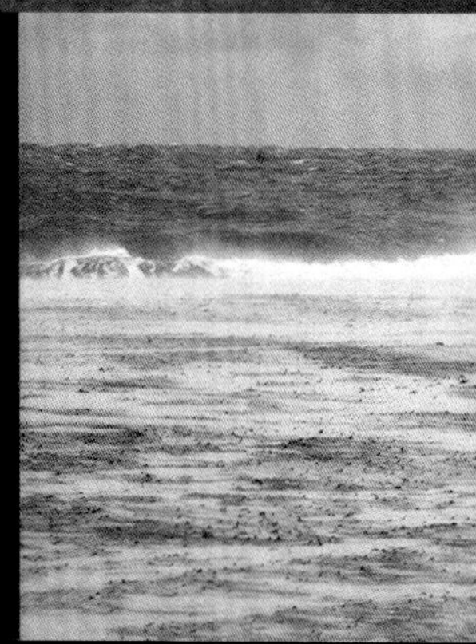

“When I think about death, I feel like I may have already died. I have these experiences that are like being in a lucid dream, as if I’ve already matriculated through death and its codices. If you look at it from a scientific perspective, matter and energy can’t be created or destroyed, so it makes sense that after death our energy persists in some form and subsequently attenuates.” —G

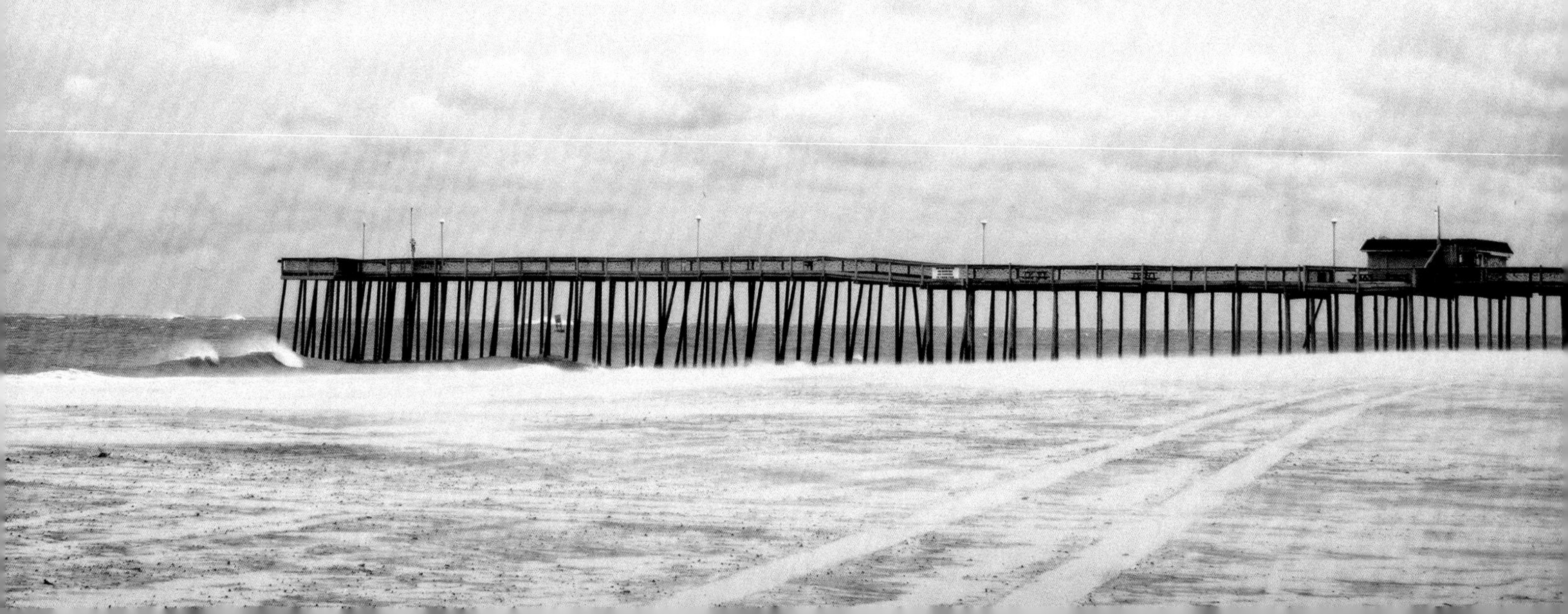

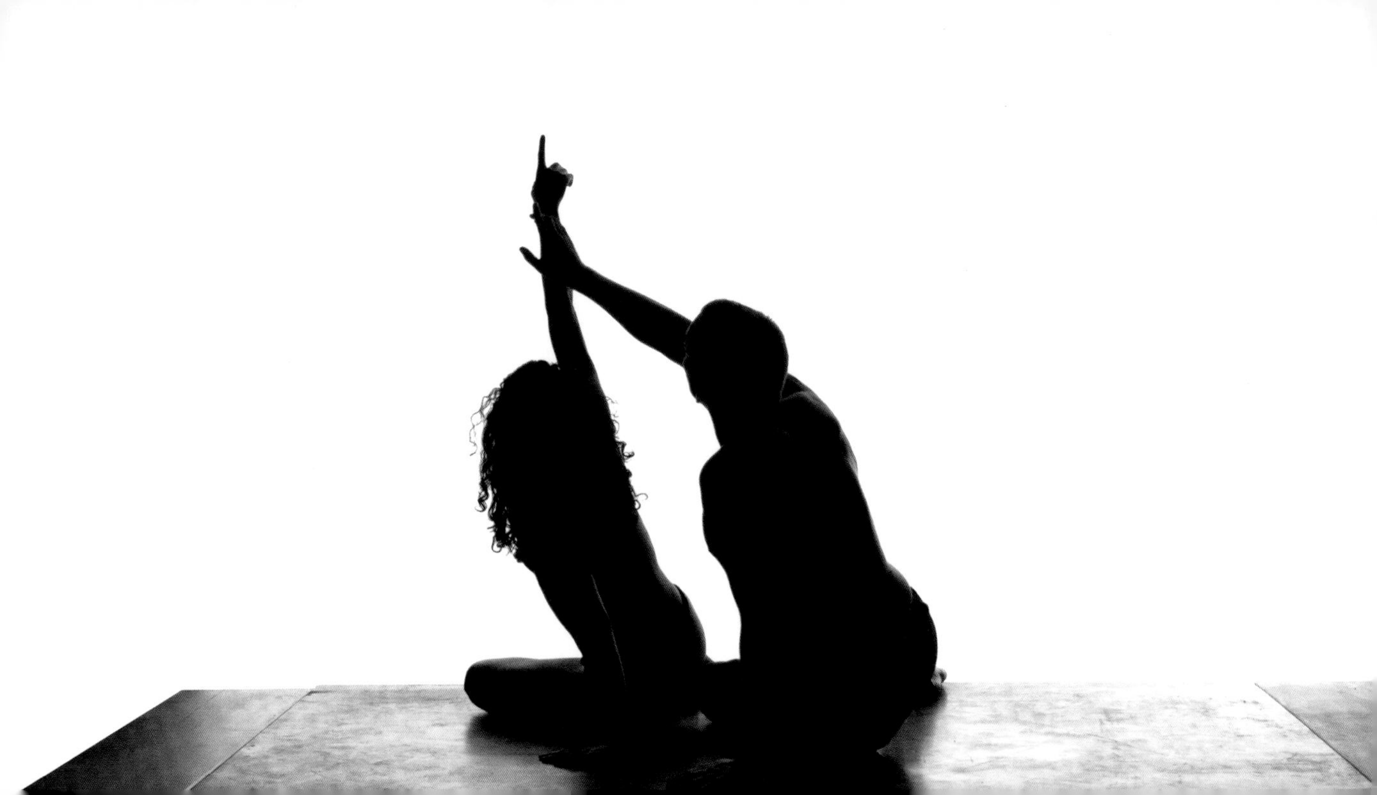

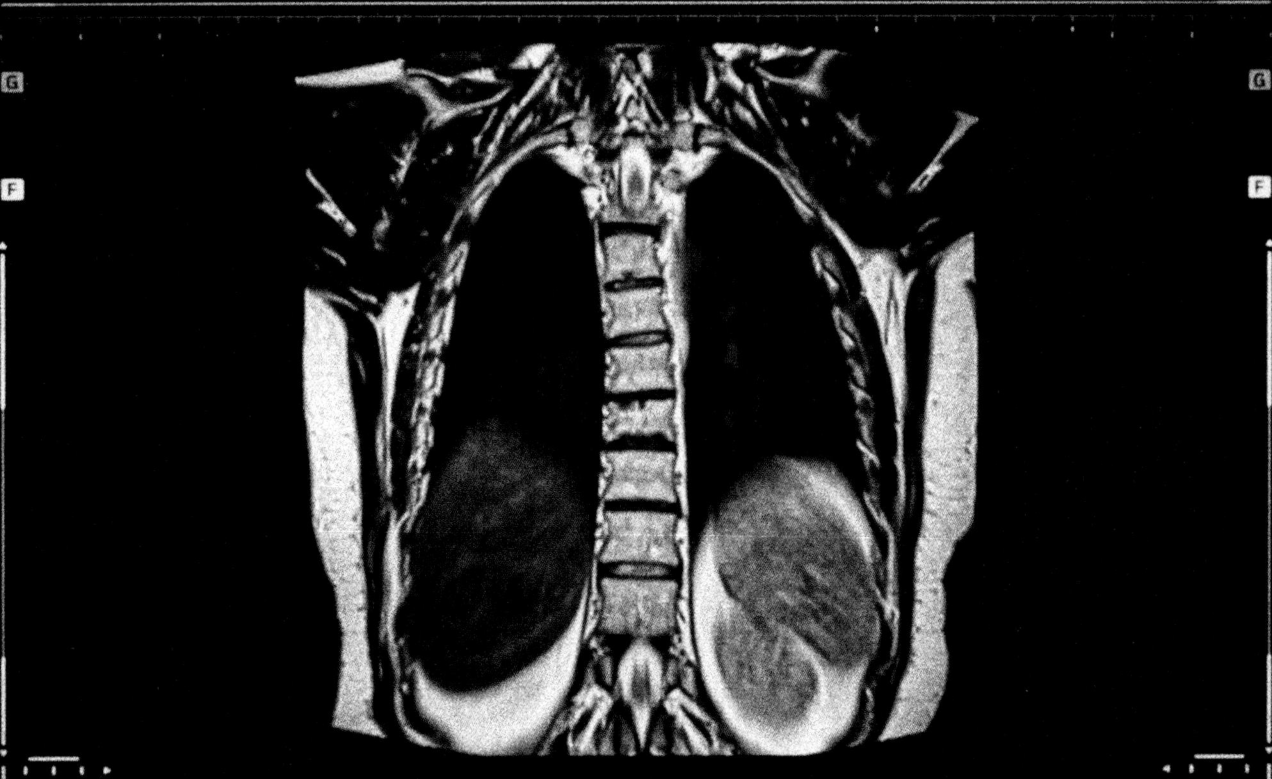
G
F
G
F

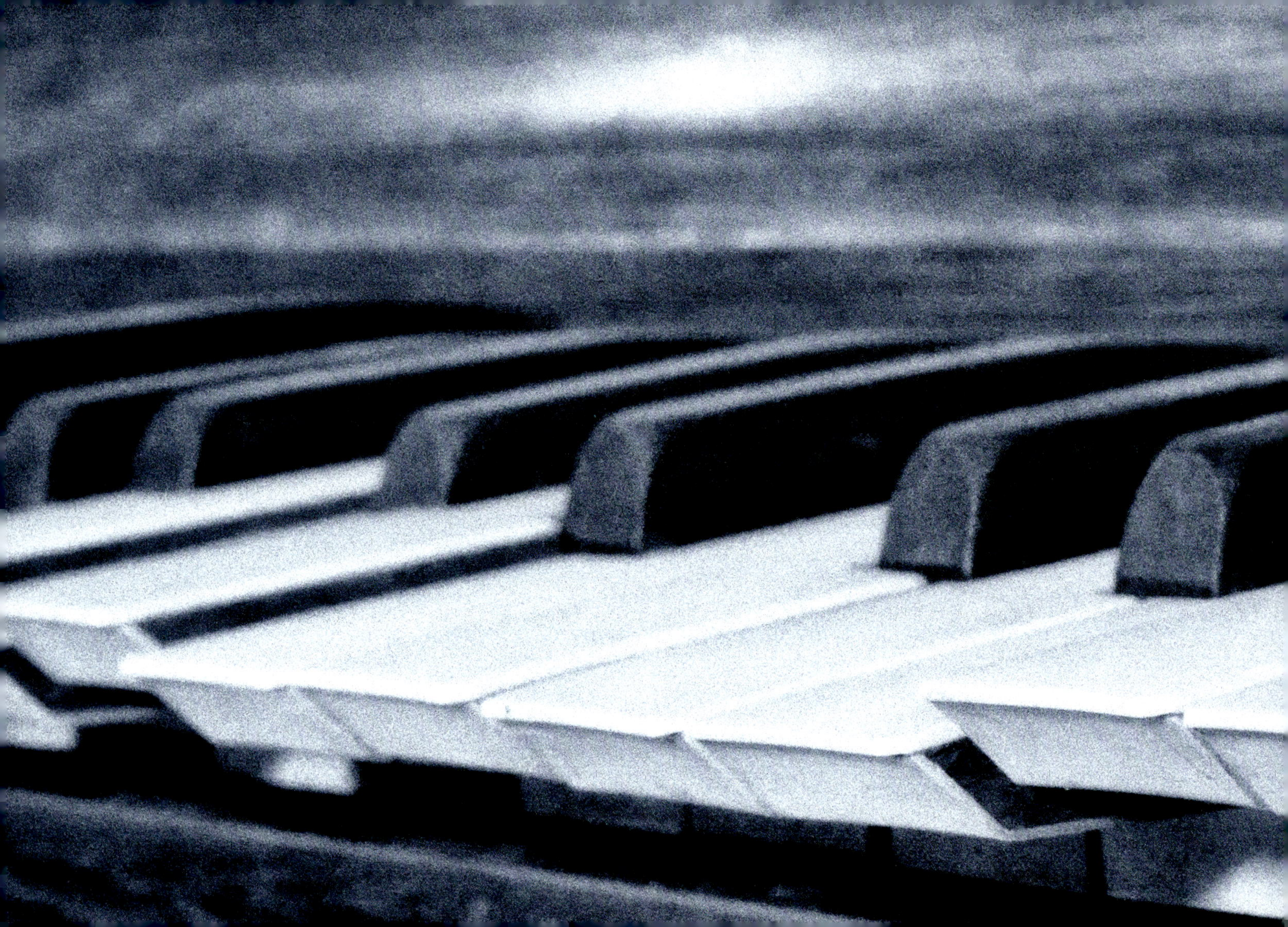

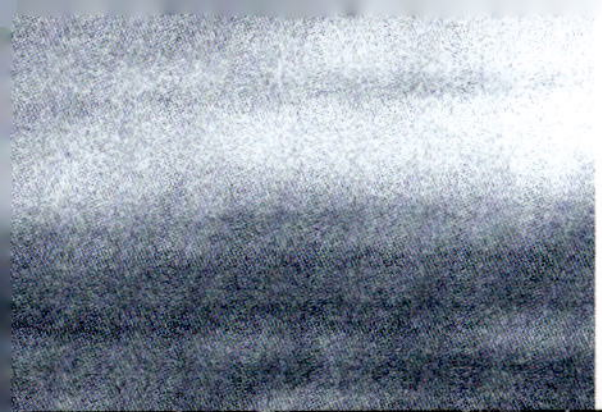

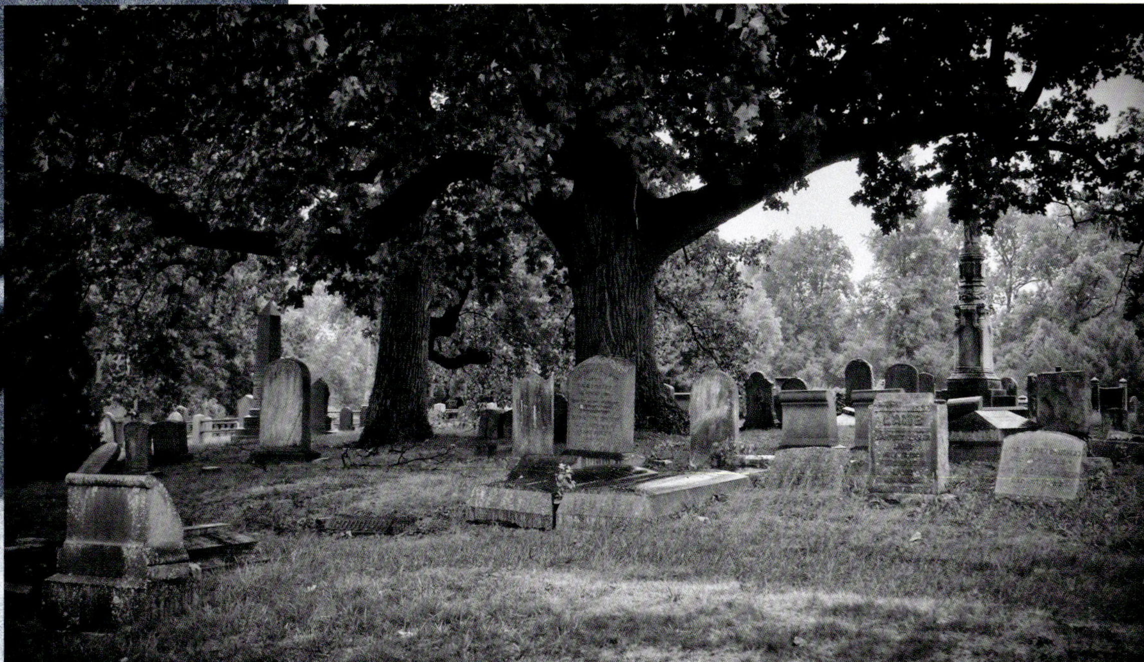

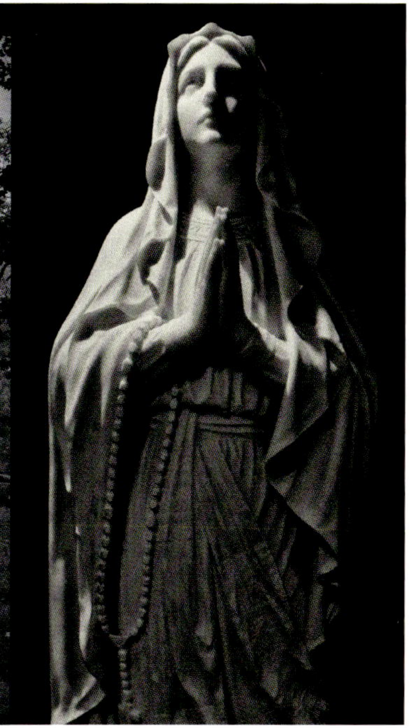

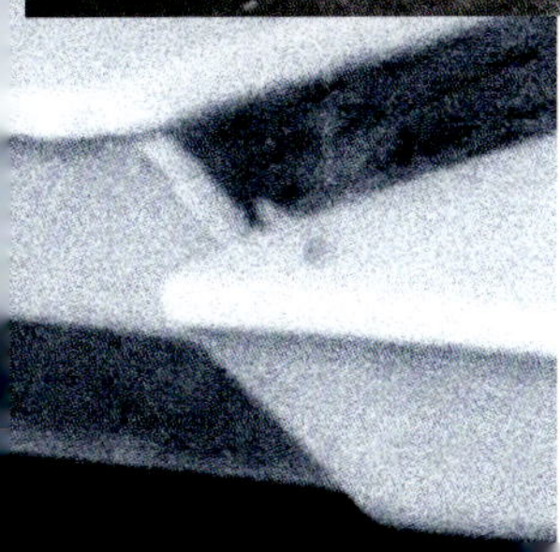

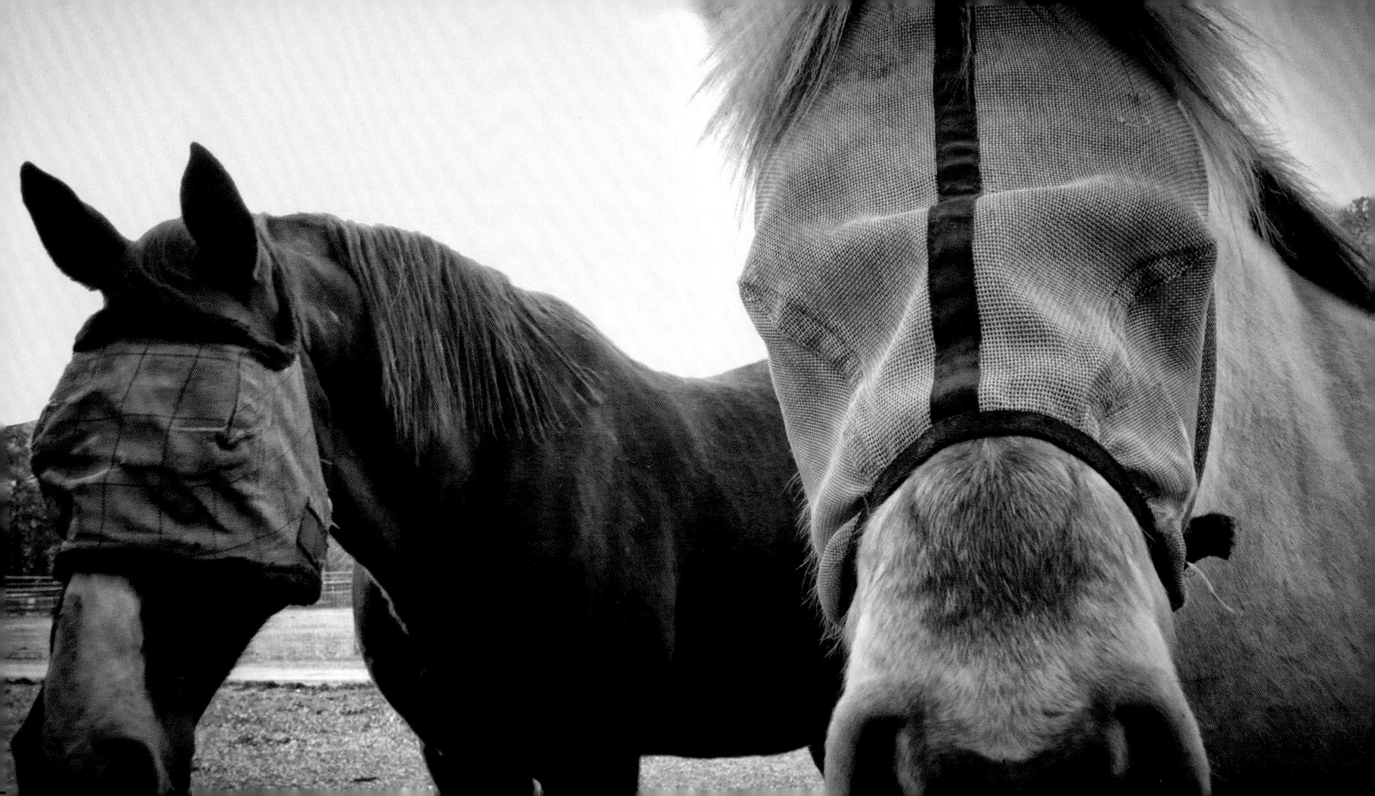

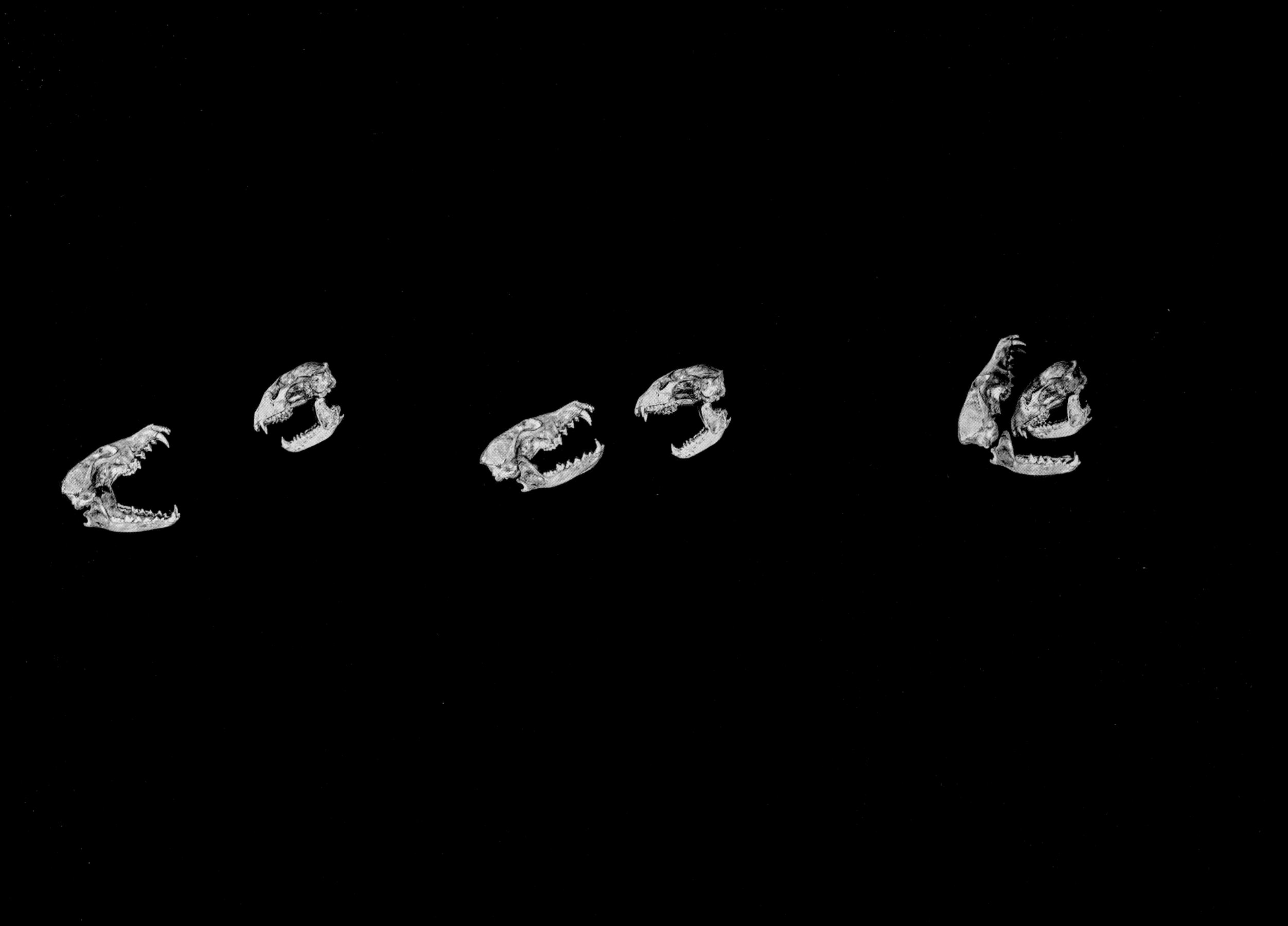

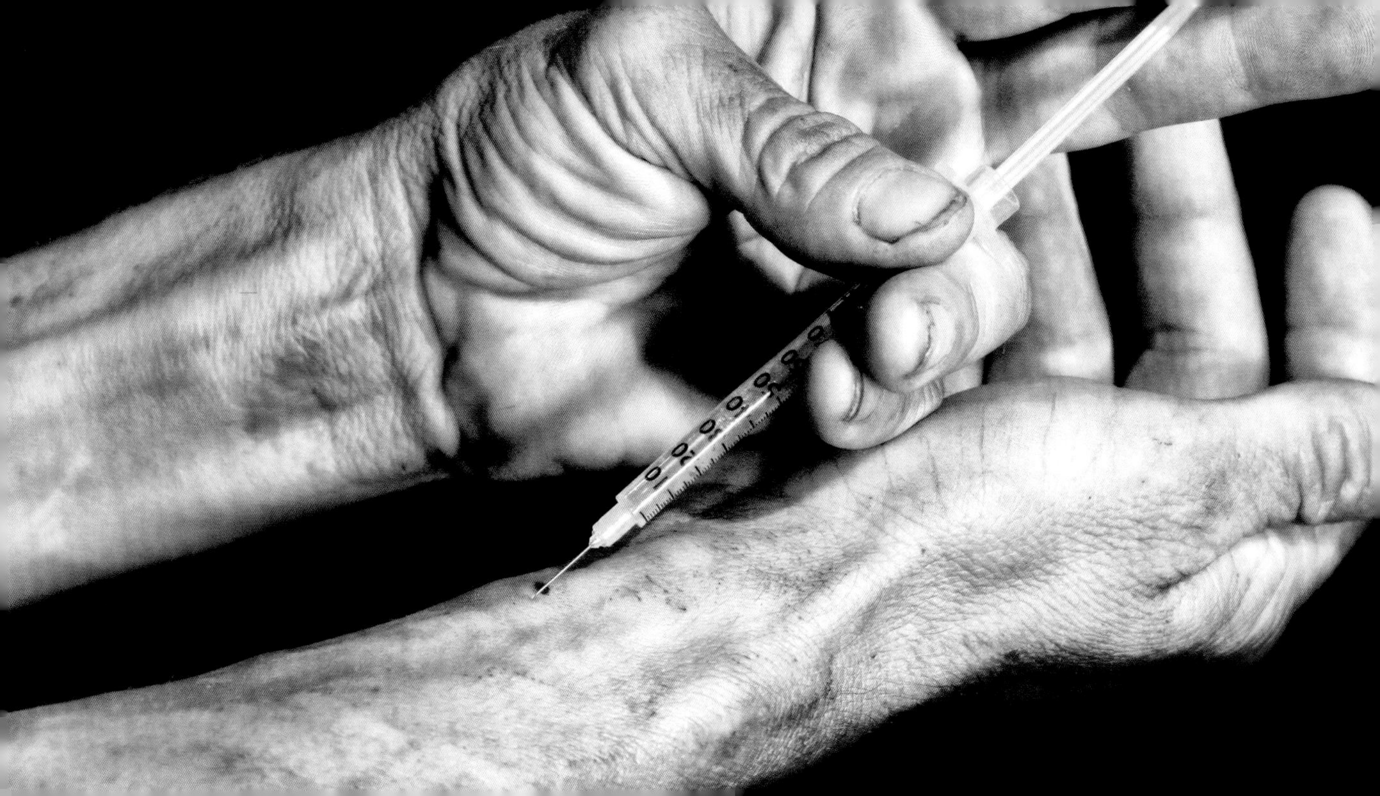

"In my experience, addiction is far and away the most fundamental human defect that could potentially exist. At the same time, I think it's a necessary force for any form of evolution to occur. What would we be if we didn't have these impulses that said, 'Try for more, do something different'? It's hard to imagine what humanity would look like without addiction. If God exists, I think he added addiction out of necessity, because there would be no means to drive the human race forward otherwise. Everyone is addicted to something." —G

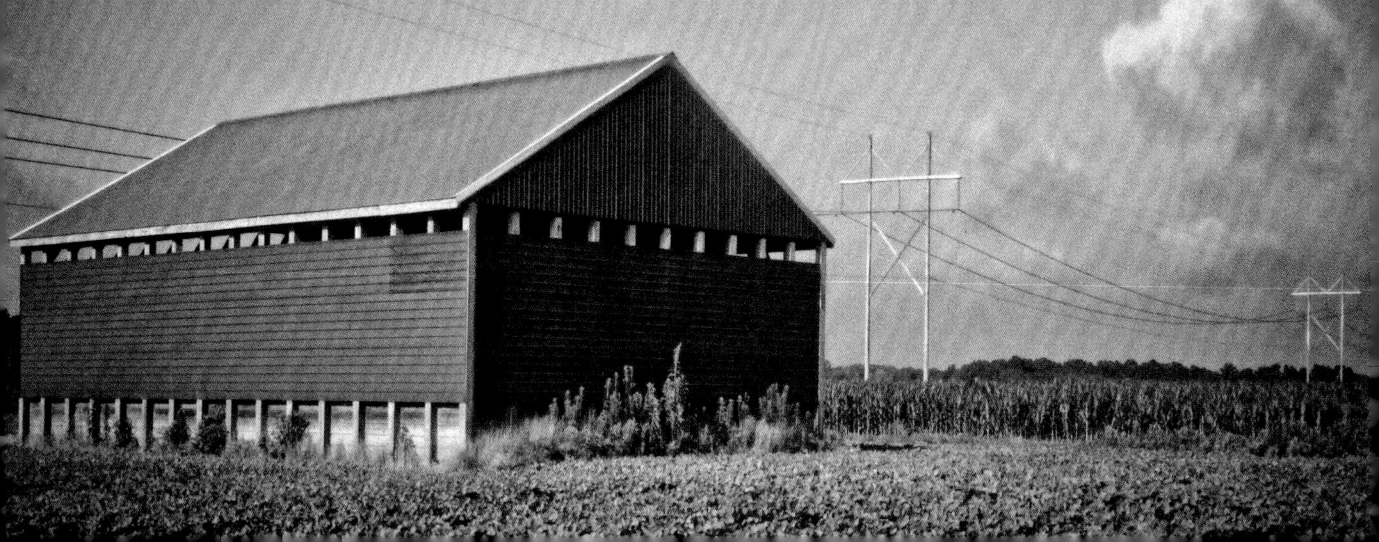

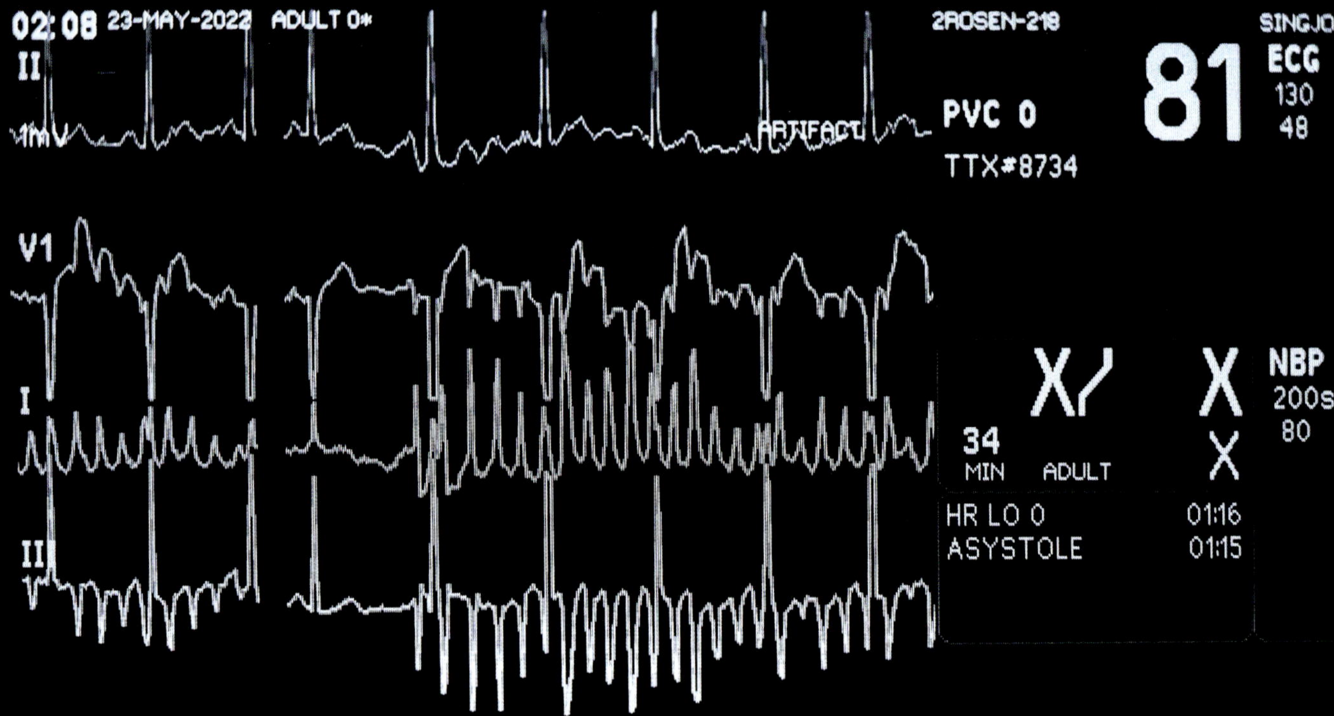
02:08 23-MAY-2022 ADULT 0*
2ROSEN-218
SINGJO
II
1mV
ARTIFACT
PVC 0
TTX#8734
81
ECG
130
48
V1
I
II
34
MIN
ADULT
NBP
200s
80
HR LO 0 01:16
ASYSTOLE 01:15

We want to find exactly how, when, and where our natural desires have warped us. We wish to look squarely at the unhappiness this has caused others and ourselves. By discovering what our emotional deformities are, we can move toward their correction. Without a willing and persistent effort to do this, there can be little sobriety or contentment for us. Without a searching and fearless moral inventory, most of us have found that the faith which really works in daily living is still out of reach.

Before tackling the inventory problem in detail, let's have a closer look at what the basic problem is. Simple examples like the following take on a world of meaning when we think about them. Suppose a person places sex desire ahead of everything else. In such a case, this imperious urge can destroy his chances for material and emotional security as well as his standing in the community. Another may develop such an obsession for financial security that he wants to do nothing but hoard money. Going to the extreme, he can become a miser, or even a recluse who denies himself both family and friends.

Nor is the quest for security always expressed in terms of money. How frequently we see a frightened human being determined to depend completely upon a stronger person for guidance and protection. This weak one, failing to meet life's responsibilities with his own resources, never grows up. Disillusionment and helplessness are his lot. In time all his protectors either flee or die, and he is once more left alone and afraid.

We have also seen men and women who go power-mad, who devote themselves to attempting to rule their fellows.

"If I could change one thing about myself, it would be to stop getting high. I use everything—heroin, meth, coke, crack—yet I'm not dependent on anything. I started getting high when I was thirteen, developed a strong taste for cocaine, and my prolific spree of burglaries began as a way of paying for it all. For me to stop getting high, I'd need to find a way to enjoy life without the presence of these external chemical communicators, and I have no idea how to do that." —G

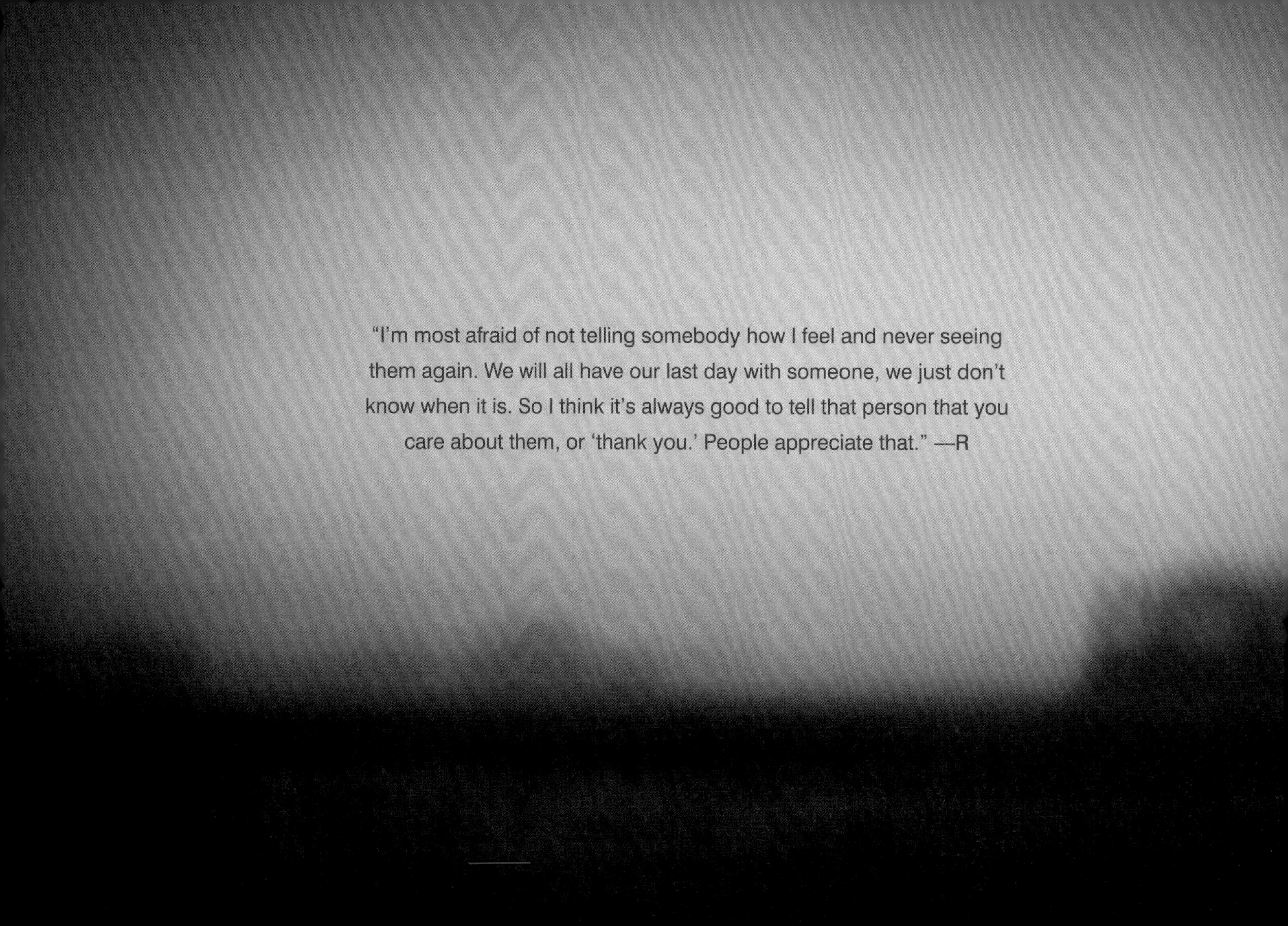

"I'm most afraid of not telling somebody how I feel and never seeing them again. We will all have our last day with someone, we just don't know when it is. So I think it's always good to tell that person that you care about them, or 'thank you.' People appreciate that." —R

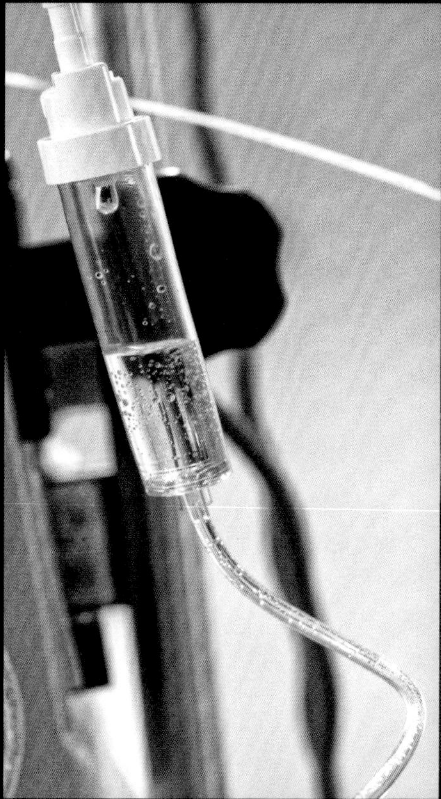

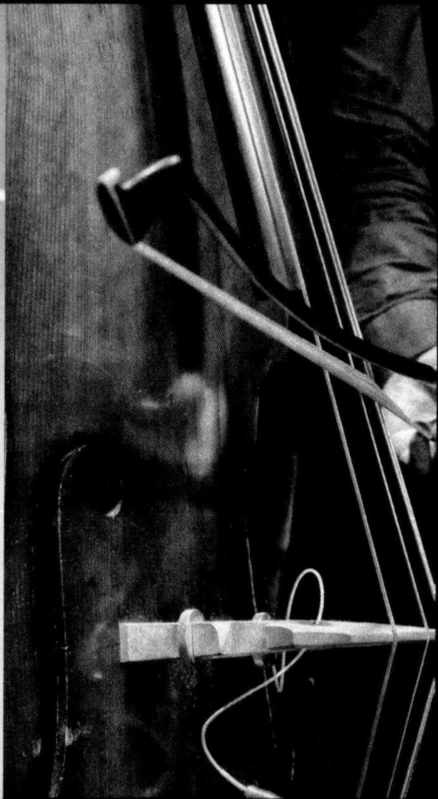

"I'm proud that love is the most important thing to me right now. Opening my heart to loving myself, and the world, and people, and animals, and the earth. I don't care about anything else." —C

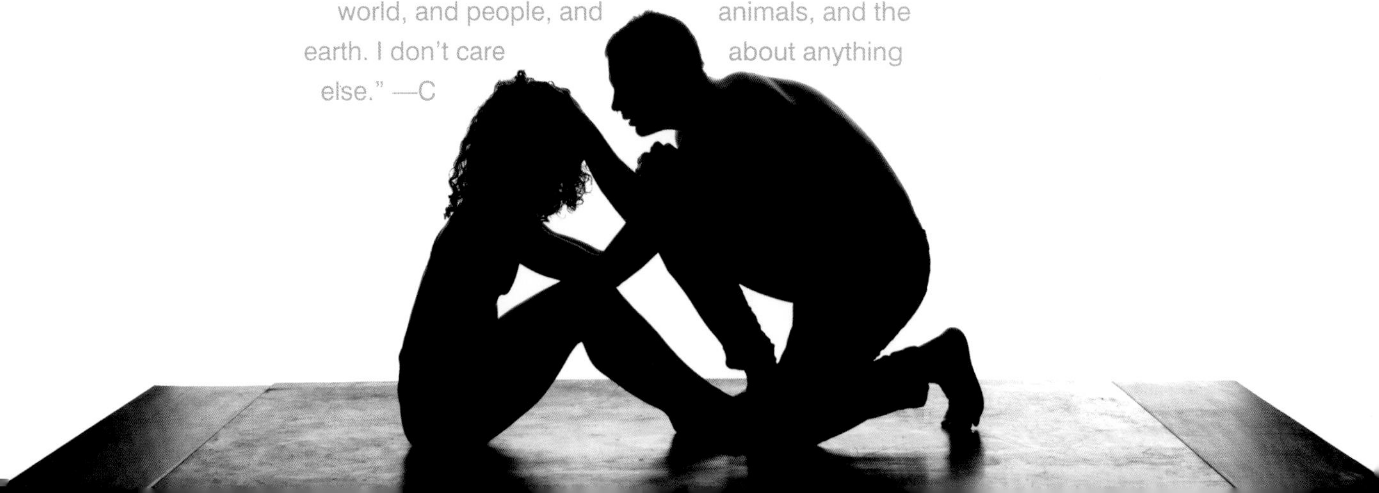

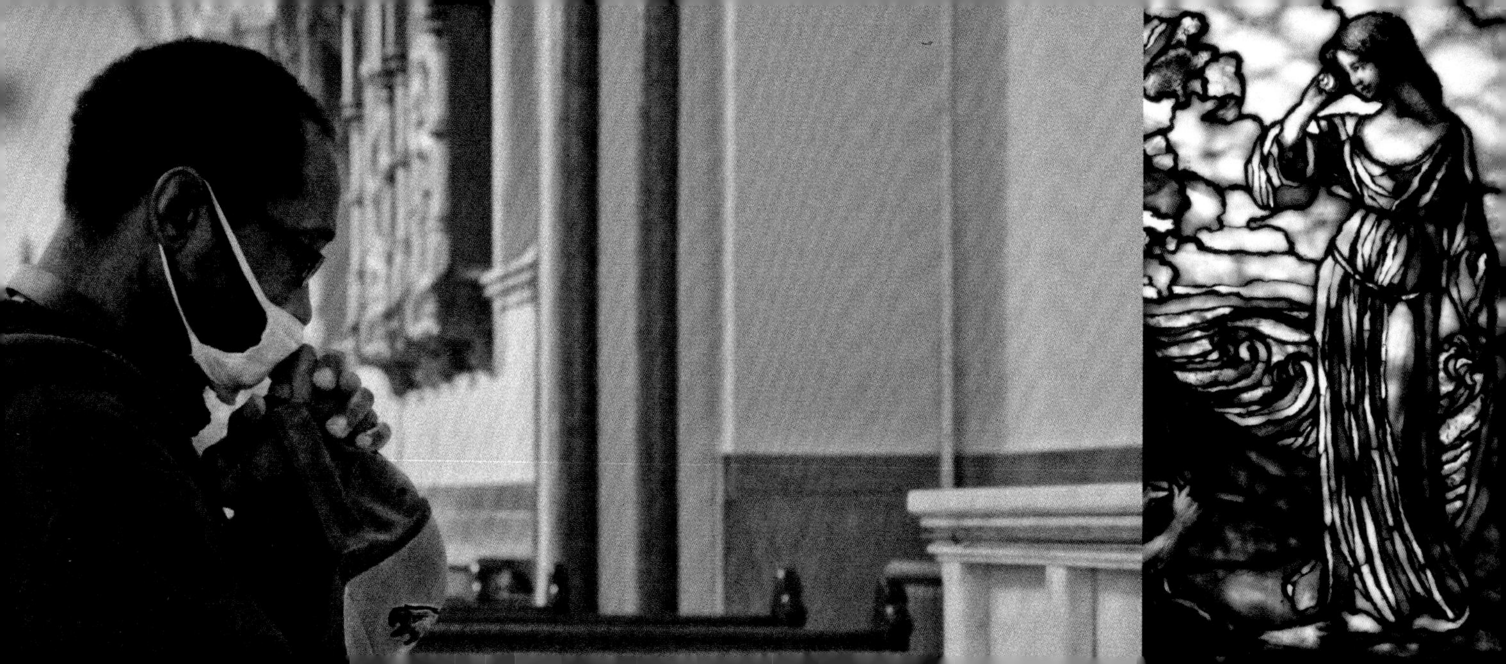

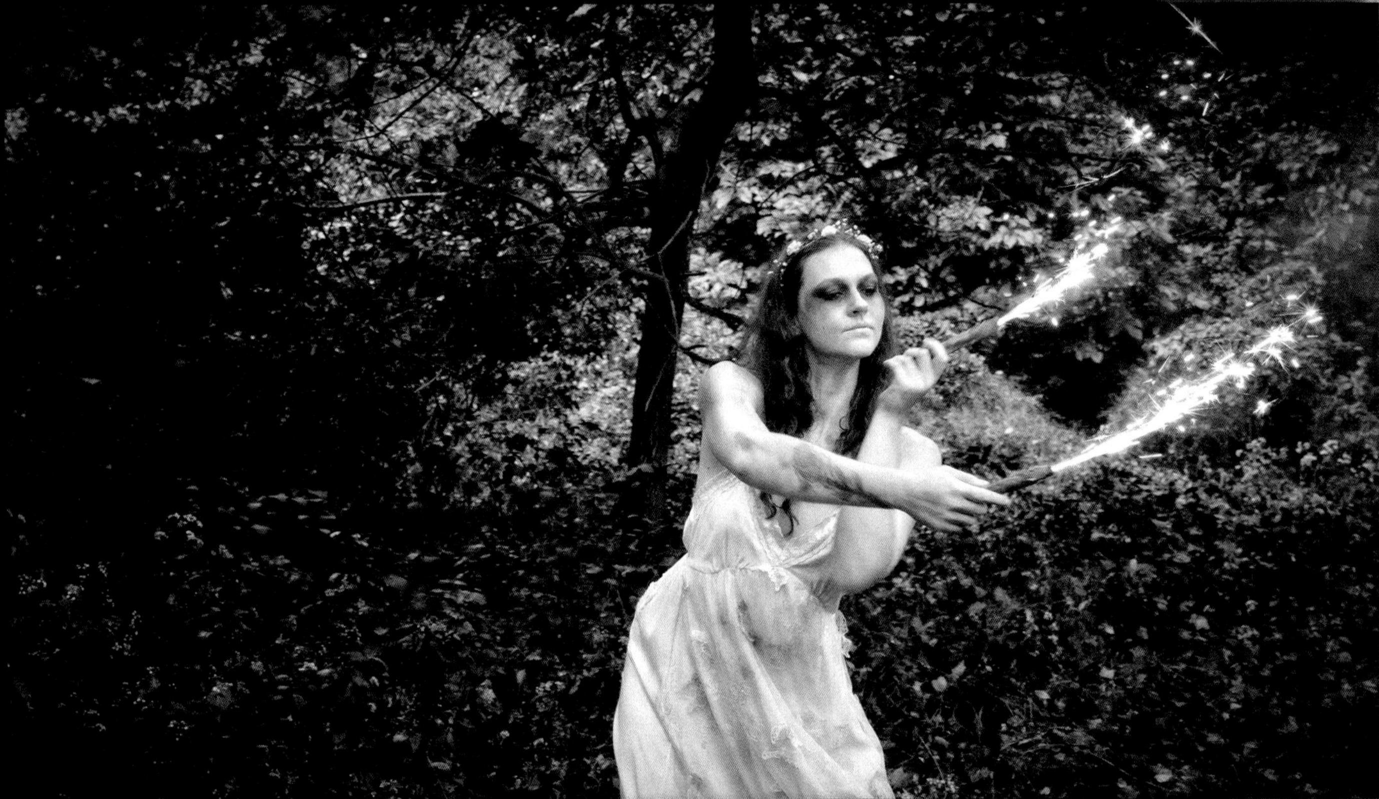

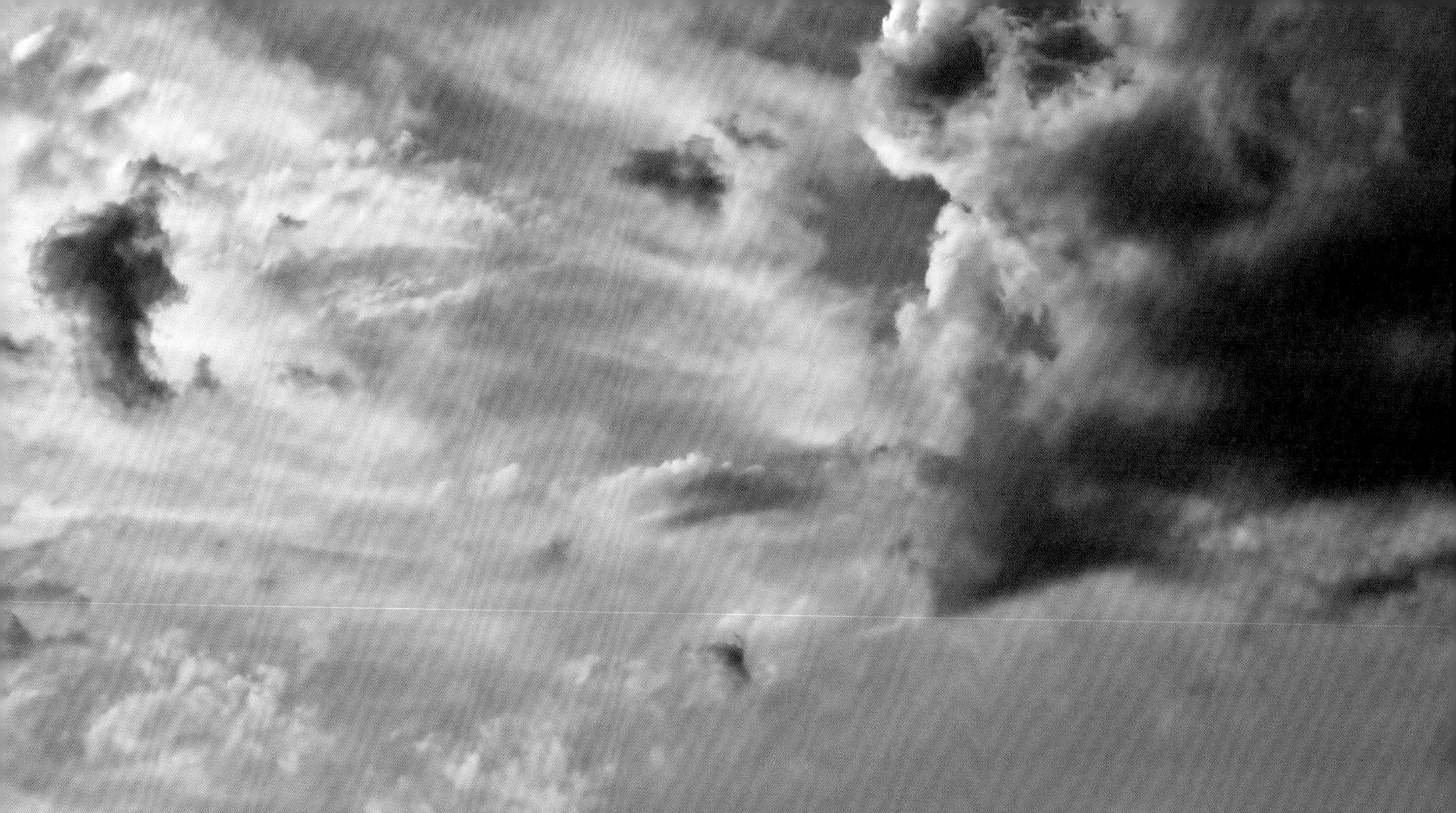

“Getting clean came after a lot of broken relationships, run-ins with the law. That was one of the turning points, watching my family cry, you know, going into a squad car and then my daughter watching me go into an ambulance, for being taken in multiple times for being suicidal. Just because I didn’t feel like I had a place anymore. Looking back now, seeing that that was the alcohol, the drugs talking, PTSD—that’s what I was diagnosed with when I got out.” —R

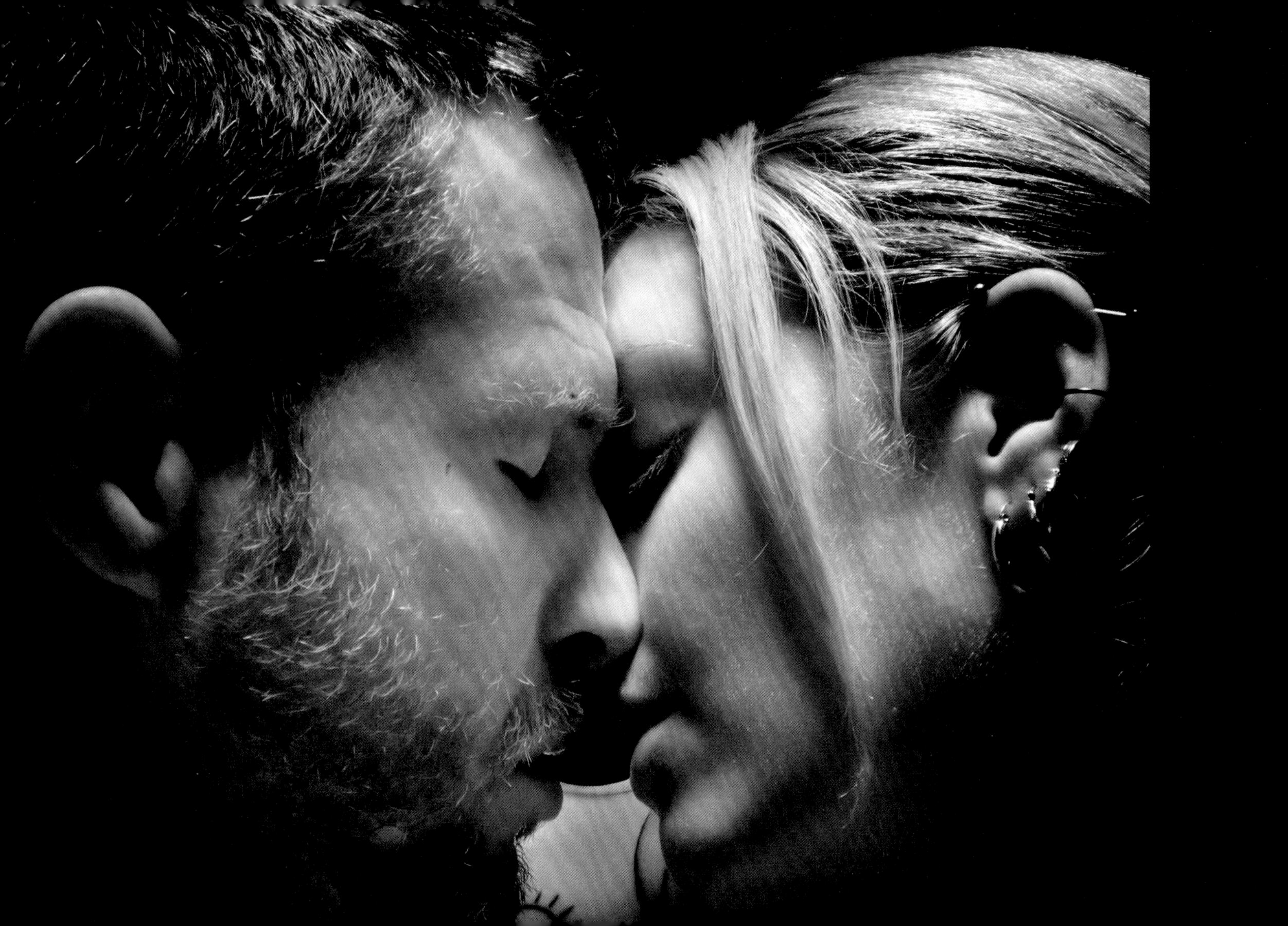

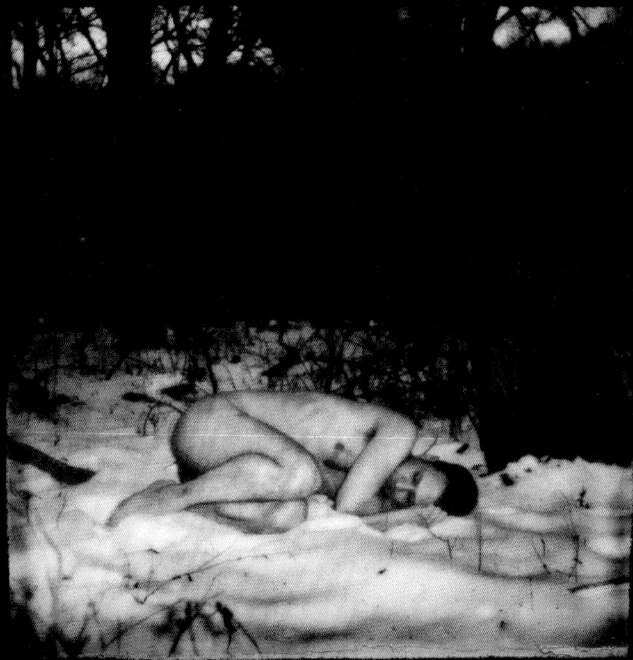

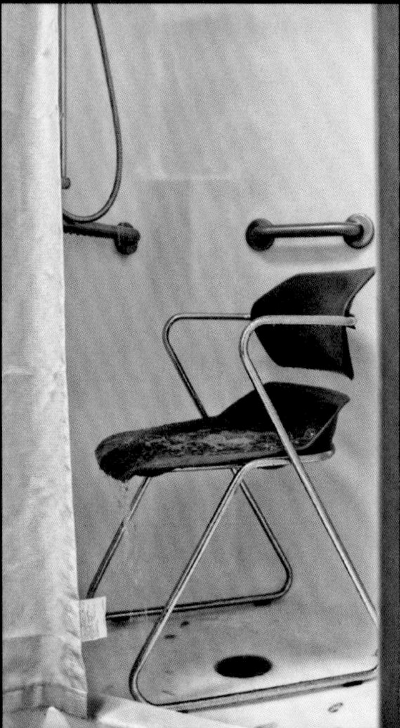

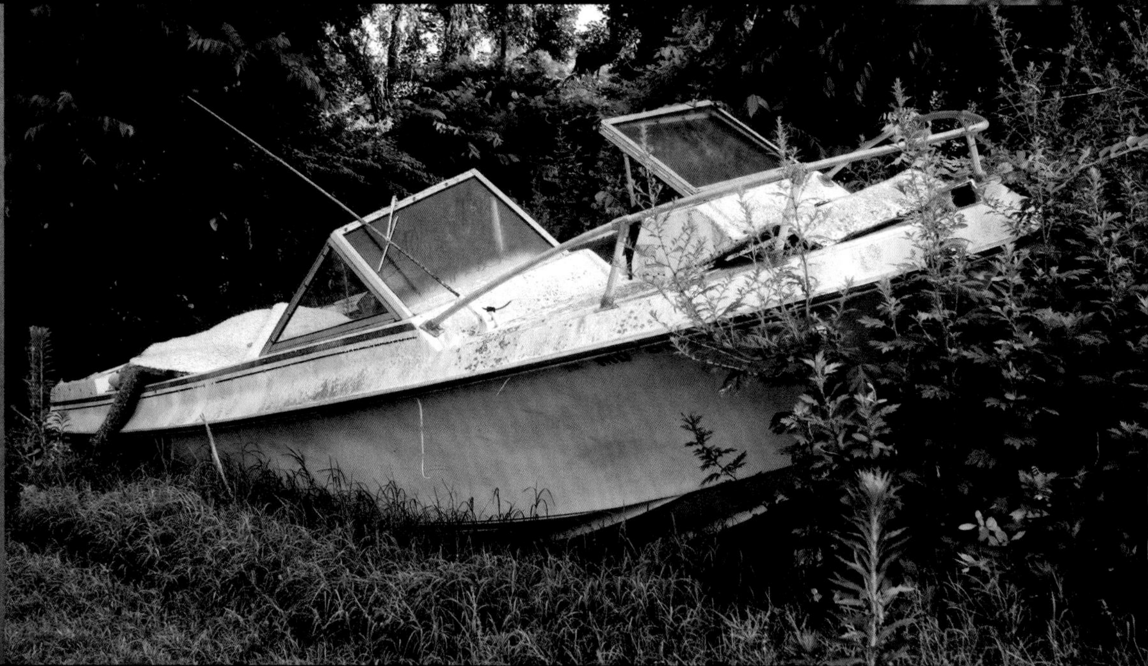

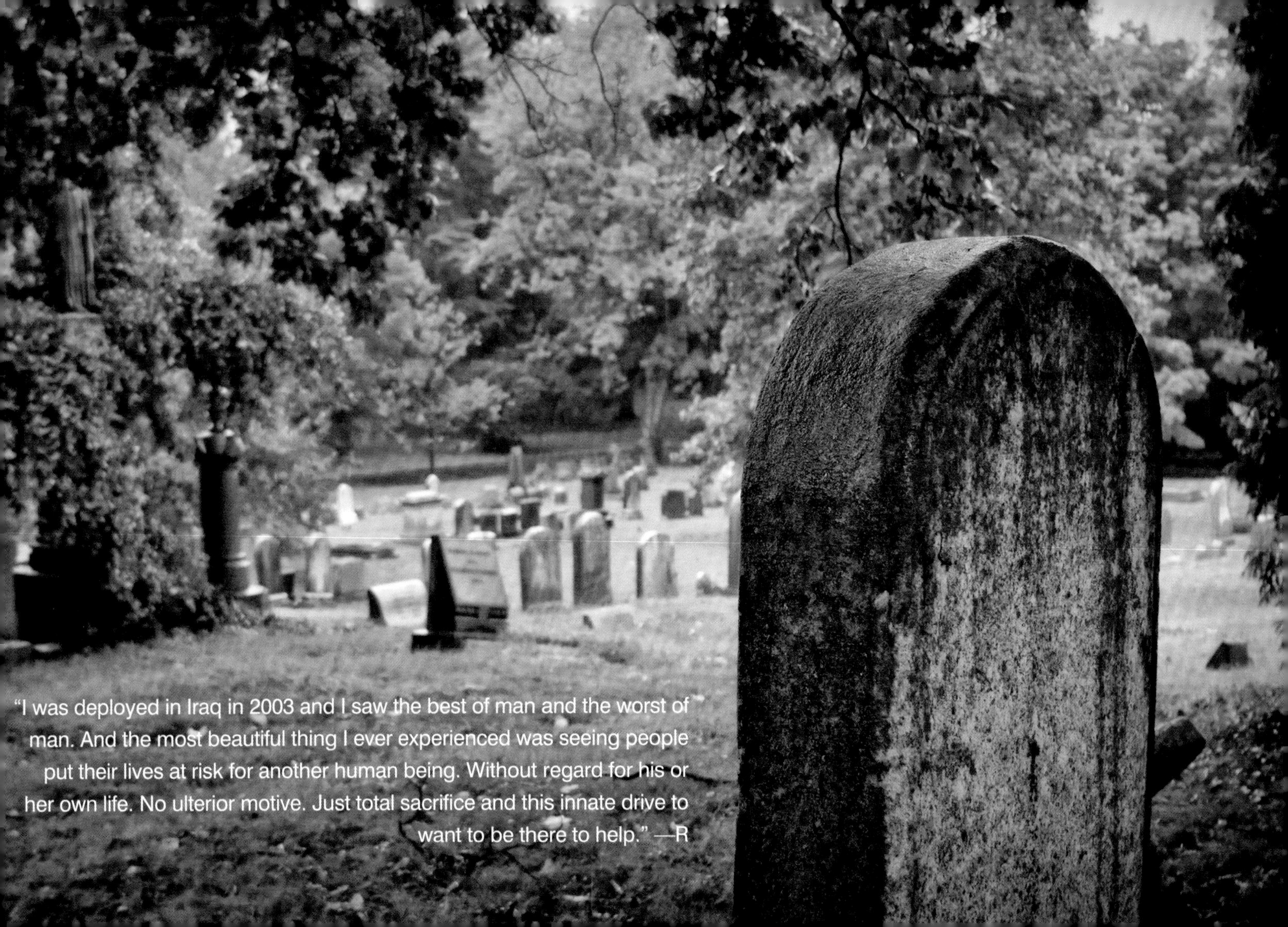

"I was deployed in Iraq in 2003 and I saw the best of man and the worst of man. And the most beautiful thing I ever experienced was seeing people put their lives at risk for another human being. Without regard for his or her own life. No ulterior motive. Just total sacrifice and this innate drive to want to be there to help." —R

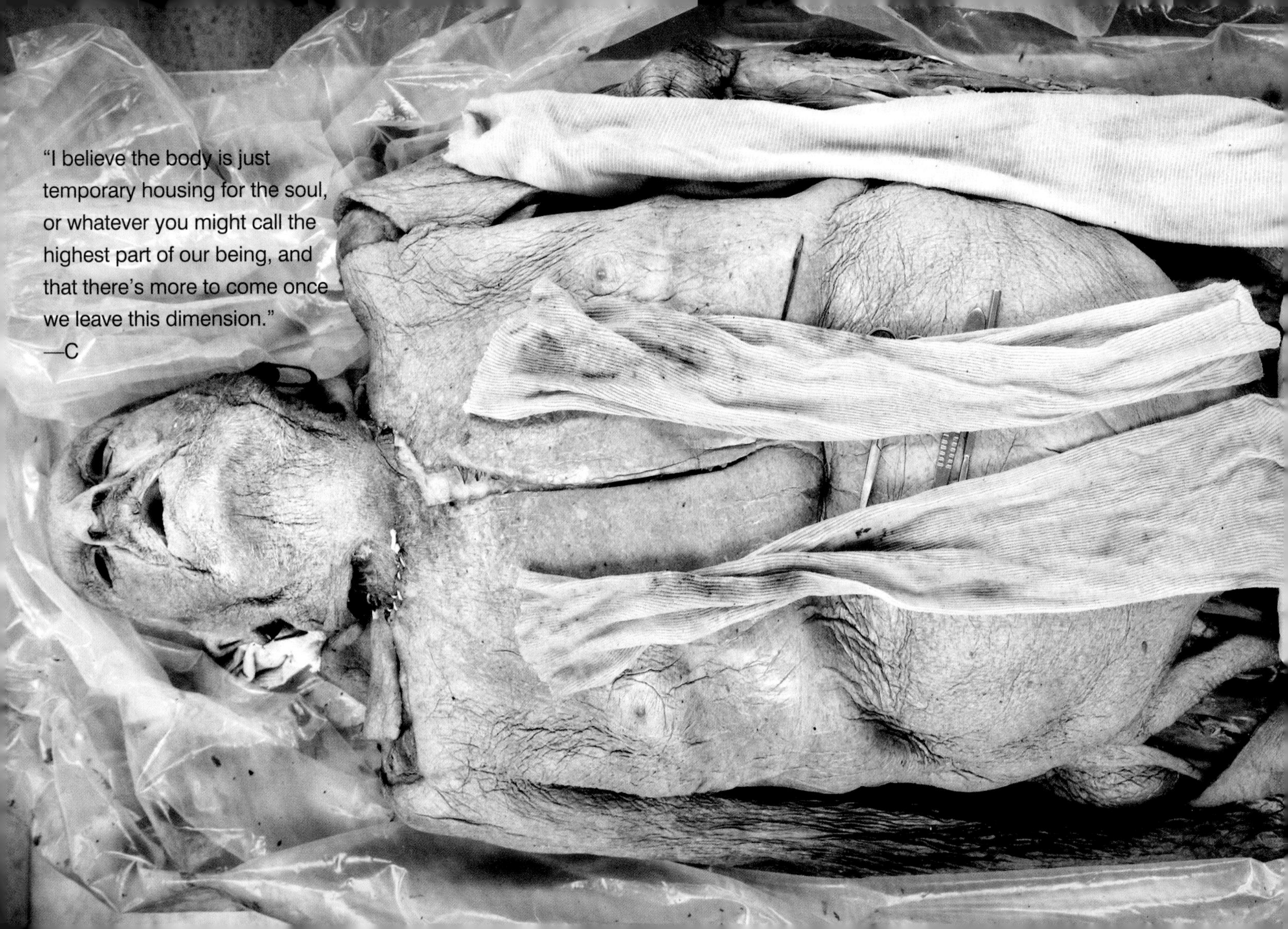

"I believe the body is just temporary housing for the soul, or whatever you might call the highest part of our being, and that there's more to come once we leave this dimension."
—C

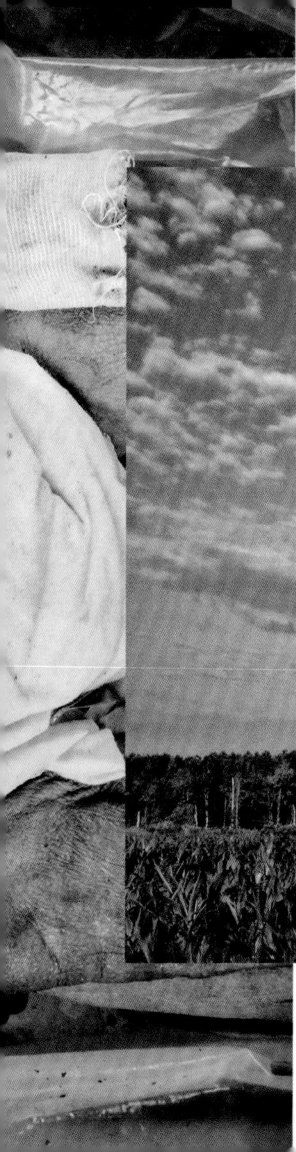

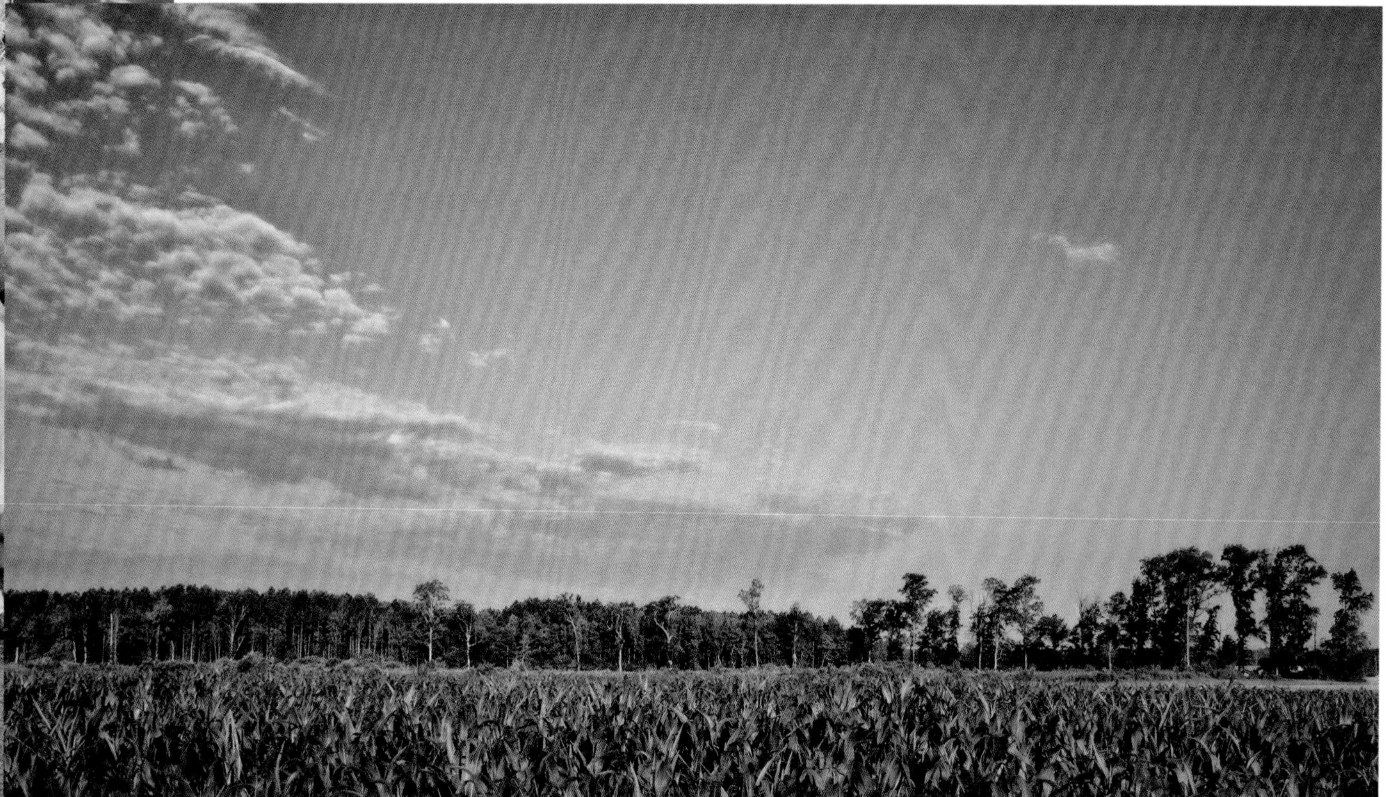

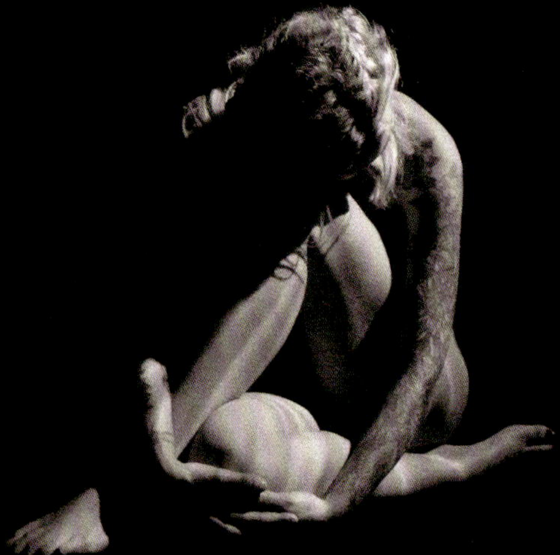

“My conception of
God has evolved as
I’ve come to better
understand the
complexity of how the
world is composed.
There’s matter, which
is of course energy,
and there are all
these different levels
of energy. We’re just
these evolved beings
that exist on different
levels of energy as
gross matter and also
very subtle matter. With
God being the highest
form.” —A

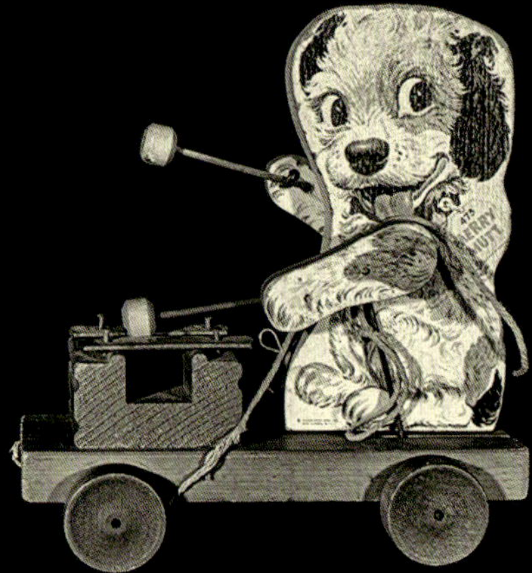

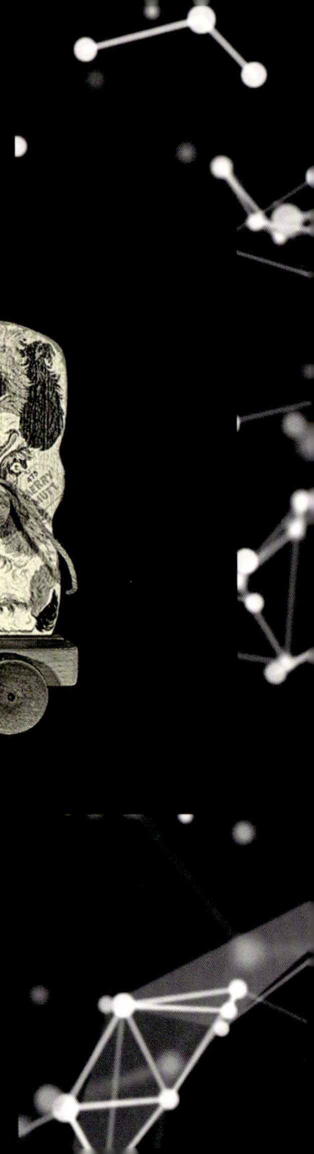

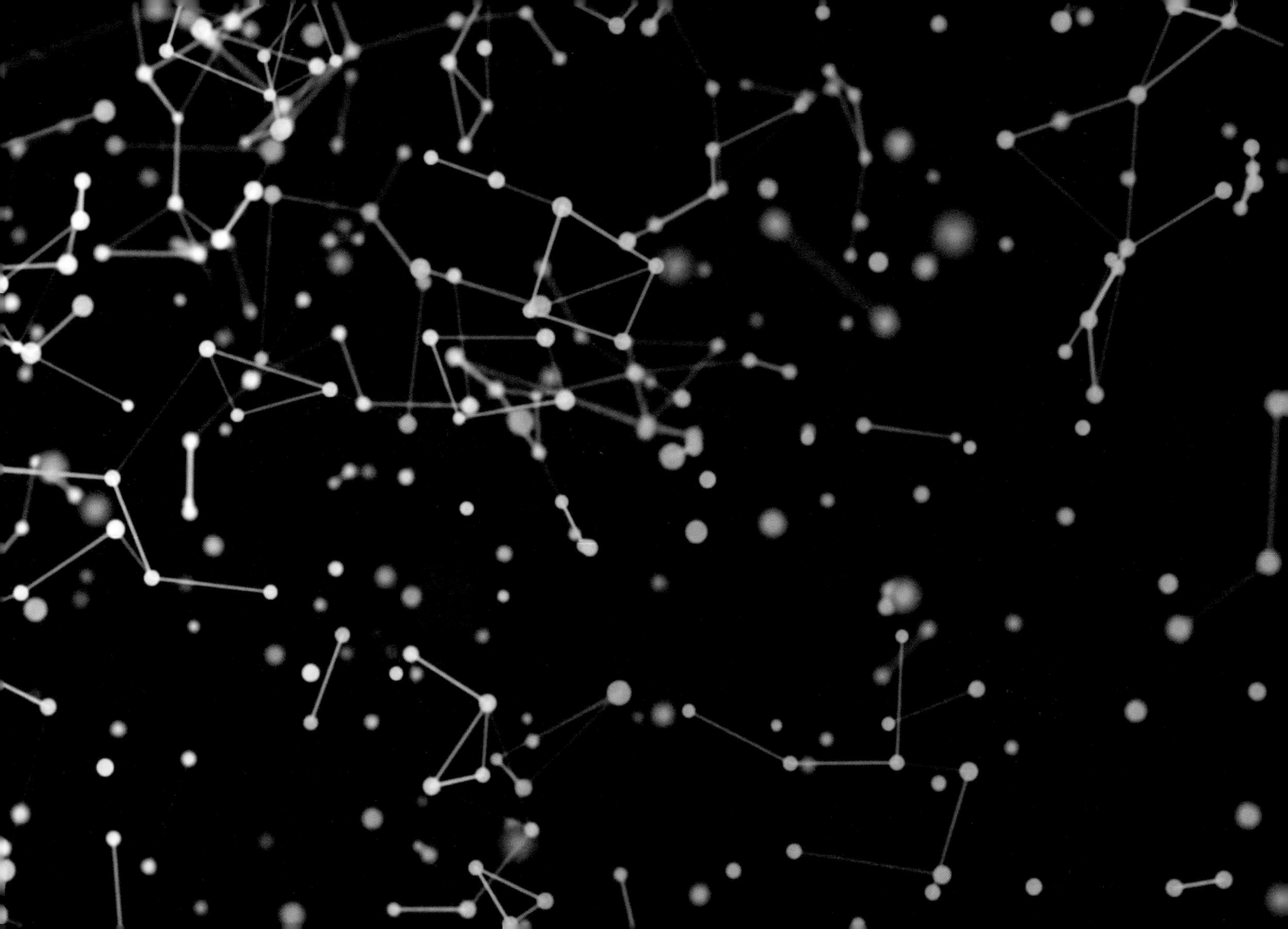

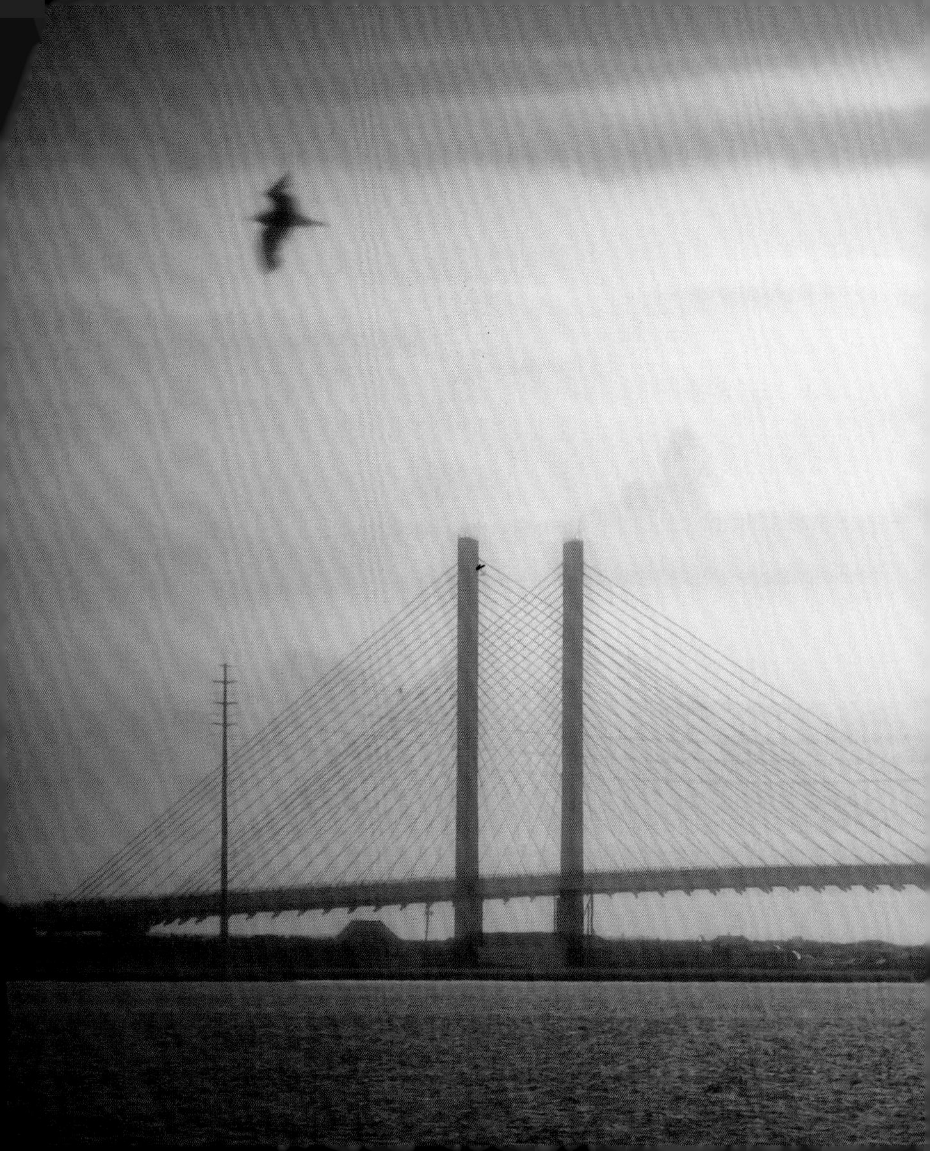

"I think of death as being the breaking of the soul's connection with the physical body, which is basically a vehicle. Death is the separation of our soul and spirit from the meat suit. And I'd hope that the next plane of existence is a timeless, constant joy, where I'm connected to God constantly and feeling love and peace with purpose." —CR

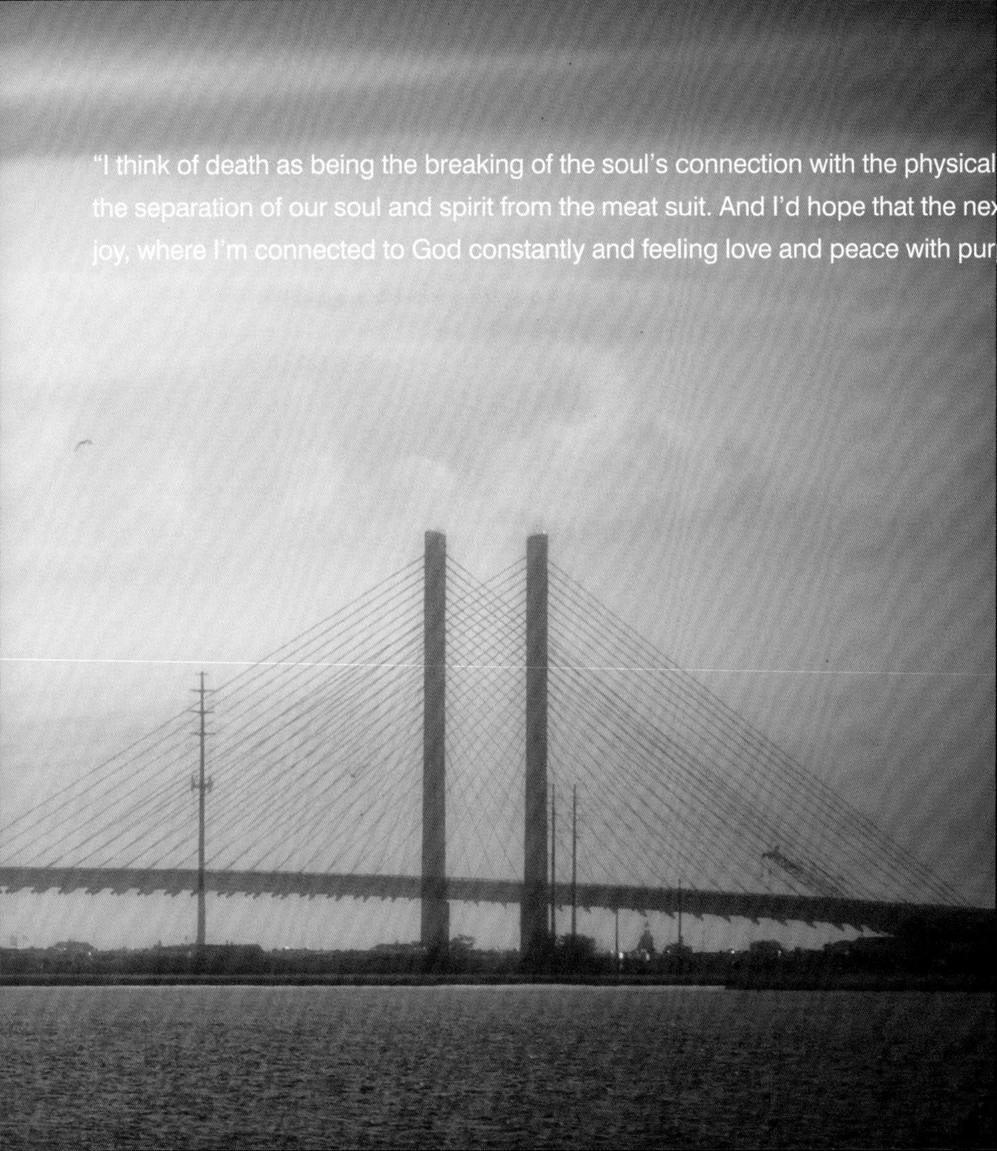

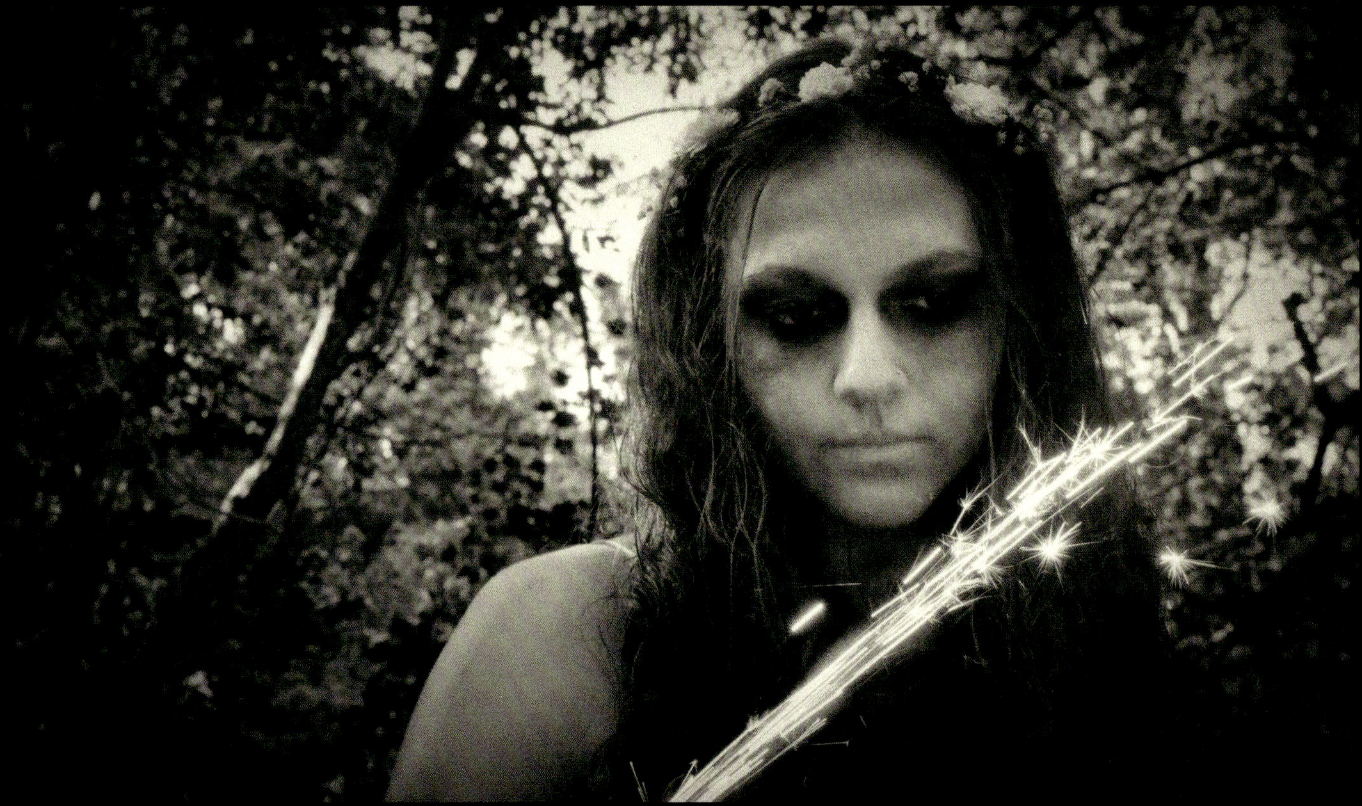

“I sometimes conceptualize death in terms of the fourth dimension. Time is kind of like a Slinky, and all the moments of the pas
when I’m in the afterlife exists. But all I can really do is live in this one moment.” —A

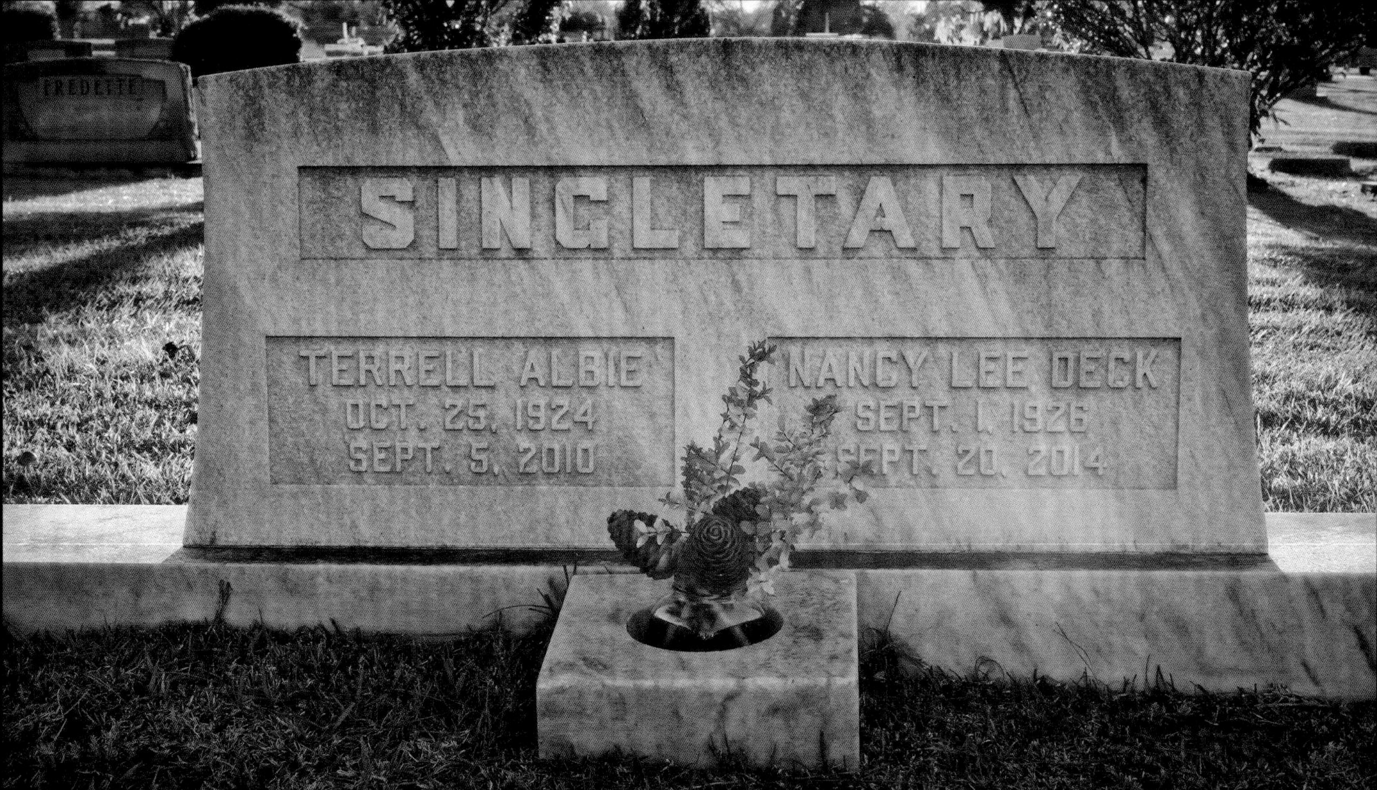

present, and future exist simultaneously, but we can only occupy one slice of the Slinky at a time. Maybe even what I'm like

TRACES OF CONTRADICTION AND CONNECTION

A mother nursing her newborn, religious ritual in a family home, storm winds on the ocean, exploding edifices, Nazis on the march, and silhouetted dancers moving in unison. These are just some of the visual ingredients and building blocks creating the structure and narratives in John Singletary's *Traces*—a video installation, book, and photographic journey through time, meaning, and purpose. Combined with a haunting instrumental score and the intermittent voices of individuals speaking about impactful and painful moments in life, Singletary's collage of black-and-white imagery speaks to the many conflicting aspects of life experience. In search of meaning and the boundaries of artistic expression through one's chosen media, the artist has comingled his profound interests in photography, philosophy, collaboration, and human connection.

Traces investigates the implications of human evolution through three distinct stages of life. Singletary's imagery begins with the first stage of life encompassing the origins of life, birth, childhood, and beauty. In these images, we are introduced to a view of the beginning of our existence as positive, loving, and joyful. Singletary then moves to a second stage of life experience fraught with anxiety, destruction, and despair. As one grows into adulthood, one sees and must process the unfairness, violence, and failures of the world around us. The imagery referencing this process includes fascist dictators, explosions, scenes of desolation, and sexuality. *Traces* reminds the viewer of their own desires, struggles, and pain in this second cycle of life. The third and final stage of life is viewed through a lens of death, resolution, and conclusion with imagery ending in tombstones and the conjuring of memory. Singletary moves through these three stages of life experience to awaken a sense of shared humanity and compassion.

In the context of this desire for empathy, existentialism's search for meaning in a meaningless world drives Singletary's image making and selection. While both attracted and repelled by religious ideology, the artist is compelled to seek answers in the cacophony of religious, cultural, and political systems imposed on us by history and contemporary society. Colliding imagery of the past, present, and the imagined, Singletary layers human behavior and purpose in disjointed and unsettling combinations, evoking anxiety, fear, and existential dread. In addition to the layers of imagery, Singletary overlaps a musical score and a variety of spoken voices sharing intimate stories and reflections on their lives. By listening to and reading their narratives, we bear witness to their suffering and celebrations as stand-ins for our own. Seeing ourselves in the stories shared by each individual, it is implied that we, too, can create meaning, despite feeling adrift. Singletary seems to be sharing his visual impressions and the intimate stories of those interviewed as a means of seeking the human connection he fears can be lost in the second stage of life. Is this questioning of purpose and becoming unmoored something to accept, rail against, or relish?

That question was at the heart of the experimental filmmakers' works whose black-and-white masterpieces inform Singletary's vision. Many Dadaist and surrealist filmmakers approached the absurd and existentialism through unconventional editing and aesthetic choices. Like Ingmar Bergman, Singletary chooses to create very long takes where the action is slowed down for deeper contemplation. Similarly, with desolate landscapes, limited dialogue, and a penchant for confronting death, the artist approaches the formation of meaning with Bergman's intensity and authenticity. Incorporating strategies for conveying the passage of time and memory from films like *Citizen Kane*, Singletary deftly uses collage, montage, and visual cues to create a nonlinear stream of consciousness. The artist's use of historical footage placed alongside imagery he shot himself creates a flashback effect familiar to us from these cinematic classics. Experiencing the constant movement of images, video sequences of war and disaster, and images of entertainment from bygone eras, we are also reminded of the torturous brainwashing scene in *A Clockwork Orange*, which has become a potent symbol of the collision of behavioral control and propaganda. In Singletary's work, these conflicting elements exist in tandem with one another to bring a sharp critique of our religious, social, and political failings.

Despite the existential dread underscored by Singletary's video editing and sequencing, the artist's enduring hope and faith in humanity are evident in the influences of still photography on his work. Focusing on the universality of human experience, Singletary takes a broad view of our similarities rather than pointing out our differences. Making these creative choices, Singletary's work approaches human connection in a manner reminiscent of the legendary photographic exhibition and book *The Family of Man*. For many photographers who came of age after the publication of this seminal book and its touring exhibition, *The Family of Man* proved that photography could communicate our most intimate and important moments in life, which were entirely universal to the human race. When *The Family of Man* was exhibited immediately after World War II, the world desperately needed a way to come together and see each other's shared humanity. Like *The Family of Man*, Singletary's images of common human experience remind us of our own humanity while driving home the power of the photographic image. Additionally, Singletary's photographic nods to Edward Weston's nudes and Richard Kagan's portraits of utilitarian tools are reminders of the indelible imagery of our mentors and idols. Combining these formal, aesthetic, and narrative strategies from the history of photography, Singletary harnesses the power of a photograph to tell us who we are, even when we feel unknown, unmoored, and disconnected. By doing so, Singletary embraces hope in the face of despair, even in the midst of investigating that which defines the depths of human suffering and dread.

With an eye on the present and future, Singletary is not only influenced by the historical traditions of photography and cinema, but is also actively defining contemporary approaches to video, installation, and visual storytelling. In keeping with artists like Bill Viola and Douglas Gordon, Singletary seeks to create an immersive experience of his time-based work while focusing on the most fundamental of human concerns. Like Viola and Gordon, Singletary has created an experiential language through video installation that requires the audience to participate in the creation of meaning and humanity. Collaboration—between himself and his subjects as well as between his artwork and the viewer—is a central pillar of Singletary's work. Every sequence of human behavior that Singletary shot was in collaboration with subject and camera. Each interview he conducted was a verbal collaboration between the artist and interviewee. Every time a viewer experiences his work, a new version of the story is conjured. Utilizing this collaborative approach and the weaving together of multiple viewpoints within the same narrative, the artist takes a specifically contemporary approach to reconstructing narrative with his dynamic presentation and use of multimedia technology.

Singletary's work combines this multimedia contemporary approach with potent and influential symbols from the past, yielding a surprising and emotionally charged work of art. *Traces* presents a story arc from Adam and Eve eating the apple in the Garden of Eden, through modernity exemplified by technology and war, to the quiet death of family members in the twenty-first century. The artist takes us on this journey through the cycles of life and history in a search for meaning in our technology-mediated world. Through his imagery of love, hate, birth, and death, our humanity is both critiqued and elevated. Experiencing *Traces* allows us to embark on a similar search for purpose in a chaotic world, knowing that we are not alone, and that hope remains in the face of cruelty, destruction, and pain. In this emotional and existential work of art, humanity is celebrated and questioned precisely because of its contradictions, conflicts, and connections.

Amie Potsic

Keila Perez-Vega, Katherine Corbett, Nakisisa Webb, Hayley Stricker, Kristen Tanchak, Mark Danowsky, Jessica Fowler, Emma Quin, Daniel Pateman, Mikhail King, Mayumi Tomii, Elizabet Perez-Vega and Danilo Perez-Santos, Yonnie Simon, Chris Strobel, and to the anonymous individuals who shared their lives, stories, and hearts so fully in the creation of this piece.

Bean, portrait of John Singletary by Kristen Tanchak.

Traces installation photograph by Rick Wright.

A heartfelt thank you to some special individuals, mentors, and past collaborators:

Richard Kagan, Amber Malmstadt, Cait Stewart, David Markham-Gessner, Justin Kutner, Andrey Kolyada, Nate Carter, Megan Hannon, Rebecca Kanach, John Carlano, Stephen Perloff, John Ignarri, Joe Roeloff, James Oliver, Megan Schuster, Jason Hartman, Alberto Giardinni, Kelly Planer, Amie Potsic, David Graham, Geoff Berken, Mike Joniec, Arthur Danek, Kyle McKay, Chris Smirnov, Marc Leto, Joel Silver, John Reformato, Kevin Miller, and everyone at Daylight Books.

This book is also dedicated to the loving memories of George Joseph Keeley, Stephen Conolley, and Dyngis Singletary.

TRANSCRIPTS

Transcriptions of conversations
between John Singletary and
anonymous participants that took
place in Philadelphia,
PA, in 2022.

INTERVIEW BETWEEN JOHN SINGLETARY AND "A"

— November 9, 2022

JS: Could you tell me something unique and special that you remember about your childhood?

A: I think I was miserable as a child. One brother broke my nose and my other brother broke my front tooth. I was molested by a neighbor. And a pedophile. So, special and unique. You know, it's funny, when I hear other people talk about their childhood, you kind of get that warm, fuzzy feeling. And I always just felt like, well, that's really nice, and, like, I was inside this bunker looking out at other people and it's like, oh, that's a nice experience that 98 percent of the world has had.

And I've just finally agreed that I'm going to just not agree to agree. I don't know, agree with who? Agree with myself that I'm just going to talk about it. You know what I mean? It's like I'm giving myself permission to say, "No, it really sucked," and it was hard and it was painful and it was lonely. And stop pretending. You know, it's like Mother's Day. My mother was horrible, my father was awful. And so everybody always around Mother's Day and Father's Day, it's like, "Oh, Mother's Day!" Like, we all have this universal feeling, like, aren't mothers wonderful? Well, mothers can be horrible.

JS: What would you say your earliest memory is, even if it's really abstract?

A: I think my earliest memory was my mother yelling at all of us to pay attention, because I think it was like the lunar landing or something. And I remember I was a kid, and her saying, "Pay attention, this is important, watch the television." And I think it was related to somebody maybe landing on the moon, I have no idea. But it was like, something important was happening on the television related to the moon and astronauts, and we were all supposed to pay attention to it.

JS: So when you were a child, what did you imagine doing with your life?

A: Escaping. I just remember, there was this painting that my parents had on the wall. And I remember thinking, someday, I am going to be out of here. And I just remember thinking I never wanted to go back. And, staring at that painting for some reason, and being like someday, I'm going to look at that painting and I'm going to be in a different place. And feeling like I just wanted to get there. So I didn't really envision what I was going to be or do or as a job. I just remember wanting to be away from there.

JS: If you could name one thing, what is the most beautiful thing that you've experienced?

A: Gosh, this is so trite to say, but I've managed to have three children, and I think it's just this gorgeous, beautiful feeling when we're all together. Like, there was this moment—we were living down in Washington, D.C., for a while—and it was just this funny moment when we were driving in the car, and it was like this happy moment. We were coming back, they'd all been swimming at the public pool, and we were all just feeling happy. And we were driving by a McDonald's. And like, we don't really eat McDonald's food. But all of a sudden it was like, they had this ad for this thing, it was like, the Cherry Berry Chiller. And I was like, "Oh my God. Does anybody want a Cherry Berry Chiller?" And my kids were all like, "Yeah, we want a Cherry Berry Chiller!" And it was just funny. It was just a funny moment.

And you know what? Actually, they decided they didn't want the Cherry Berry Chillers, because there had been this bird that had fallen out of a nest, and they had picked up the bird and they had put it in the nest, and they had hidden it from me, because they didn't think I would want them to have saved this bird. And even though they wanted the Cherry Berry Chillers, they were like, "No, we have to go home to the bird." And then they had to explain to me why on this rare occasion, they were saying no to something so unusual as a Cherry Berry Chiller. And it was because they had to go home, and they had this bird. And I was like, it was so sweet. Because they were all in cahoots on saving this bird.

JS: How would you personally define the word "grace" as exhibited as a human quality?

A: That's so funny you ask about grace, because "grace" is one of those words that I've always grappled with. Like, what does it even mean? And I guess if I put it into human terms and not, like, God terms, you know, I think grace is like, moments when our humanity comes through the surface. You know, when instead of us being in our roles, like, "Oh, I'm this and that's the pizza guy," or "I'm this and that's the postman," it's like, grace is when our humanity comes to the surface, and we are able to communicate as human to human.

I'll give you an example, like, okay, we were at the dollar store with my kids. And the line was really long, and this lady was obviously having a really bad day. The line was really long and people were impatient and I was the next person in line. And I just remember, I started to cry for some reason on her behalf, because I could feel her pressure and how she wanted to get it right. But she kept making the mistake. And I just leaned over and I said, "You're doing a great job. You're doing really well." And it was like, she started to cry, and I started to cry. And it was just that moment where, I wasn't an impatient customer and she wasn't a messing-up cashier. It was like we were both just coming together. And it was just bizarre. And it wasn't, like, sobbing, we weren't sobbing. But it was just like, life is hard. And we all just do the best we can, you know?

JS: What would you say that the most disappointing thing that's happened to you has been?

A: I think the most disappointing thing that's ever happened is I was married for twenty-two years, and I believed that if my husband and I … I believed that if I could just move and create the right mix of home, country, job, stability, that he would stop being a workaholic, and that he would find pleasure and "enoughness" in being at home. We moved three countries and many, many jobs and houses, and he still couldn't. It was like he was still fixated on what he needed to get out of the job. And the most disappointing thing was that no matter what I could do—home, job, place, country, money, everything—none of it satisfied. And he couldn't untie himself from that fixation, and I realized I was his great enabler. And my enabling wasn't enough to enable him to stop being addicted to work.

JS: So what are your thoughts about and experiences with addiction?

A: Well, you know, I was a workaholic, too, and that was why we got along so well. We were both in our parallel play of addiction, right. He was going to do his work; I was going to do my work. And we were both like, supportive. And then we had a child. And my child, my first son, had some health issues. And I realized I couldn't palm the kid off on a nanny, or a daycare the way I thought I was, and I was like, "Fuck!" I had to really, like, I had to serve this other person, and I couldn't be a workaholic in the same way that I was before. So it was really hard. Like, an addict does not want to stop being an addict, [*laughs*] you know what I mean? I had to change and learn. And I went into it kicking and screaming, and it was the greatest thing I ever did, you know. Because it really forced me to stop, slow down, be a mother. Otherwise, I would have been the same mother my mother was: angry, disappointed, pissed off at having kids. Like, "What do you mean? You kids are keeping me from my job." And it was, like, the greatest thing that ever happened.

So my experience with addiction is, there are a lot of addictions, you know. I had a whole food thing happening, and then I flirted with alcohol. And it's really just, there's always that temptation to deal with the other thing, you know, deal with your anxiety or your inadequateness or whatever it is, and deal with that through the addiction, rather than sitting with, "Well, what are these intrusive thoughts, why are they coming?" Or whatever format it comes to you in. I mean, so, oftentimes addictions come in the form of intrusive thoughts, like, "Well, instead of doing this, I'll do this. Oh, I'll have food or I'll have alcohol or I'll go to work, and that will make me feel better." Instead of learning to sit with the intrusive thoughts, and sort of saying, "Well, why are these coming? Let me deal with them."

JS: It's interesting because I'm thinking about, like, in having the child there was something outside of yourself. And they talk a lot in twelve-step programs about a power greater than yourself and the necessity to realize the existence of such.

A: Yeah, absolutely. I think having a child, you know, he had some health issues, so that really pulled me out of myself, and then having twins. But I'm like, "Oh, okay, I've now mastered this kid, and he's two, and he's ready for a nanny. I'm going to go back to school." And then it was like, boom, twins, you know. I was like, "Oh, I got this thing. Let me go back to work." And then twins really threw me for another loop.

JS: Do you feel like the experiences that we have in life are random, or do you feel like there's an underlying purpose?

A: Well, is it that a random event happens and then in retrospect you ascribe meaning to it? You know what I mean? And then I wonder, does it even matter? But I don't know, and that is a baffling thing. I'm just grateful. I'm just grateful that, you know, having a son with some special health issues was enough to make me be like, nobody is going to take care of him the way I'm going to take care of him. I need to change course. Or twins, like, holy shit. That's like the triple strike. It's like [*imitates an explosion*], you know, whoa, start over again.

I don't know. That question, is it random, is it predestined? Oddly enough, sometimes I go to these Bible study groups because I think it's really interesting, because I'm too lazy to read the Bible on my own and I don't have enough context to really understand it, so I'm always grateful that I can go to a class and somebody explains it to me. And it's kind of like this whole idea of predestined, is it really predestined? Because then you get into the question of, well, is there really free will? If it's all predestined, how is there free will? And what I heard that was really interesting was somebody said, predestined can just mean that you have the capability of having free will. So you have the capability of hearing, let's say—this is now getting biblical about it—hearing God's call. That's what's predestined. "Predestined" is that you have that innate ability. Not, like, oh, God's figured out your whole path. And I thought, "Well, that's really interesting. That's a different way to think about predetermined." You've only been predetermined in the sense that you have this capability.

JS: So what is God to you?

A: I think about God as this sort of universal flow, like, that is going in a positive direction. The Hindus call it lila. Lila is child's play. And it's like this: there's this video on YouTube about these wolves that were reintroduced into a park; I think it's in Colorado. And there had been this overpopulation of wolves. So the wolf population disappears, all these deer take over, they eat every single thing down to a nub, right? All of a sudden there's nothing left but stalks. And this is a true story. So then some park rangers introduce, I think, fourteen wolves, and then the wolves start living there. And that means that the deer go back to the sides of the mountains. And the deer stay there, and the grass grows, and trees start, and streams start. Because, you know, the roots of the trees enable the ground to form rivers.

Anyways, it's a long story. But when they look at this evolution over time, it's like, that to me represents God. There is no way that engineers would ever be able to invent that level of complexity, of grass and trees and a stream that then becomes a river, that then has salmon, and then the bears come. It's like, to me, that is God in motion. It's like this ever-flowing propensity for things to just, create and recreate, and grow with greater complexity and greater beauty and greater collaboration. You know, we think of nature red in tooth and claw. And when nature actually evolves, it evolves toward greater complexity. And it actually requires greater cooperation. Otherwise, we'd be single-celled organisms, you know what I mean? And in fact, we're actually more and more complicated organisms. So that to me … I don't even know how to describe that in a sentence. But that to me is sort of God; God is this constant flow of goodness that in a snapshot, you look at and say, "Well that's shitty. Why did somebody step on that entire anthill and kill all those ants?" Or, "Why did a hurricane come and kill all these people?" But at a greater distance you can see that, somehow, it's moving toward a greater complexity and evolution, toward a somehow greater good.

JS: How has your conception of God evolved or changed over the years?

A: Have you ever read the book *The Autobiography of a Yogi*? So I just find it fascinating. It's kind of evolved in this sense of, sort of a greater complexity of understanding how the world is composed, you know, there's matter and matter is of course energy. So there's all these different layers of, you know, gross matter. And then as you sort of look in the world, you get to these higher and higher levels of more and more subtle energy. And so we're just these evolved beings that exist on different levels of energy as gross matter, and also as very subtle matter. And with God being the highest form.

JS: Do you think that the whole concept of romantic love is a biological or sociological construct by which to propagate the species, or is it a profound human necessity?

A: Well, it's a necessity from evolution's point of view. I think that love—that can start as, you know, romantic love—is actually one of the highest forms of expression. And I think that, it's almost like if you look at this same concept, right, of gross matter, like, we're here in a physical body, and that we also exist on these multiple different planes. You could just have, you know, there's sex, which is just this combining of the gross matter, or the whatever, physical plane. But that we exist on all these other different levels. And that when you have two individuals who are communicating and fitting together on that really subtle plane … It's like Rumi, the thirteenth-century Muslim mystic, Sufi poet. And you think about that beautiful phrase, "Out beyond this world of right and wrong, I'll meet you there." Or, he has a beautiful phrase, which is, "My heart and your heart are very, very old friends." And it's like, when you meet somebody on that other plane, *that* is extraordinary. You know what I mean? To me, romantic love in its highest evolution is that.

JS: Tell me something special that you remember about a time when you were in love.

A: I feel like, sometimes it's texting; sometimes it can be so weird. It can be texting with somebody who you feel like you're in that space. Like, they can be physically somewhere else, completely far away. And yet, you're right there in that moment. There's this wonderful book; I can't remember who it's written by. It's called *I and Thou*. And the idea is, most relationships with people are I–It: it's transactional. Like I was saying before, "Well, I'm the customer and he's the pizza delivery guy," where we just see people in our roles and it may be transactional, right? Whereas an I-Thou relationship is where you come without preconceived notions. Where you're actually seeing that other person for who they are, and it's happening in real time. So you're naked and vulnerable, and that person is naked and vulnerable, and you are meeting each other in that space. Whether that's happening over text, or over the phone, where you're in that naked, vulnerable place, where you can't control that person, you can't predict that person, and you're just meeting them there. That's being in love. I think, when you're at that place of just true, as naked a revelation as you can be in terms of revealing yourself to another person.

JS: So what would consider the most intimate experience that you've had?

A: I think it's that. I think it's being in that communication space. You know? Where it's just of being completely myself.

JS: What is the relationship between intimacy and sexuality for you personally?

A: For me personally, I mean, that would be the most awesome thing in the world, for sexuality to be an expression. I don't know if it's the ultimate expression, but it could be the ultimate expression of intimacy. Because intimacy, I think, is that unguarded moment where two people are allowing themselves to fully be seen. And with sex or sexuality, I think that would be an ultimate expression, but I still think there's inhibition or there's still guardedness or there's still fear. So I think sexuality *can* be the ultimate expression of intimacy. But I think intimacy lasts a lot longer, and can be expressed in lots of different things besides sexuality.

JS: How important is monogamy to you?

A: I think it's really important, because in order to get to those levels of intimacy, that requires so much trust, and it's not a journey that's taken quickly. Because I think in order to be that vulnerable, it's not all pretty. You know what I mean? Seeing people's weak sides and their ugly sides and … you know, somebody once described, like, when you're looking for a mate, you want that guy who's going to hold your bag for you. You go into the X-ray for like, some awful cancer treatment, and you want the guy who's going to sit there in the waiting room holding your bag. And that's—oh, I'll get all choked up—just the idea that somebody would be willing and want to be there, not guilted into it: "Will I need a ride home?" But actually willing to see you through all of that.

JS: What do you think in your life gives you the greatest sense of purpose or happiness?

A: Well, it's so trite again to say it, but I love being a mom. And especially given the childhood that I had, and to see my kids flourish, and to see them be vulnerable with me. You know, when I was growing up, I could never tell my mother about my period or anything, and we never went bra shopping, so I would steal my bras from the people I was babysitting for, or I would shoplift deodorant. And with my kids, it's completely different. We can joke about things like that. And it's so funny. And it's just so lovely. You know what I mean? And intimate. It's back to Cherry Berry Chillers. And them being able to have their little cabal and say, "Well, we've got to tell you about the bird."

JS: Looking back on the trajectory of your life so far, what would you say is your biggest regret?

A: Oh. Gosh. You know, I really don't have … I mean, I have some. What came to mind was, I hired somebody who was really awful in the UK for a top job, and he *totally* was a disaster. And that was uncomfortable; that put a lot of people in an uncomfortable position. Because he was just a terrible manager and then I had to fire him. And I made the decision too quickly. And I learned a lot about that. Maybe not divorcing my husband more quickly. But then again, you don't know until you know.

JS: If you could change one thing about yourself, what would you change?

A: Oh my God. You know, in Chinese medicine there's yin and yang, right? And in personalities. So in Chinese medicine the yang of a personality is like the doer, and the "got to get it done." And the yin is the willingness; there's a feminine quality, to like, let it all unfold. I am not good with yin. I am not good at letting things unfold. I am a yang.

One of the things I love about the Hindu religion, or Hindu faith, is this belief that we live in four chapters. That in our youth we're learning habits, you know; not knowledge, but habits are most important. And then we go to this householder phase. And householder is kind of making your mark and acquiring things, acquiring money, acquiring status, maybe acquiring a relationship, acquiring kids perhaps, acquiring maybe a home. But it's acquiring. It's like this feeling you need to make your mark, and in order to do that, sometimes, you do need a certain tunnel vision. And then you start to transition to a different phase in life, which is sort of the phase of life where I am, which is more of a forest dweller. And it's like a twenty-year period—you know, if you're so lucky to live that long—where you really get to focus on what is of value to you. So I've been able to do that with my children and now I'm focusing more on this like, I want to help people with weight loss, with addiction, with stuff like that. And it's like, these are my values. Then you go to a different phase in life. So, you know, I think sometimes it's an evolution.

JS: So we go through all of these phases, then, inevitably, we pass. So what is your conception of death?

A: It's interesting, did you ever read the book *Dying to Be Me* by Anita Moorjani? Okay, there's like multiple different things. Sometimes I think in terms of the fourth dimension, and the fourth dimension is that time is kind of like a Slinky. So if you look at time and you include the fourth dimension, it's like time is, you know [*imitates chopping sound*], and we're just in this one slice of the Slinky or the salami, right? So you and I are here today. But, twenty years ago exists simultaneously; we're just elongating the salami. And you know, the endpoint, like when I'm ninety-five or whatever, exists. And so I only have—because of time being spread out like this—I only have the ability to go through slice by slice by slice by slice. But actually, really, all of these phases exist, so even though I'm only here today at fifty-eight, well, what I'm like at ninety-five is there, and what I'm like at maybe the afterlife is there, and it's actually all happening at once. So if I were to lean forward I'd be ninety-five, and if I lean this way I'd be this way. But really all I'm able to do is to live in this one moment.

So is there an afterlife? I don't know. Maybe there's this period where … you know, one of the reasons I love to wear these [*rattles her bracelets*] is because they remind me of the sea. So it's like, we come from the sea. We're like a bucket, and we have our shape, and we're still seawater. And someday we're going to go back into the ocean, right? So I just feel like, you know, I'm here, I'm in this bucket, I'm going back to the sea. Will I live in the sea for a while and then come back again as another bucket? Or do I just actually stay in the same bucket? That is a long way of saying I have no idea. But I see it as this real fluid continuity.

JS: And does the idea of death scare you?

A: I've read so many near death–experience stories that it scares me only in the sense of, man, do I want to suck as much lemon juice out of the lemon as I can while I'm here? While I'm in this bucket, I want to really *be* in the bucket, you know what I mean? And experiencing as much as I can.

JS: What would you say that you're most afraid of?

A: What I'm most afraid of is, you know, my kids are going to graduate, my daughters are seniors. And I think what would scare me is not living this next period of my life to the fullest. I mean, I've had a great run, and it's been wonderful and I love it. I've done good things with my career, and I've done great things with family. And I want to have this next phase be like, super, extra great. And I'd really like to meet somebody and totally fall in love. And travel and do amazing things together, with that person. Not having that would be my biggest fear.

JS: Do you experience anxiety?

A: Oh, absolutely [*laughs*].

JS: And what does that feel like for you?

A: It depends on the day. You know, yesterday I was having this massive anxiety attack. Because as a creative person, I feel like there's this new creative phase inside me. And I'm trying to figure out, how do I give birth to it? What does that look like? And my anxiety is, "Oh my God, how do I get this out? What does this look like? What do I do? Does it take this format? Does it take that format? What am I doing? I'm not making progress. It's not coming out. I don't know." Like, that's where I start to spin.

JS: Along similar lines to the question about grace, how would you personally define "integrity"?

A: I was just thinking about integrity today, isn't that weird? You know, Gandhi defined happiness as when what you think, say, and do are in harmony. And I think integrity is the same way. I think it's when what you think, say, and do is in harmony. Also, I would bounce that up one more level. So if you have a sense of God and purpose, integrity is living in alignment with that, and making decisions and actions and living in alignment with that.

JS: We're living in a really crazy time and I think there's a lot of misalignment in so many different ways. What do you think is the biggest problem facing society at the moment?

A: I actually think the greatest problem is this [*gestures to phone*]. Because I think that what's happened is that this is a dopamine delivery device. It's an addiction. And it's a socially acceptable narcotic that has put people to sleep. So everyone is checked out, and we're not doing the work of being alive, which is to think and feel and sense and grow and expand, and we're becoming these inert zombies. You know? That, instead of this being a tool, it's a trap. And we then become victims of this massive addiction which is being visited on an entire generation and population.

And the fact that this provides us with our own optimized world, that's been optimized to be angry because of, you know, outrage media. Like, everything is—you're constantly being fed a drip feed of media which plays on your emotions for aggression and being aggrieved, because that's the thing that people engage with. So you're constantly forming this hyperindividualized worldview—which is, you know, I'm sure you've seen *The Social Dilemma*—so everybody is existing within their own hyperindividualized bubble.

JS: What role does your ethnicity or gender play in the construction of your own personality, whether that's internally or socially?

A: Well, you know, I'm obviously like this nice, middle-aged white woman. And it's funny, in typical white fragility, "whiteness" fashion, it didn't occur to me that there was anything particular about it. Because I was just assuming, in that kind of fish not seeing the water kind of way, that this is the way things are. Not realizing, of course, that I'm seeing things from this sort of white-privileged position. So, you know, I think that's played a role in the sense of this assumption of "whiteness is the way," you know, and trying to be more open about that.

And I think as a woman, certainly that's played a role. I mean, in jobs that I've gotten or jobs that I haven't gotten. I grew up in Alexandria, Virginia, which is kind of right outside of Washington [D.C.]. But it's also got this Southern twang to it. So growing up, there was always this overlay of like, the good old boys. And I really wanted to, you know, in high school, do something with my life. I didn't want to just be like, "Hey, little lady." And so that's one reason why I felt like it was important for me to go north and get out of that Southern mindset. So I've definitely always had an awareness, and I've been lucky enough to be very kind of ambitious in my career, and see that you can go so far, but at a certain level it tends to be, you know, all men.

I remember having this interview. And every single person I interviewed with was a man. And every single person in the office is, the secretarial pool was all women. And I just remember asking this guy, I was like, "Well, there aren't any women in senior-level positions." He was like, "Well, you know, we're trying to hire for that," i.e., that's why you're here, lady. So, I'm always very conscious of it. And there are churches. I even go to a church, I attend a church somewhat regularly, which I would never want to join. But they don't even let the women be pastors. They're not allowed to be elders. So, I mean, there's a tremendous misogyny. And especially having daughters. You can't go running, you can't go jogging, you know, because my daughters have been almost kidnapped. They were out walking one night and some people came up with this van and tried to pull them into it. So, like, human trafficking shit really does happen. My daughter was roofied. I mean, this stuff just happens.

JS: What are your thoughts about suicide?

A: I just feel really sorry for people who are in that dark a space.

And I feel like some lucky people never feel that dark. But I think there's a spectrum of, you know, feeling balanced and [having] mental wellness, and feeling hopeless. And unfortunately, I think there are a lot of factors that can compound to make people feel that way.

JS: Have you ever felt that way?

A: I think I've felt really bleak in my life, you know, and I have felt despair. But I've never felt the active desire to end things. I have felt very unclear about how this is going to end well. Like, this is really ... I'm in a dark space, and I don't know how I'm ever going to get out of it. But never like, I'm going to then take the active step of saying I want to exit. But I feel like I can understand how people get there. I really can. And I think we live in a world now where it's so easy to make a decision very rashly. I think we live in a very isolated world. And I don't think enough mental-health resources are readily available.

JS: If you could be anything or have anything or embody anything, what would you choose?

A: I don't know. I guess I would probably wish this for myself and I'd wish this for anybody else, it's just less second guessing. You know, speaking for myself and I think in a lot of people, there's a tendency to take one step forward, and like, three-quarters of a step back, if not two steps back. It's like, "Well, how could I? How could I think about that? Really, can I do that? No, I can't do that. Here are 10 reasons why I can't do that." And I feel like, you know, if we could just live much more the way nature intended. Because trees don't second guess themselves, they just absorb the sun's energy and they just grow, you know. Maybe they lose a limb in a storm and they just keep on growing. And they don't obsess, "Well I'm now an ugly tree." Or, they don't say, "How could I?" I think that's what I would love to change about myself and I think a lot of people would love to change that about themselves.

JS: Can you give one example of the human spirit at its best?

A: I mean, we're all doing this; we're all just stumbling forward. And I think we're at our best, in the human spirit, when there is no path and you sort of just say, well, there's something inside me that propels me to go into this unknown realm, and just try. Especially when there is no path. You know what I mean? Everybody else can just kind of stumble along and do what everybody else did. But to create something new? That's the human spirit in action.

JS: And what about at its worst?

A: Well, that's when you've been given a gift like Donald Trump has been given a gift, of being somebody who's able to really strongly influence people, and to use that for your own corrupt means. You know. There's this wonderful scene I remember seeing and somebody was reenacting a moment apparently in Abraham Lincoln's history, and I don't know whether it was true or if it was like some movie, some 1950s' black-and-white movie, where there's a mob and they were gonna do something and attack people. And so it was, like, Lincoln—and I don't know whether it was true or not—talking to these people, and sort of calming them down, and bringing them back to their better angels, so to speak, where they put down their pitchforks and they went home and they didn't attack. And I think, you know, that's the human spirit at its best. We all have darker impulses, right? It's easy to be like, "Rah, it's the other guy" and that's what Trump does. He whips people up into this state, he brings out these awful, aggressive, mean, othering, and violent things. And he encourages people to be their absolute worst. And it's like, to be given the gift of that level of influence and power and to use it to such negative means ...

JS: The final question that I have for you is, do you feel understood?

A: Do I feel understood? I think I feel pretty well understood. I think when I find that super other person who I hope to marry, you know, in a monogamous relationship and create that, like, real period of intimacy, I feel like then I will feel fully understood. I feel like my family understands me pretty well. I feel like my best friends understand me really well. I wouldn't say I feel fully understood, yet. But pretty close.

INTERVIEW BETWEEN JOHN SINGLETARY AND "CR"

—October 27, 2022

JS: Tell me something unique and special about your childhood.

CR: I made friends with Bob. He was my best friend growing up, and I knew when I met him that he was gonna be my best friend for life, when we were just little kids. And I remember my mother saying, "Oh, you have a new best friend every other week." She could be a little sarcastic sometimes. And I said, "No. Bob's gonna be my best friend." And I knew it; I knew it like you know the water's going to be cold. Before I knew what it was, I would say I knew he was a soulmate, before I knew there was such a thing.

And then another thing I'll share is my grandmother—this is a bit of a sidenote, but it did affect the rest of my life—she told me when I was younger that she had an out-of-body experience. I didn't know what that meant until she told me her story about going into the light and hovering above the room and then hearing God's voice. And that story, that experience she had, I believe set a solid foundation for the entirety of the rest of my life. That one story, that one experience she had gave me faith at times when I had none.

JS: What's your earliest memory like?

CR: Well, I remember my parents fighting a lot. I remember at the apartment complex, I remember, I was so little, but the couch of a little friend—I had a girl *friend*—her couch had these velvet bumps on them, and I used to hold them like they were breasts. And I remember saying that these were boobies [*laughs*] when I was little. And I remember Richard, a fella named Richard, I remember him sneezing. We were all in a baby pool and he sneezed, and to my little-boy eyes, the snot that came out of his nose—I still remember it and I'm fifty-one years old—it looked like it was twelve inches long.

JS: When you were a child, what did you want to do with your life? What did you imagine doing with your life?

CR: Chasing criminals.

JS: Like a detective or a cop?

CR: Yeah, I used to chase people down with my bicycle if they ran the stop sign.

JS: If you could only choose one thing, what's the most beautiful thing you've ever experienced?

CR: Young love.

JS: Tell me about a time that you were in love. And what did that feel like?

CR: I remember my first love, she would lie on my back when we would take a nap. I always like pressure on my back, it just always, it still feels so good. And I remember her crawling on my back and falling asleep. She fell asleep, and I was listening to her breathe and I was feeling the rhythm. I could hear her heart, the sound of her breath, and the up and down of her body while she breathed, asleep. And she felt so warm. And I just remember—I was young, I was probably late teens, early twenties—and I just remember feeling so peaceful.

I think it stems from, maybe a little bit of … I used to nap when I was a little boy next to my father. We would listen to WPEN on the radio. They would play older music. And I felt so safe and loved. And I think it's one of my fondest memories because it wasn't too long after that, my father seemed to stop liking me. And that stuck for a long time. So the early memories, those two memories, I felt protected and loved, and I felt in love, and protective, and just in a cocoon of joy.

JS: Do you believe that romantic love is simply a biological or sociological construct by which to propagate the species, or is it a true human necessity?

CR: I think romance is often confused with infatuation. I think people mean one when they say the other. I've come to the point where I believe that true love—not in the Hallmark understanding of those two words together, but true love—is a commitment that supersedes understanding, time, space, and definition. I think romance is a tactic for the propagation of the species and to prove one's intentions. But love and romance are not the same thing.

JS: So is monogamy important to you in a relationship?

CR: It is now, yeah.

JS: But it wasn't at a certain point?

CR: It was when I was young. And then, it became less important when I was young, dumb, and full of cum [*laughs*]. And now I feel like if someone loved me dearly, and only wanted to be with me and only wanted me to want to be with her, that sounds pretty damn beautiful to me.

JS: What do you consider the most intimate experience you've had with another person?

CR: I'm a generally intimate person and open-book type of man, type of person. So for me to be intimate and answer this question in a way that stands out among all of the intimate experiences of my day-to-day life … I'm assuming you're asking about with another person?

JS: Yeah, something that you shared with another person.

CR: There was a long stretch of time where I was struggling with something that almost, I would say, other people would have killed themselves in my situation. Some other people. And there was a woman who was there for me every day that I called her, when I needed to talk to someone. And she was open to hearing everything I had to say, and never once judging me. Never once a selfish moment. So it was a long stretch of selfless, intimate moments that helped me realize how important support is, in life, on this planet. But that was a stretch of intimate moments that lasted for months, and ultimately years.

JS: How would you personally define the word "grace" as exhibited as a human quality?

CR: To be full of grace, I think, is to be pure of heart, pure of intention. Almost childlike, with tender palms, glowing eyes, and a solid constitution of spirit. For me that is a graceful person, how a person can appear graceful, and move with a fluidity that we might call graceful. But to be full of grace, I believe, is maybe even the burden of perfection.

JS: So what are you most afraid of?

CR: Being a mistake.

JS: And do you experience anxiety?

CR: Yes.

JS: And what does that feel like?

CR: Nail scraping. A constant feeling of, something's wrong. Lack of peace. A cage that can't be opened. Even in a fit of laughter, deep true laughter, anxiety can be the anchor. Anxiety is an ever-present—when it's present—oily coating and electric stabbing of a nagging, cruel, hateful entity. Anxiety is the lack of connection with God.

JS: And what is God to you?

CR: God is a name that we give the constant, conscious, creative force. God is our life force. The father of all fathers. The love of all loves. And the energy that makes up everything. What God is *not*, is the selfish creation of man. Anything that is love, and beauty, and power, and truth, and a gazillion other unnameables, that is God.

JS: How has your conception of God changed and evolved over time?

CR: My conception of God has changed to increase the inability to understand God, after listening to, at this point, probably over 100 near-death experiencers describe God. It's the most indescribable love and compassion that, if I had experienced this love or compassion and connection, I wouldn't be able to say these words without sobbing right now. So my little monkey mind can only come up with this.

JS: Have you had any experiences that you cannot explain rationally?

CR: Yeah, but I'm not sure what "rationally" means anymore. If I were to use the term "rationally," as in the normal—by normal I mean very average, the way most people in my life, I think, might see the world, or, maybe not my life, but ...

JS: I kind of mean logically, like, what we accept conventionally as, "This is possible, this is not possible."

CR: I feel like the people who might say no to such a thing are asleep. Or in denial. I've had countless experiences like that, I mean, every time I get a message in a dream. I will say this. When I receive audibles, which doesn't happen often, but when I get audibles, in the beta state, when I've been woken up by voices that are female [*sighs*] ... when I have those experiences, I am mystified. I am blown away when it happens because I know that I'm being communicated with and I am so frustrated, and I feel like I must be doing something wrong to lose that connection. I must have done something to break the chain, turn the channel. So yes, I've had countless at this point.

JS: If you could only choose one thing, what do you consider that you're most proud of?

CR: Being kind and generous, in general.

JS: And what would you consider your biggest regret?

CR: It would be an overall, long stretch of my life where I believed I was humanist. I was living for myself, and I think I must have missed a lot of opportunities and messages in that time. And maybe a lot of love.

JS: If you could change one thing about yourself, what would that be?

CR: I don't want to sound cliché, but I have difficulty feeling good about decisions and taking action on them. Committed action. I would like less of that and more ability. Like, for instance, when I decided I wanted to learn photography, I committed, and it felt spiritual; it felt like I was doing exactly what I was supposed to be doing. I miss that. So I regret that I can't seem to muster that again, that passion for something.

JS: How do you conceptualize death?

CR: Death is the breaking of the soul's connection to the physical body, which is basically a vehicle. It's a living bio suit for this third dimension that we live in, this planet, this physical planet. So death is the separation of our soul and spirit from the meat suit.

JS: And is this frightening to you?

CR: It's frightening when I contemplate that maybe I will take my failures and fears with me, and live in the next plane of existence in those fears, a product of those fears. Basically, the fear I have of death is going to what some people might call hell. A place where my spirit is the opposite of with God and with joy and with the connection of those that I love dearly, and desperately. It would be away from all of that, in a place of regret and shame.

JS: If you could speculate, what is that next plane like?

CR: The bad would be—I'm going to use a physical plane example—but it would be a 24/7, cold, empty, hopeless situation on the negative, if that were to happen. But I don't want to dwell too much on that possibility. I do know of people that have come back from those experiences, from near-death experiences, and they've said, "You don't want to go there." I'd like to think the next plane is a timeless, constant joy and purposeful existence, where I am connected with God constantly, and feeling love and joy and peace with purpose.

JS: Do you feel like the events that happen to us in life are random, like we're spit out of some particle collider and it's all just random happenstance and chaos? Or is there some kind of underlying order, or structure, or purpose to the things that happen?

CR: I would say I'm still evolving that. But at this point in my understanding, I would say some of them are planned and some of them are collider. Collider-spitting, random experiences. I think it's both.

JS: What are your ideas about or experiences of addiction?

CR: I think addiction can be a false fail-safe. Addiction is a surrender of power. I think addiction is either a conscious or unconscious relinquishing of one's power and giving oneself a challenge that sometimes can be nothing but a headache. And, at the worst, a destruction of life's purpose, a failure to honor one's commitment on the deepest possible levels to have a purposeful learning experience, life connected with God. I think addiction has many faces. And I think addiction can be such a sneaky bastard, we don't even know it's happening. And I'm not even speaking ... I mean, drugs and alcohol are the obvious two, but I think there's many addictions that people could be quite clueless that they're even wrapped up in, a pattern of purposeful destruction. A pattern of the relinquishing of one's power. That's what I think addiction is, at least in part.

JS: How would you personally define "integrity"?

CR: Lack of selfishness. A commitment to humility. The ability to accept one's mistakes; to accept one makes mistakes and to learn from those mistakes.

JS: What do you think the most significant problem is that we're facing right now as a species or a society?

CR: Well, the most pressing for me is, somehow, we gave our collective power away. I would say, not just here in the United States but in most countries, if not all countries of the world—like the entire globe—gave away their intuition; they gave away their ability to reason and think for themselves. And we gave control to people who don't deserve that control. We have sacrificed our God-given, born right, to be born free, to people who would oppress, deny, and destroy.

JS: If you could only choose one thing, what comes to mind as a representation of the human spirit at its best?

CR: A loving embrace. A loving, eyes-closed embrace that lingers.

JS: And what would you consider to be the most disappointing thing that's happened to you?

CR: My father's desire to be right.

JS: How do you associate intimacy and sexuality? Or rather, what role does sexuality play in intimacy for you?

CR: Well. I think that's the Shangri-la, when sexuality is, if we're talking about sexuality shared with someone else, I would say when those two come together, when sexuality is an expression of intimacy. When it is a blending of the loving, spiritual connection superseding the physical. I think that's the Shangri-la when you can express intimate, deep love with someone, and sexuality can be a part of that; it can be the icing on the physical cake. But you can't live just on icing.

JS: If you could have anything or be anything, what would that be? What would you choose?

CR: I guess they would both be the same thing. I would love to have my own family. You know, wife and a child or two that, even if I adopted, I felt a unity, where we all felt a unity where we supported each other and every day was a positive choice, and it was a real positive choice. Not a therapist's suggestion but a heartfelt desire to be each other's best, best love.

JS: Do you feel understood?

CR: No [*laughs*]. Maybe by some people but in general, no.

JS: What are your thoughts about suicide, and have you ever considered suicide?

CR: Yeah. I had a very lame attempt when I was in high school. I'm grateful it was lame. I think that suicide is a—I mean, this is a cliché but some clichés are beautiful—it is a permanent solution to a temporary problem, most of the time. I know someone who committed suicide because he was diagnosed with a mental disorder that was going to get worse. I think suicide is a breach of contract. And I think that, based upon research that has been done with people who have had near-death experiences, suicide is a no-no. Because you have jumped off of your agreement. And I think, based upon things I've heard, suicide is [*sighs*] a self-imposed prison sentence, for lack of better words. And that's why I would never attempt it again, and I'd like to think that I can, in one way or another, overcome whatever it was that was giving me the thoughts to do it. And I've had long stretches of suicidal thinking.

INTERVIEW BETWEEN JOHN SINGLETARY AND "G"

—September 8, 2022

JS: What is the most beautiful thing that you've experienced?

G: The most beautiful thing I have ever experienced was a time when I was in Wyoming with my grandfather when I was quite young. I told him I was going to climb a little bit when in truth I was going to be aggressive as hell and try to get up this mountain.

And I made it up that fucker. When I got to the top I was totally exhausted, so I yanked off my sweatshirt and lay down to catch my breath. When I looked over I realized there was this snake and he was utterly huge—I'd have to say about nine feet—and I was small, so I was terrified. So I climbed down to get away and this bison came running around the corner like God itself, he was so magnificent. He was perfect, without a scratch or flaw, and I'm thinking, "Oh God, this thing is going to rip my head off." And yet we maintained this composure, locking eyes for almost three minutes. He was such a magnificent specimen of joy and life, I've never seen anything like it before or since. People have downplayed bison, like they've been written out of the history books, like this is some big dog. But if you ever spend time standing next to one that's seven feet, five inches, it's no big dog. These experiences of the divine in normal, daily life are something that happen every day and people don't seem to realize or notice most of the time.

JS: Tell me something special about your childhood.

G: You know, I was really fucking bent on being seen as erudite and someone who would ... I was the kind of guy you would see stealing the *New York Times*, the newspaper. I wanted people to see that I was far apart from the exact nature of what people were like around there.

JS: You wanted your intellect to be noticed and respected?

G: Very much so.

JS: What made you happy as a kid? What was your favorite thing to do?

G: My grandfather would give me gold and silver coins for reading pages from *The New Yorker* and the *New York Times*. He would give me very generous rewards, and in return for those rewards, I would really go to the meat wagon.

JS: The meat wagon?

G: Yes, I'd make sure I really had it down.

JS: And did you enjoy doing this?

G: I enjoyed it as much as I enjoyed what I was getting. I loved gold and silver. I was really greedy as a kid.

JS: When you were around that age, what did you imagine doing with your life?

G: I'm not sure if it's quite [far] back enough, but I really liked the idea of becoming a theoretical physicist because I found the combination of mastery over physics and mathematics together to be extremely fucking fascinating and deeply meaningful, special.

JS: What is God to you?

G: I've spent a significant portion of my life mistakenly living as if I am God. I have been one of the most prolific cat burglars in Philadelphia's history, probably over 500 burglaries, and each of these crimes says the same thing: it's a way of telling the world that I am God.

It's not something I thought about consciously, but to go into someone's home and feel that it is my right to dig through everything that they own, what am I telling the world?

It was a detective who actually illuminated this way of thinking and asked if I use the toilet in these homes. And I'm thinking, "Where is he going with this?" He described that every single major criminal he'd spent time with had shown him evidence that they felt that they were in fact the deity, that they were running things. I'd never considered such a perspective. There must be something correct about this as it is a constant attempt to restructure someone else's reality.

JS: How has your conception of God evolved or changed over time?

G: I don't really have a clear concept of these things. I have certainly pacified my views, as I no longer feel I'm in charge or have control over anything really. It's actually quite rewarding, as there are a lot of aspects of reality which are so awful and that I am dreadfully thankful not to have any authorship over.

People would ask me this question when I'd tell them I'm a Buddhist and I would often get the question, "Does this mean you will be in hell or something?" I would explain that I would be happy to be wherever the Buddha is, as he is an example of living the belief of not doing any harm to anyone. However, whoever the great creator is, he doesn't seem to be able to slow down with this constant slogging of poor humanity. And if you were God, how would you become God? There would still have to be some quasi god; there's always a retrograde and it doesn't solve any problem, it just elevates the issue, which is not helping anything. If I were God, how would I know?

Really, I am just grateful for the things I receive, and I have no understanding of the means by which I receive them. It's utterly beautiful and I feel so fortunate.

JS: What are your thoughts about death?

G: This may sound bizarre, but I feel like I may have already died. That I am living some sort of reincarnation. I have these experiences that feel as if I am in a lucid dream, as if I had already matriculated through death and its various codices. If you look at it from a scientific perspective, matter and energy cannot be created or destroyed. Then it only makes sense that after death our energy must persist in some form and continue to attenuate as time goes on.

The way in which this happens I have no idea, and I don't think that the question is useful or knowable, however it works. Achieving immortality, that is the essence of the ultimate human dream.

JS: Have you had any experiences in life that you cannot explain rationally?

G: I don't understand the vast majority of the things that have happened in my life. At the beginning of life it all seemed so clear and I had a deep appreciation for the world ahead of me, yet what happens when experiences just continue to accumulate and they stop representing anything cohesive? It's as if I'm watching the manifestations of nature as it moves through, but I'm not really making the selections here; I'm not qualified to do that.

I often express the opinion that I'm immortal, but who's going to believe that? No one in my crowd for sure.

JS: What are you most proud of in your life?

G: I don't think that I'm very proud of anything I've done in my life. I have not managed to do anything that I am really proud of. If there is such a thing as death, I would like to be able to turn around from whatever platform exists beyond and feel it was worthwhile.

Because, what am I leaving for my daughter? Nothing really, and that's not something to be proud of. I've had a slow-building drive over the last year where I've become more and more intent upon doing something that makes a mark on this world, and largely that is because of my daughter.

When I was ten years old they got a hold of me and said my biological father would like to talk with me and I said, "Fuck him." At the end of the day, I realize I never gave him an opportunity, and if I get this opportunity from my daughter I'd like to be able to present something worthwhile.

JS: What's the most disappointing thing you've experienced in your life?

G: I think you believe I'm better than I am. It's like, the people that got ahead, they were relentlessly persistent even if they were dumb as rocks, even if they were relentless about plasticware.

My inability to make the choice to step forward and father my daughter, it's lifelong; there's no escape. She seems to have mastered the very talents and abilities that I found so valuable, and I don't know if that's hubris or sad in some way, but she's going to be the one that goes to an Ivy League school, and after all the skull scrawling against the concrete walls, I'm not going to be that guy that works for MIT [Massachusetts Institute of Technology]. That's going to be her and maybe that's a manifestation of evolution in some way. It's as if she took the strengths I've passed along and mastered the things that I couldn't. She will present to me vicariously, her entry into a doctorate program and all of these programs of excellence that I felt were so critical in defining who I was yet failed to achieve. But she will not fail to achieve these things.

JS: If you could change one thing about yourself, what would it be?

G: I would stop getting high. It's been the only experience in life that has perpetually dominated my experience. I started getting high and drinking when I was thirteen. I developed a strong taste for cocaine and my prolific spree of burglaries began as a means of paying for too much of it, and I've been in and out of prison my whole life. Currently I'm homeless. I have warrants out for my arrest. I use everything—heroin, meth, coke, crack—yet I'm not dependent on anything.

My life story seems very long, but if you cut the jail periods out, it's really not. I always get out and find I'm not happy. Nothing I've ever done has made me feel satisfied. The eternal problem here is that I am never happy.

I used to live across the street from John Singletary and that guy was crazy.

JS: I'm John Singletary.

G: Right, of course. I mean that other John. Well, you are crazy as well, but he was a wild son of a gun. He dragged me all over

Narberth doing everything stupid imaginable. It didn't take long before I began to capitulate to the desires, which is weird because when I moved in I felt like I don't do that and people who do are fucked up.

JS: What have your experiences with addiction been?

G: Addiction is far and away the most fundamental human defect that could potentially exist. Although, at the same time, I believe it is an endemic and necessary force for any form of evolution to occur, because who would ever make the effort to change if there wasn't the desire to be better? If I didn't have the desire to fly, I could never develop wings.

It has this bizarre, double-edged effect in that way. If I did want to know what it felt like to move very quickly, I would just walk. What would we be if we didn't have these impulses that said, "Try for more. Do something different"? It's hard to imagine what humanity would look like without addiction.

JS: Do you think addiction is an inherent impulse?

G: If there is a God, he added addiction out of necessity because otherwise there would be no means by which to drive his species forward. Everyone is addicted to something.

JS: Could you stop getting high if you wanted to, and do you?

G: I could stop getting high any day. It's not a problem. For me to want to stop, I'd need to find a way to enjoy life without the presence of these external chemical communicators and I have no idea how to do this.

JS: How would you define the word "grace"?

G: Grace is being able to exhibit kindness, decency, love, and joy while accepting the inevitability of pain and suffering.

JS: And how would you define "integrity"?

G: Integrity is the ability to exhibit a solidity of belief, ideal, and kindness in a manner that is unconditional.

JS: What are you most afraid of?

G: The unknown. The things that I cannot appreciate or control, or being unaware of the most frightening possibilities. I used to have this recurring nightmare in which I would wake up on my uncle's boat and be confronted with an entity that demanded a question about weighing the value of life and the value of existence. I could never find the right answer.

JS: What do you feel is the most intimate experience you have had?

G: In many ways I do everything I can to avoid feelings of intimacy, although I can see my relationship with the needle to be very, very intimate. Sexual relationships cause me so much physical discomfort. I don't like being touched and would never want to subject someone to that.

JS: Do you feel that "intimacy" and "sexuality" are interchangeable as words?

G: I think this is a largely American construct. Sure, sexual behavior can be an expression of intimacy; however, intimacy extends far beyond sex. I very rarely feel the kind of carnal lust that seems to drive society on such a fundamental level.

JS: Do you think that monogamy is important in a romantic relationship?

G: I don't think it has to be. It's not something I would insist upon personally.

JS: Do you believe in romantic love?

G: It could be merely a biological or sociological construct by which to propagate the species, or romantic love could be a profound human necessity. It is very hard to know.

When I moved to Philadelphia I began to collect various other types of fancy baubles. I think the reason is that this made me feel that with these I could somehow provide security, because the old life was gone; there is no fixing that.

JS: What is the biggest problem we are facing as a species?

G: Selfishness. The utter lack of ability to consider the well-being of any third party, which is both shortsighted and maniacal. As a human being I don't think I'm doing anyone a service by shifting perspectives. Sometimes I'm a great guy, and other times I'm really not a good person. I need to learn how to be present and consistent in each moment. I try to be a better person with each moment that passes.

I had a friend that passed last week from an overdose, and one of the things she implored of me was to make sure that each moment that passes offers the most to the next moment. I don't always succeed at this but I know it's important. If I can do it 70 percent of the time, I would be a fantastic human being.

JS: If you could be anything or have anything, what would it be?

G: I'm tempted to give a rather wild answer, but when I really think about it, just as I have needed the time I have needed over my life, so has everyone else. I think I'm okay with just being me. Allow the rest of humanity to continue growing into what it will ultimately become anyway. There's no real thing I want; there's no person I'd want to take over being. Ultimately you're just back at zero anyway.

JS: That's so interesting, because many people in society would choose or spend most of their lives trying to escape themselves or become someone else.

G: Correct. But if you gave some fool what they wanted and came back in twelve hours, if you came around at 6 p.m. and not 6 a.m., do you think they'd still want it? I think most people would step off their initial conclusions quite quickly. Who really wants to be someone else? For what?

JS: A lot of people, man.

G: I guess, but it's foolish, do you know what I mean? If you go down that road it's really time to hang it up.

JS: Do you think about suicide?

G: I make these references to hanging it up all the time and I think it's time to stop doing that. I have no right to choose when to stop living. What I really mean is I am tired of living the way I am. And that is some way from wishing your existence was terminated, but for some reason or other this is often how I express my dissatisfaction. I should be more cautious with words. Many people are not able to parse the language efficiently.

I think everyone has the right to commit suicide and I will maintain that until the end of time, but I can't see myself ever doing that. As much as life may bring me pain and suffering it can always get better, so as long as I don't terminate it, I'm in good shape. I don't think most people think about it with the degree of being close to actually equating the behavior, and it would entail that everyone suffers in equal measure.

JS: Do you feel understood?

G: Perhaps by some but in truth, I'm not sure I have the capacity to understand myself. I wish I did.

INTERVIEW BETWEEN JOHN SINGLETARY AND "C"

—November 8, 2022

JS: What was something unique and special that you remember about your childhood?

C: That my parents had foster kids in our home. Starting when I was about ten years old, and I was the number-three child. At the time I think there were two, three others. So there were already six of us. And then my parents started to do foster care for children that had the worst start in life. They had been either attempted to be killed, or were starved, tortured. Children came into our home when I was ten years old. That was different.

JS: What was your earliest memory, even if it's very abstract?

C: I remember the woods next to our home. And there was a creek. And I remember going into it and it being a very welcoming place, a safe place, and a place to explore and discover.

JS: And what gave you the most sense of joy at that time?

C: Something about the creek and the water, and stones, and earth, really resonated with me.

JS: What did you imagine doing with your life when you were a child? What did you want to do?

C: I remember because—I did a one-woman show on this—I had a diary of mine from when I was probably around this nine- or ten-year-old self. And I started to really like boys. And so I did have in this diary that I was going to be an interior designer. And I was going to marry this guy, Andy, that I'm still friends with. So I think somewhere along the line I was going to be an interior designer.

JS: If you could pick just one thing, what do you think is the most beautiful thing you've seen or experienced in your life?

C: Seen would be in nature. I really dug the Grand Canyon. The Grand Canyon was gorgeous. And the Colorado River and the sunset. That was probably beautiful because of the whole experience of it. I can say more about that, in that I had to hike about a mile out from the camp. And my friend that I was hiking with, she was in her first trimester of pregnancy, so she didn't want to go and I had to go by myself. And I was walking and walking and walking, and it was up and down, and no one was around and I was terrified. Was I going to be able to get back? So that arrival. And there were people there. So not only the beauty of the land, but also just the beauty that I was in the right place at the right time.

JS: What is the most beautiful moment you've had or experience of just being alive?

C: I wouldn't say there's just one, but most of them have been spiritual experiences that … there's so many of them that have occurred. There was one when I was nineteen years old, when I was really heading in a wrong direction. And I had this experience of healing.

I had a cast on my left arm because I'd smashed it roller-skating and I experienced this healing sensation. There were other people around. I was prayed over. And there was this woman that seemed to know everything about me. And I felt very known and seen, and it was in 1979, in July, in Ocean City, New Jersey. And I would probably say that was one of the most beautiful experiences I've had.

JS: What do you think the most disappointing experience that you've had is?

C: That I've never had a child. I miscarried when I was in my thirties. And I've never been pregnant any other time. And I really wanted to have a child.

JS: What are you most afraid of?

C: There are some things about the spirit realm that really scare me [*laughs*]. Really scare me. And I have had some experiences. But I haven't yet gotten to the point of conquering my fears on that. That's an important one; that's up for me right now. I don't understand it. But I do truly believe that there are powers. Principalities. Rulers of darkness. And, um, early on, when I was eighteen, nineteen, I had an experience, when I lived in New York City, that was really wild. And I felt that there was a clear, "Make your choice now, light or dark?" That power was coming through me, and I had to choose. I chose the light, by the way.

JS: Do you experience anxiety?

C: Oh, sure. Yeah. I've become more aware of it the older I get. And I believe that because of the world that we live in, and the constant barrage of information—these little devices we carry around that call to us, and people expect to have us at their beck and call—there's been an awareness on my part that I'm going to need to unplug way more, way more, to bring the anxiety down. Because there's so much going on with just about everybody that I come in contact with.

JS: And palpably, what does that feel like?

C: I feel it physically; I feel it in my heart area. I feel a buzziness in my nervous system.

JS: Forgetting the religious and dictionary definitions of it, how would you personally define the word "grace" as exhibited as a human quality?

C: I believe grace is holding space for somebody. It is the deepest listening that you're possible of giving to that person. And it could be more than one person at a time. I do it better one-on-one. I've done it in small groups. Where your ego is taking a nap—or whatever you want to say about your ego—so that you're listening and being with that other person with the purest amount of love in the listening. To me, that's grace.

JS: What kind of ideas or experiences do you have surrounding addiction? And I'm not just talking about the way we think of addiction in terms of drugs or alcohol.

C: So I have a lot of experience with addiction, both as I grow up, and then, being aware of my own patterns, starting at a very young age—teenage years—when I started to have behaviors that weren't really going to work for me in the long run. So choices, choices, choices. I was making choices that were maybe what my friends were doing, things of this nature. I grew up where every self-help book—there was a lot of self-help stuff going on in the '70s—so everybody was wounded, or some kind of an addict, it seemed. And I have embraced the need for transformation. So addiction is when you can't transform out of the ruts and the patterns and the behaviors. But I believe everybody needs to transform. I don't know why. I do not know why we're human, I've been having lots of thoughts about that lately.

JS: What role does your ethnicity or gender play in the construction of your identity?

C: Alright. So if I were to say what my basic philosophy of life is, I believe—this is where I'm at—each one of us is our soul, is love and light. Then we're in a body. I'm in a white woman's body. The way I get perceived or treated, or what's expected of me by society, that's just ongoing. And because I grew up being able to question things … I was in seventh grade when I became very fascinated with the National Organization for Women and what was going on, and what it meant to be a woman. I was given a lot of permission to express myself creatively and articulate what my thoughts were. I didn't really feel held back when I was younger, being a young girl or woman. I was told by my father, as an actor, "Hey, you don't ever have to do a casting couch." So there are things that I was taught along the way that, because I'm a woman, you're going to have to navigate things a certain way. Because I'm a woman, I have frequently been told that the way I say things, or the way I present myself, I'm not always, like, nice. So all along there's been pushback because I'm independent. I didn't get married until I was fifty-three. I have been my own person. I married somebody who's a strong person in themselves. And because he's Black and I'm white, we get treated all kinds of ways by people. So it's very much a part of what I have to navigate, more as I get older than I did when I was younger. Now I think about it a lot more.

People have gotten more outspoken about their prejudice, their philosophies. I believe there's one human race; I don't even say I'm in an interracial relationship. It might be a word to some people, but I think that once you start saying that there are different races, then you can say, "Well, this race is__." We're one human race and we have different ethnicities. I mean, why can't people just get that?

JS: So what do you think is the most significant problem facing society right now, or facing the human species right now?

C: I think just boiling down to the fact that people are so disconnected; they're disconnected from Creator, they're disconnected from themselves, they're disconnected from other people. The devices and the social media, that is not a connection. Being that I've been a massage practitioner for over thirty years, I have had connection that is both physical and spiritual at the same time. And that's what sustains me through all the things that I have to encounter in life. Even just this morning, I found out a young twelve year old got murdered by his cousin with a gun. You know, this is kinda like just every day these horrific things are happening, that if there was more connection, true connection with oneself, with the love that we are, and we were able to connect with another person from that place, from an open-hearted place, then the world would be very different.

JS: You mentioned "Creator" in there. So what is God to you?

C: God is Creator. God created this world, this planet, beyond. I absolutely do not know anything, except the only thing I can say, that I can rest in, is God is love.

JS: How has your conception of God changed or evolved over your life?

C: It's a conundrum, my relationship with God right now. Because I've had religious indoctrination, not from my parents so much, but places that I've put myself, and I've been in a process of dismantling indoctrinations of God. And just experiencing it, just experiencing God, just being led, just being guided. Just being ... I watched the lunar eclipse with my husband between four and five today. And I had this real knowing about part of my shadow side, you know, the anger that I have, a lot of anger. And I have to let go of it, I have to let go of some of this anger. Some of it's toward God. And I hadn't been angry, or aware of my anger toward God until recently. And some conversations I've been having in the middle of the night, of like, this world. I'm disappointed, really disappointed in humans. But I'm disappointed that humans were created [*laughs*]. In some of the ways that humans are. So I have a relationship with God that's developed over many, many years. Consciously started when I was little. Nothing too deep. And then sometimes I feel like I'm not deep enough in that relationship, and then sometimes I'm very, very deep with others. But that's just all part of it for me.

JS: Have you had any experiences that you have trouble explaining rationally?

C: Sure. The experience that I was mentioning before about the healing that I had when I was a teenager. I had these pins in my hands, and it was very painful. My friend was joking, she was like, "You're a drug addict"— my doctor gave me Percocet—and I'm like, "Oh, you can't call me that. I'm just not gonna take it. I'm not an addict." Right? So the pain was pretty intense, and the healing that occurred in this wrist—I mean, I've had no pain, ever, and people said, "Oh, you'll have arthritis, probably, and pain." And even the doctors have said that. So I guess the whole healing process that I have sought to understand, or at least engage in, a mind, body, spirit healing process in the course of life, God is all in and through that. I don't even like to use the word God sometimes, because, when I say "Creator," I believe we are creators made in the image of Creator. The most beautiful parts of being a human. That's when I say, "Oh, that, that's God."

Now, what about the shadow parts and all these other parts? There are so many things that are not easy to explain. I mean, I was T-boned in a car and I thought I was going to die and I didn't. That's easy to explain; the car saved me. But there are lots of things that, when I get together with other people that are open spiritually, we don't have to explain them. We just experience them together. And I love that. I really dig that. Because, you know, the left brain, the meaning-making part of ourselves, I do it well. But I love the mysticism. To me, it's so important that we go there, into the mystical dimensions. Again, you have to be discerning, though.

JS: At this stage in your life, looking back on everything, what would you say that you're most proud of?

C: That love is the most important thing to me. Opening my heart to loving myself, and the world, and people and animals and the earth. That love is the most important thing to me, and I don't care about anything else.

JS: And what would you say is your biggest regret?

C: That I didn't stay at Emerson College in Boston. That I was so intent to go to New York City that I left Emerson after one year, my freshman year. And I look back on it and it was such a small, nurturing college, with excellent teachers and instructors, and I was a big fish in this wonderful pond, and then I went to New York City and I lost it all. Including my mind.

JS: If you could change one thing about yourself, what would it be?

C: That I would not have such, *such* white skin that I can't be in the sun. Like, it's melanin-impaired skin that would be … predisposition to skin cancer and stuff in our family.

JS: I've been thinking about death a lot recently, because one of my friends passed in a very intense way. How do you conceptualize death? What are your thoughts surrounding that?

C: I've been with people when they've passed. I believe that this body is just temporary to house the other really … words are really hard sometimes. You can call it the soul, or whatever is the highest part of our being. So I think when we get to leave here, whenever that is, there is more after this. I don't have the answers, I don't think anybody does. I know lots of people like to think they have all the answers. But I believe that everyone has their time. And I've been doing a lot more accepting of death. I, too, have had a lot of loss recently. I make temporary mandalas; it's a ritual to accept and be with and honor a person, or being or entity, that's gone on to the next dimension. I have, even though I'm very open to mystical experiences, and I have lots of friends that have way more mystical experiences than I have, there's that part of me that's super practical and grounded. So some of it has to be intellectual: "I believe that there's something else." But I really don't know, and I am a little bit afraid about the way I'm going to leave this body.

JS: You kind of answered my follow-up, which was whether death was frightening for you.

C: Not the not being here. It's the way that I go out. Some people really have to suffer. Some people suffer *horribly*. That's part of the thing because there's a war going on. Ukraine is part of where my family is from. Kyiv, my grandfather was from there. And I just have felt such a … it's really been a tough year, with just how much loss there has been, and the war, and the fact that, I believe that the polarization that's going on, and the way that people are with each other and the lack of love, that anything could happen. To me. At any day. And some of the anxiety—you asked me earlier if I was anxious—it's because I'm anxious that my husband's a Black man. I'm anxious because I don't know what could happen to any of us. The way people drive, they're not conscious. No one's conscious enough to be able to say, "I'm caring about you on the planet." So I have a little bit of fear and I'm just dealing with it. And, um, I believe that when it's my time to go, that I will be taken to wherever I am supposed to go next.

JS: And what are your thoughts about suicide? Have you thought about suicide?

C: I have contemplated not wanting to be here on the planet. And I've had to tell people, when I'm honest with them, "I don't want to be on this planet anymore. This is too hard. This is terrible." But I assure them that I would not disrespect Creator. I would not do that. I just … that's a hard no for me. I've seen people kill themselves over a long period of time, close to me. That's been heartbreaking. So if anything, it's intensified my desire to live fully, and to love more fully. To be more of a servant of love. And to make sure that I'm living fully, here. So I would not commit suicide, and it breaks my heart for how much someone has to be suffering to do that to themselves. It's heartbreaking. I would love to be able to love that person so that they wouldn't do that. I would love to be able to make a difference. But people do it. And I'm not a person that … I don't make the rules. I didn't make the rules for any of this, gravity, or the way things work, so I don't believe in judging other people. I really don't. I mean, there's a difference to me between judgment and discernment. Discernment is just navigating. I just believe I'm supposed to navigate this world and the spirit realm, which I believe exists. I haven't had experiences like some people. Some people have the coolest experiences [*laughs*]. Some people have had the scariest experiences. I feel like, the suicide thing, you know, people have hard things that they say about people that commit suicide. I mean, I have no idea. I just know that they must have been suffering so much. And that breaks my heart. And that's all I know. Like, why would I get into saying, like people do, like religious people do ... I don't think we have all the answers, that's the whole thing. As humans. But I get very perplexed when people ... I suppose it makes them feel comfortable on some level, to think they have all the answers. I'd rather be uncomfortable and just say, "Okay, I'll keep it really simple."

JS: How would you personally define "integrity"?

C: Being true to yourself. Integrity is keeping your word to yourself, to Creator if you have a relationship with Creator. For instance, I realized as I'm watching this lunar eclipse, I need to let go. I need to release anger. I know I do. I need to release anger about these things that I have no control over. And either they have happened or they're currently happening. Having integrity is that you make a commitment to something higher, and you do what you can to focus your energy on fulfilling that commitment. Whatever it may be. I mean, integrity also involves caring about the planet, caring about other people, caring about animals. Loving.

JS: What's a memory or feeling that resonates with you about a time that you were in love?

C: I think of being in love as more of a romantic thing. So, swept up, wanting to be with the other person, getting some fulfillment or some rush or some feeling of euphoria. I mean, I've had that in my life, but I don't seek that out as much, at all. I've had relationships where I've been in love, but then I realized—probably through finally getting married when I was fifty-three—that the most important thing about love is it's a constant choice. It's choice after choice after choice.

JS: In terms of the whole idea of romantic love, do you feel that it's merely a biological or sociological construct by which to propagate the species? Or is it a profound and deep human necessity?

C: I think I read something a long time ago that romantic love and the attraction and the sexual desire for another person, to be with another person, to have sex with another person, to feel them—you know, you're in them, they're in you, you're enmeshed or one or whatever. Yeah, definitely, that keeps people having humans on the planet. And, I had heard that that's our trick. You know, we get tricked into being with this other person, and then you learn how to love them.

JS: Do you feel that monogamy is important in a relationship?

C: See, you can have sex with other people or you can have really deep relationships with other people. So the word monogamy, what does that mean? That you're just with this other person and you don't have any other? I mean, there's lots and lots of people.

JS: What does it mean to you?

C: For me, I think it means—because I'm married—not to have a sexual relationship, or even a really, really close intimate relationship emotionally with another person. But I do have really close friends that I've spent lots of intimate time with. Women, mostly. So, like, I don't really know what monogamy is, you know. Everybody has their own definition of it. I discussed these things with my husband before we got married, so we're not having sex with other people. I think it's important that I don't have really deep, intimate relationships that will take me away from having him be my priority. Love, conscious. Through the difficulties, through everything. So he's one person that I've chosen to be like, "Okay, I'm all in." I've watched shows about polyamory and things like that, and I'm like, "Oh, that looks hellish. That looks like just a hellish experience right there" [*laughs*]. And people explore it and do that. But I had enough experiences before I married him. I don't need to be polyamorous. I mean, it can be, "Okay, well, I didn't have sex." That's what people say, like, to me. The stupidest things. "Oh, I didn't have sex with her!" Okay. But you can be so intimate when you dance with somebody. You can be so intimate when you talk to somebody. It really has to do with where your heart is. Now, that's why there's different kinds of love. You know, there's romantic love, and then there's spiritual love. I think because I had these experiences when I was younger, of spiritual love, and I also sought to develop that. And I had to ask these questions about love and monogamy and relationships, you know. I went through a lot of my life without romantic love. It was hard as shit. It was really hard.

JS: What do you think the most intimate experience that you've had is?

C: Most intimate? Well, I just think that the man that I'm with now, I've been the most vulnerable with. I've been the most open. So I think for intimacy to occur there has to be authenticity and vulnerability. That's not easy for most people. And I've been really … it's taken me a long time to be vulnerable and authentic as a regular thing.

JS: How would you associate intimacy and sexuality? Like, what's the correlation between those things?

C: It's easy to have sex with anybody without being intimate. I mean, you can just enjoy the pleasure part of it without having any emotional intimacy at all.

JS: What role does sexuality play in life overall, or in your life?

C: Sexuality for me is about me connecting with my own body first, and being in love with my own body first. And knowing how my body likes to be pleasured first. That can be any number of sensual experiences. I love them all, as you can see [*gestures to surroundings*]: candles, aromatherapy, warm things. You know, touch. I think all of that is really important. I mean, I think they're on the list of needs that we have as humans. There are more than most people even know for thriving. And I believe it involves way more sensuality than people give to themselves. So for me, that's the most important thing. And then if I involve myself, hopefully I involve myself with another person who's also able to do that, also able to love themselves, and that they're coming to the other person with, "Oh, I want to bring you pleasure. Oh, I want to bring you healing. Oh, I want to bring what *you* need. Does this feel good?" You know, from a generous place. People have a hard time with that, for any number of reasons. So I've accepted in my life that I've had sexual experiences that have been seemingly devoid of any kind of real intimacy. And I've been very defensive; I've been a very protected person in the course of my life. So for me to drop my guard and to love … I feel that, even though I'm older, I feel very young in the thing that we're talking about. Because the more that I'm able to love myself, then I'm going to be even more available to have intimacy. Which I already have, sexually or not. I have more intimacy with people now than I did ever before in my life.

JS: What would you say is something that is representative to you of the human spirit at its best?

C: That's an important question. Just riffing, I feel it's people who volunteer and give their lives in a selfless way, however that shows up. When you know that ego isn't driving somebody and that they're coming from their strengths, and wanting this world to be better, and wanting there to be connection and community and unity. So I can't say that I've ever seen just one thing. But I know when I see an artist that presents that, or a sacred activist that is doing that beautiful thing, I get moved. I feel the human spirit. So there are any number of things. Music. It is different when it's coming from ego and it's presentational, versus coming from the human spirit or human heart. And it could be anything. It could literally be a garden, or someone presenting a flower. If it's coming from love, and it's coming from that highest part of ourselves, then I get moved by that all the time.

JS: And what would be the human spirit at its worst?

C: Destroying another human being. Taking over their life, their identity, or their body. Torturing. Taking what's not theirs, but empowering themselves or others to destroy their people groups, or the earth. It's going on all the time. It's hard for me not to see it right now.

JS: If you could choose to have or embody one thing, what would that be?

C: If I could embody one thing, I would be radiating love that would make such a difference. But I would just *be* love. That's what I'm hoping for, for the rest of the days that I'm on earth. That when people are in my presence …

JS: And the final question is, do you feel understood?

C: By a few people on the earth, I do, at this time. I'm even in the process of understanding myself, so I can't expect other people to completely understand me if I don't understand myself. I've had a few people that have held up a mirror to me, that have allowed me to see myself and understand myself. So even if they don't completely understand me, they understand aspects of me, and help me to see what they think that I should see. Whether it's something that needs transformation, or something that needs to be celebrated.

INTERVIEW BETWEEN JOHN SINGLETARY AND "R"

—October 16, 2022

JS: Tell me something unique and special about your childhood.

R: Well, I grew up in Chicago, born 1982. It was just a different time then. You played outside; there was no technology. It was a lot different, you know. There were more gangs, it felt like, versus now. I feel like I was made to grow up faster. *I was* the oldest of five. I felt like I was made to be more mature. Left home alone with my siblings more, you know [*sighs*]. It was like, I think compared to now, there was a lot more on my plate. There was more expected of me. There wasn't as much of a concern for safety or anything like that.

JS: So you felt a lot of responsibility?

R: Yeah, it was a lot more responsibility.

JS: What were the kinds of things that made you happy?

R: What made me happy was really just being with my brothers and sister. And just having time outside. Not really focusing on anything but just being with them, family, really. Because those were the values that were instilled.

JS: And when you were a kid, what did you envision doing with your life?

R: When I was a kid, growing up in the city of Chicago, I wanted to be a police officer. You know, typical kid. I really wanted to do that, because that's what I saw: boys wanting to be, you know, police, firemen. But yeah, that's really what I was drawn to.

JS: If you could only pick one thing, what do you think is the most beautiful thing you've experienced or witnessed in your life?

R: I think, when I was in Iraq, deployed in 2003, seeing the best of man and also the worst of man. And what I mean by that is, seeing a man put his life at risk for another. I think that's the most beautiful thing anybody could witness. No regard for his or her life. And just pure, raw emotion. You know. And then seeing the best of humanity. Wanting to help. With no motive; no ulterior motive, I should say. Just wanting to help and be there for somebody. I think that's probably the most beautiful thing I've seen. And I have seen other scenic things. I used to live in Germany, in Europe, for three years. And I've seen beautiful things like that. But nothing like another human helping another human because of the innate drive to just want to be there to help.

JS: And what do you think is the most disappointing thing that you've experienced throughout the course of your life?

R: Probably the most disappointing thing is watching young life taken before they could flourish in life. That is probably the saddest thing. And watching a parent grieve for their child. That's probably the toughest thing to see, you know. That I carry with me because it's something I don't want to experience. That's very hard, hard on the soul.

JS: Without thinking about the dictionary definition, how would you define the word "grace"? Not as in, "By the grace of God," but grace as exhibited as a human characteristic.

R: I would define grace as giving somebody a second chance. Looking over their deficiencies, defects. Looking at them as who they are. Not looking at their past, but giving them a second chance.

JS: What role does your gender or ethnicity play in constructing your sense of identity?

R: Well, I feel, being of Hispanic, Mexican heritage, I feel that what was instilled in me from my father, and my parents—and being male—is having to be head of household, strong. Having to carry, you know, a lot of weight, family weight, and having to have answers when needed. That's a lot of weight to carry. But it's been great for personal growth. But also detrimental at the same time. That sense of responsibility, duty. It can be difficult as well, because part of Hispanic culture is to be tough, and not show weakness.

JS: What is the most intimate experience you feel that you've shared with another person?

R: Probably the most intimate thing I've shared with another person would be, probably my experience with childbirth. Watching my first daughter, my first kid be born. You know, that was a very exciting experience, an intimate experience. That's a … man, it's an experience to watch that. One, because I was experiencing a lot of emotions, because I came back that day when my daughter was born—I had just come back from Iraq from my tour leave. So my ex-wife had just gone into labor, just when I landed. So when my flight landed, I arrived to frantic in-laws saying, "We gotta go, we gotta go, we got a police escort." So I had a police escort from the airport to the hospital in Harrisburg, and I walked right into the room where my ex-wife was in active labor. So I had like, a lot of emotions going from deployment—I was on my third deployment, and it was very, very brutal, my third deployment. So I had that weight on my head and shoulders. And then to come into something as beautiful as childbirth. And then telling somebody about that. How do you go from death and violence to life? You know, and how beautiful that was, too. I was defused immediately once I held my daughter. That was just like, I just felt instant relief. That moment where, I felt just love, pure love. You know, I actually felt something for another human being, you know, like I felt my life was going to take a different direction. So telling somebody about that for the first time, telling another first-time father about that was really cool. And then hearing other dads talk about that.

JS: You were talking a lot about being in the military, and being deployed in Iraq and the things that you'd seen. That must give you a really firsthand view on death. So what are your thoughts about death? How do you conceptualize it, and is it something that frightens you?

R: Okay. As far as death, when I was nineteen, I deployed to Kuwait [in] 2002. And then, obviously in 2003, March 19th, the war kicked off. I was pretty scared, you know, once we crossed the border. Once we hit first contact with Iraq enemy forces, of course, I was scared shitless. Once that was done with, and I encountered my first dead body, I was terrified. I felt like … you know that feeling when you get caught doing something wrong, you know, that rush? That's what it felt like when I first saw this dead Iraqi. And that's the last time I felt that rush. After that I didn't feel it anymore. But it was surreal. It felt like everything got dark and that's all I saw. But he was still; his body hadn't hit rigor mortis yet. But seeing that body for the first time, I froze, you know, I couldn't move. I was, like, stiff. And no matter what I told my body, I couldn't, I couldn't move.

But after that experience, you know, we didn't have much time, we had to move again. We had to keep going. But somebody took a picture; I actually have that picture at home. After that, I had no more fear. Because I saw more. It was like an everyday thing. Once that initial shock was gone, I wasn't scared of it anymore. It became part of just, every day. I didn't see an American casualty until toward the end of the deployment. And that was more scary than seeing an enemy, what we were told was an enemy, you know, the Iraqi. And that was scary to see because that was the first time I felt mortality.

JS: So are you afraid of death?

R: No, not in the traditional sense. I'm afraid of what I'll leave, of leaving my kids unprepared. Like, am I doing enough? Okay, let me backtrack. I'm trying to right my wrongs. Because I truly feel like I did a lot of wrong. And I'm trying to make up for it. You know, as an addict, and as a soldier, I carry a lot of guilt. And I'm trying to make up by doing good deeds. Not broadcasting any of it, just doing things. And, by that, if I happen to face stuff, after seeing a lot of people go … I'd rather not go slow. Because I've seen the fear, and the processing that goes with that, with the fear. It didn't look fun. You know, knowing that it's coming. I'd rather it just be "lights out." But not having things prepared, saying what I have to say to my kids, making sure they have those lessons that I want them to have. That's the only thing I fear. I feel like at thirty-nine I've had a pretty good run.

JS: What would your personal definition of integrity be?

R: Integrity, that's actually one of the Army values. Doing the right thing, even when nobody's looking. It's hard to do for a lot of people. You know, for me it was easy to do, and then I found myself struggling with it. When I was down on my luck, I found myself struggling with integrity. But now, I find myself clinging to that; that's all I have, you know, because it's like your credit. That's what you have, integrity. When you don't have anything else, you have your word. That's it. Like, you have no money, you have no possessions, but if you have integrity, you have everything. Because then people will be like, "Hey, you can trust that guy."

JS: Do you experience anxiety?

R: Yeah, very much so. That's why I have my service dog, Remus. He helps me through a lot of it. Now, anxiety comes in different forms; you experience, like, panic attacks. But before it usually sets in, I remove myself from the equation. Remus senses it, and he'll sit up, and he'll place his paw on my thigh. And usually, right when it's coming in, and I've removed myself from the situation, I usually feel like a room is caving in. And then I'll start feeling like, I don't know, like a whole bunch of eyes are looking at me, you know, and everything starts spinning. And it's just, sometimes it's unbearable. But yeah, to answer your question, yes.

JS: What are you most afraid of?

R: I'm most afraid of not telling somebody how I feel and then not seeing them again. Like, we're all gonna have our last day with somebody, we just don't know when. And we go through life, you know, taking a lot of things for granted. Not saying goodbye, you know: "Oh, we'll see them again tomorrow." "I'll just message them tonight, I'll text them. I'll text her." Or, "I'll call them tomorrow." And then something happens, you know. The unthinkable. I think it's always good to tell that person you care about them, or "Thank you," you know. Even if it's out of nowhere, I've noticed that people appreciate that out of nowhere, and people always ask you, "Is everything okay?" Yeah, things are okay. You know, just, people like to be validated, just out of nowhere because, yeah, we get caught up, doing things out of muscle memory, just getting out of the grind. But it's nice to tell those people that, "Hey, I appreciate you doing this for me daily," or "I appreciate you checking in; I appreciate you texting me." Because all too many times … like, for example, I used to get texts from my friend, all the time, and then all of a sudden it just stopped. And then, you know, and then he's gone. And I took that for granted. I just never … I just didn't respond. I was too busy. I felt like I was too busy. And now I'm just like, I'm not busy. Like, I try and get back to texts and say, "Hey, I'm kind of caught up right now, but I saw your message." You know. So yeah. It's just I'm afraid of not saying what I need to say to people.

JS: What have your experiences with addiction been?

R: Well, I started after my deployment, 2003. I wasn't really a big drinker. But that's how it started. I started drinking in 2003 after my deployment. Not knowing why, I had alcohol poisoning at Fort Stewart, Georgia. And right after I got out of the hospital, I started drinking again. And I started developing a habit of drinking and that's what I was known for—from 2003 all the way, I started progressively getting worse with drinking. It started just, [as] blackouts, you know. Then I started fighting my friends, then I started, like, emotional crying. And then I started abusing prescriptions. Because in active-duty Army you get piss tested; you piss in a cup and then it comes back, so you have to time things right. I got smart and started figuring things out. "I gotta make friends with this guy." You know, to figure things out. Then you figure out prescriptions that have a short half-life, so you don't get caught up. But when I got out of the military I found a whole bunch of stuff. Like, I became a really bad alcoholic, discovered coke, discovered pills, everything, man. I met one guy from up in Mansfield where I used to live, Wellsboro, and he introduced me to a smorgasbord of stuff, and it was off to the races.

JS: And you're clean now?

R: Yes.

JS: How did that come about?

R: Well, that came after a lot of broken relationships, run-ins with the law. That really was one of the turning points, watching my family cry. You know. Going into a squad car, and then my daughter watching me go into an ambulance, being taken in a couple of times just for being suicidal. Just because I didn't feel like I had a place anymore. Looking back now, seeing that that was the alcohol, the drugs talking, PTSD—that's what I was diagnosed with when I got out.

JS: Looking back on your life so far, what are you most proud of?

R: Oh, man, that's a hard one, man. I think I'm most proud of … oh man, that's tough. That's really tough.

JS: Is serving your country something that would be up there?

R: Yeah, I mean, I would say that because of the way my kids brag about me; they're really proud of me. I mean, I'm really proud of my kids. My family is really my biggest, you know, my pride. Military service? You know, I absolutely love, love serving the country. I did it for fifteen and a half years. I really can't narrow it down. I think, you know, family, service, and contributing as much back to society as I can.

JS: When you look at the world right now—I think we could probably both admit that things have gotten crazy over the past two and a half years, since Covid—what do you think is the most significant problem that we're currently facing, as a culture or society or species?

R: I mean, there's numerous issues, cultural, economic, and what-not. I think right now we have to, as a society, get over this issue about race. You know, we have got to work together, and realize that we're not to be pitted against each other. That there is strength in numbers. That we're more alike than we are different. You know, if people would stop touting our differences, and bring up our likenesses, and see that we can work as a team and get things done, the world would probably be a better-off place. But people want to bring up our differences, you know, and highlight those differences and say, you know, that, pretty much what I'm trying to say is, everybody wants to be unique and bring it out. Like, I get it, we're all unique, and this and that, but, you know, there's a time and a place for that. There are too many groups for everybody to have all this uniqueness. Like, this is the United States; we all have a common goal to be American, and let's get this country back where it's supposed to be and let's stop fighting. When you try and be, like, very unique, you end up excluding a lot of people. So then you'd like, for example, you have us two in here, you'd be like, "Oh, this guy's brown, this guy's white." And then, you have that dog there, and, like, all these other people. Someone will always be like, "What about me?" Somebody will always be excluded and you're not going to make everybody happy. But when you share what is alike between everybody, everybody's included. And I think if people were to look at it that way, you know, "Hey, we're all alike. You have a nose just like me! You have ears just like me! You have hair just like me!" You know. We're focusing on all the wrong things, like skin color and all that. You cut us all open, we're all bleeding red. We all have the same internal organs. You know, we should be going off of personal character. I think that's what we need to be focusing on and then get together and let's work on issues together.

JS: What role do you feel sexuality plays in life, or in your life?

R: I think, currently, how it is set in society, I don't think it should have any say, really. It shouldn't really be brought up, I don't think. It should be behind closed doors. You know, I don't think it should have any factor to do with anything. I think it's being brought up too much. You know, I really don't care what you do. As far as people wanting to make that a thing, more power to you. But I don't think it has any weight in society, like that, that wasn't, you know, it doesn't matter to me. It doesn't matter to me what you do. Do I care? No, I don't care. But I think if it holds weight to you getting your employment, or a position and they hold that as a factor, then I think that's wrong. I think it shouldn't have anything to do with anything.

JS: Tell me about a time that you were in love.

R: I think the last time I felt that butterfly feeling was actually with my current wife. You know, I didn't think I could feel that again. I felt it in 2002, when I met my first wife, and I was with her for ten years. I thought that I couldn't feel that feeling again. And then when I met my current wife, you know, she was the first one since that got me to feel that emotion. Because one thing that I deal with is not feeling anything. You know, like, it's hard for me to feel something. It's tough, you know. Like, I try, and feel, kind of. But I only feel, like, certain things, you know. If I connect with somebody, I can feel that. But, other than that, I feel like, I don't know, like nothing. If it's a strong emotion, then I feel that. But it's either, like, anger, or that love. Like when I see my kids, I feel that. But that love, I felt that with my new wife when I met her, because she saw me not as a soldier; she saw me for who I was. Soldier stuff had nothing to do with anything. And I think that's why I felt something. Because for the longest [time], I felt like I can't shake off this addict stuff.

JS: Do you believe in romantic love, like, as a thing that we need? Or is it just kind of like a biological reaction by which to propagate the species?

R: I think it's something that we do need. Because [of] companionship. You know, it's nice to come home to somebody. For a long time I came home to nobody. And that was a miserable existence. It added to my misery, especially when I was down low. Like, I'd come home and it would make it worse. I just heard, you know, things. Not actually heard things, but, my mind was my worst enemy. And now, coming home to somebody that's actually happy to see me—for the most part—and encourages me, and sometimes when I'm down, will pick me up. This doesn't go for everybody, but when you find somebody that is actually willing to do that, that knows when you're not right, and that can pick you up and put you back where you need to be, you know, and encourage you or send you that text, or call you randomly, I think that's really motivating. But when you don't have that, you just continue to decline slowly and not even realize it. So I think it's necessary to have that romantic aspect in a relationship. Because it also helps with your mental health, you know, and to help you not slip back down into the abyss.

JS: So for you, is monogamy something that's important in a romantic relationship?

R: I think so. I prefer monogamy myself. Because I don't ever want to be away and have to wonder, "Is somebody else taking care of what I'm supposed to be taking care of?" I like to have my own space, my own spot, my own family, you know, my own thing. If there's too many players, if there's too many people involved, there's too much room for jealousy. There's just too many variables there. If it's monogamous then there's—for me, anyway—there's very little room for miscommunication except for what *we* go through. So there won't be any jealousy, or "Where are you at?" You know, you can focus your time on one person.

JS: What is God to you?

R: Well, I'm Christian, nondenominational, so I believe in Jesus Christ. So I believe he's the one true savior. That's where I stand with that. I also respect other people's opinions. You know, it doesn't have to be what I say, because that causes friction. I don't believe in forcing opinions on anybody else. That's the surefire way to cause arguments and not get cohesion with people. The best way to present a higher power is to say, "Hey, you believe what you want, this is what I believe in. If you're willing to listen, hey, you're willing to listen, and if not, hey, you know, whatever. But that's what I believe in."

JS: How has your conception of God changed or evolved over your lifetime?

R: When I was at war, I wasn't very religious or faithful. It wasn't until I saw a lot of chaos and death that I kind of changed a little bit. At first I was angry, you know, angry with God. Seeing the chaos, seeing children die. Seeing a lot of innocent people die that I feel weren't supposed to die. But then, I don't know the plans. I don't know why things happen. But it's not up to me. Our brains are supposed to make sense of everything. But it progressed a few years to now, from 2003, where I was angry—and I've been baptized, like, three times since then—to 2022, where I'm now more at peace. Where my understanding, or my relationship with God, is better. Where now I feel like he is tapping into me to help others. You know. And I'm still trying to understand. I'm not saying I'm full-up religious or anything. I just feel like I'm still discovering.

JS: Do you feel that the events that happen in life are random, like we're just in this kind of random particle accelerator? Or do you feel more that there's an underlying purpose and order and structure to things?

R: I believe there is no meaning to life. I believe that our purpose is to *give* meaning to life. So we're born with a blank slate, and I think that's why a lot of people have big problems, trying to find *the* meaning to life. But really, we are supposed to *give* meaning to life. And, when people figure that out, I think they'll be better off.

I truly believe that a lot of people make themselves miserable, trying to figure out the meaning to life, when really, you give it meaning, you know. Whether it's family, whether it's wealth for you, whether it's finding that adventure, you know, jumping off a cliff or whatever. Whether it's influencing people to do the right thing. Whatever your purpose is, you give it that meaning. That's for you to figure out. And that's why you're given all of this stuff in life, you know, you're given the path. And then when you figure that out, like, that's the beautiful thing. All of a sudden, you're like, "Oh, I know my purpose." For a lot of us it takes a long time, and I think that's what drives people nuts, is trying to figure out their own meaning. And it doesn't come later for a lot of people.

JS: Have you had any experiences in life that you can't explain rationally?

R: I think meeting some people that I felt like I've known before. You know, like, they have this … man, I just got goosebumps [*laughs*]. Just meeting some people that I just have this strong feeling, like, "I've known you before." And then that strange déjà vu, sometimes, it just comes and it feels so powerful. Like, have I been here before? And I've read about it, you know, sometimes it just feels like a trick. But is it really?

JS: If you could have anything, or be anything, what would you choose?

R: At this stage of my life, if I could have anything, I think I'd have a place for kids that come from single-parent homes to go after school. Like, for every city to have one. Because I think kids are very underrepresented. You know, a lot of traumatic things happen to kids, and that's why they grow up to be, as adults … and I don't think they talk to anybody, really. By the time we figure out something's wrong, it's too late. And they end up going through the system, homes, things like that. And I think there's something that can be done if we identify these children earlier. I have the idea; I just don't know where I want to go with it. But, I would like to have something like that, you know. Identify those populations early and then have, like, an intervention.

I think parents nowadays aren't very well equipped; there's not a lot of resources. The other day I was at Sheetz, over here down Maynard, and I saw this lady in there with a toddler, four years old, and she was just freaking, was slamming her down in her stroller, you know, because she was screaming. And I'm like, "Lady, calm down." But she was forcefully, like, putting her down. And I don't butt into anybody's business, you know, like, ever, but it's the first time I felt like I had to do something. But it was just, like, because the kid was getting on her nerves.

JS: Looking back on things, what is your biggest regret?

R: Okay. My biggest regret is people that say they have no regrets [*laughs*]. I used to say, "No regrets," and that was a big load of shit. So what I would say is, not being close with my siblings. I think that was a big mistake. Because I left when I was eighteen and I just really didn't keep in contact with them. So now we're kind of like … and I make up for that now with my kids. I tell them hard. You know, stick together. You guys are all you got. You know, and that's important for me, for them, in case something happens to me, that they have each other; family is important. Because I don't have that. My mom gave me shit yesterday, she's like, "Why don't you talk to your brothers?" And I was just, I didn't have an answer, man. And I do feel regret. You know. I just don't know why. And I'm the oldest.

JS: If there was anything right now that you could change about yourself, what's the biggest thing that you would change about yourself?

R: If I could change, and I had the power to, I'd probably want to be a better father. And by that I mean I would want to spend more time with my older three kids. You know, have them here more often. Because I see the power that a male role model has, that it's healthy for them. That's what I would want to do.

JS: The final question that I have is, do you feel understood in the world?

R: No. Not at all. I feel there's a lot of negative connotations, being a veteran with PTSD, and also having addiction. That's going to be hard, and having a record. Because when I do talk to people that actually know my past, and I say what I want to do, it's kind of hard to overcome that. It's, you know, "Oh, he's an addict. Oh, he was arrested before, multiple times. Oh, he's got PTSD." So how am I going to gain the trust, you know? That's a lot of barriers.

So I feel like my actions have got to do more than my talking. Even then, people are always still going to talk, so that's why I say I don't have to explain my actions anymore. Because those people, no matter what I do, they're always going to look at me that way. So I feel like I've got to work twice, three times as hard as my peers because I have to overcome that perception. So that's a struggle.